Architecture of High Performance Computers

Volume II

R. N. Ibbett and N. P. Topham

Department of Computer Science
University of Edinburgh
Edinburgh
Scotland EH9 3JZ

Architecture of High Performance Computers

Volume II

Array processors and multiprocessor systems

Springer-Verlag New York Inc.

First published 1989

Sole distributors in the USA and Canada
Springer-Verlag New York Inc.
175 Fifth Avenue
New York, NY 10010
USA

Published by
MACMILLAN EDUCATION LTD
Houndmills, Basingstoke, Hampshire RG21 2XS
and London
Companies and representatives
throughout the world

Printed in Great Britain

ISBN 0–387–91353–X

Contents

Preface   **viii**

1 Introduction   **1**
   1.1 Parallel hardware structures 2
   1.2 Taxonomy of parallel architectures 3
   1.3 Summary of the book 4

2 Array-processor Architecture   **6**
   2.1 Design Issues 7
      2.1.1   Array processor organisation 8
      2.1.2   ILLIAC IV — a distributed-memory machine 11
      2.1.3   BSP — a shared-memory machine 12
   2.2 Performance issues 15
      2.2.1   Scalability 20
   2.3 Summary 21

3 Interconnection Networks   **22**
   3.1 Characteristics of interconnection structures 23
   3.2 Network routing functions 24
   3.3 Network topology 29
      3.3.1   Static networks 31
      3.3.2   Dynamic networks 35
      3.3.3   Multi-stage networks 36
   3.4 Summary 42

4 Practical Array Architectures   **43**
   4.1 The ICL DAP 43
      4.1.1   System architecture 44
      4.1.2   Array architecture 45
      4.1.3   PE architecture 48
      4.1.4   Instruction set 52
      4.1.5   Performance 56
      4.1.6   The DAP-3 58
   4.2 The Connection Machine 58
      4.2.1   System architecture 59
      4.2.2   Processing elements 61

	4.2.3	The router	63
4.3		Summary	66

5 Array Processor Software   **67**

5.1		Array processing languages	67
	5.1.1	DAP Fortran	68
	5.1.2	CM-Lisp	70
5.2		Algorithms for array processors	73
	5.2.1	Partial differential equations	75
	5.2.2	Minimum path length	79
5.3		Summary	82

6 Multiprocessor Architecture   **83**

6.1		Design issues	86
	6.1.1	Categories of MIMD architecture	88
	6.1.2	Granularity	89
	6.1.3	Load balancing	90
6.2		Performance issues	91
	6.2.1	Speed-up and efficiency	96
	6.2.2	Extensibility	104
	6.2.3	Reliability and fault-tolerance	105
6.3		Summary	108

7 Shared-memory Multiprocessors   **109**

7.1		Shared-memory architecture	109
	7.1.1	Sequential-access shared-memory systems	111
	7.1.2	Highly-connected shared-memory systems	115
	7.1.3	Scalable multiprocessors	116
7.2		The Sequent Balance 8000	116
	7.2.1	Cache consistency	118
	7.2.2	The SLIC	118
	7.2.3	The SB8000 system bus	121
7.3		C.mmp	122
	7.3.1	The small address problem	124
	7.3.2	Locks and synchronisation	125
7.4		The BBN Butterfly	127
	7.4.1	Overview of the Butterfly	127
	7.4.2	Butterfly processing nodes	128
	7.4.3	The Butterfly switch	130
	7.4.4	Performance	132
7.5		Summary	140

8 Message-passing Multiprocessors   **141**
   8.1 Design issues for message-passing architectures 143
   8.2 Transputer-based systems 146
       8.2.1 Architecture of the T414 147
       8.2.2 The T800 floating point transputer 156
       8.2.3 Constructing multi-transputer systems 158
       8.2.4 The Meiko Computing Surface 160
   8.3 Hypercube multiprocessors 165
       8.3.1 Cosmic Cube and the Intel iPSC 165
       8.3.2 The NCUBE/10 166
       8.3.3 The FPS T series 167
   8.4 Summary 167

9 Multiprocessor Software   **169**
   9.1 Languages for multiprocessors 169
       9.1.1 Ada 170
       9.1.2 Occam 175
   9.2 Multiprocessor algorithms 177
       9.2.1 Sorting on a shared-memory architecture 178
       9.2.2 Matrix multiplication using message-passing 185
   9.3 Summary 191

Bibliography   **194**

Index   **201**

Preface

This book is the second volume of a two-volume set covering the architecture of high performance computers. The division of material between the two volumes has been devised so that Volume I essentially deals with architectures in which parallelism is used to attain high performance but is hidden from the programmer, whereas Volume II deals with machines which are explicitly parallel in nature. Volume I therefore describes architectural techniques that can be used, and indeed have become widespread, in the design of individual high performance processors, whereas this volume concentrates on the architecture of systems in which a number of processors operate in concert to achieve high performance. The high performance structures described in Volume I are naturally applicable to the design of the elements within parallel processors. Volume II represents a historical progression from Volume I, describing some architectures and machines which have evolved recently and could be described as 'state-of-the-art'.

Computer architecture is an extensive subject, with a large body of mostly descriptive literature, and any treatment of the subject is necessarily incomplete. There are many high performance architectures, both on the market and within research environments, far too many to cover in a student text. We have attempted to extract the fundamental principles of high performance architectures and set them in perspective with case studies. Where possible we have used commercially available machines as our examples. The two volumes of this book are designed to accompany undergraduate courses in computer architecture, and constitute a core of material presented in third and fourth year courses in the Computer Science Department at Edinburgh University.

The authors would like to thank Duncan Roweth for vetting the section which describes the Meiko Computing Surface, as well as the colleagues and friends who read and commented on other parts of the manuscript.

Roland Ibbett
Nigel Topham

1 Introduction

In volume I of this two-volume set we examined the architectural techniques that have been used to produce high performance computers. This included techniques to maximise processor performance; for example, instruction pipelines and parallel functional units. It also included techniques to maximise the throughput, and minimise the latency, of storage structures; for example, interleaving and caching respectively. We saw how these design techniques can be brought together in the form of vector processors in order to provide a platform for very high performance numerical processing. However, all the machines considered in volume I have something in common; they operate within a relatively conventional programming model, and this means that high-level language programs written for one high performance architecture will work equally well on another, with little or no modification. In this book we are concerned with architectures for which this does not necessarily hold true, and for which new languages and new application algorithms are required. This naturally implies a greater overall design effort, but in many cases this is outweighed by the resulting gain in performance. The architectures dealt with by this book all embody some form of parallel processing capability that cannot be hidden from the user's view of the machine, at least not without the aid of compilers that are able to decompose a conventional program into fragments of parallel code automatically.

One question which must be answered is 'why do we need to consider new architectures when existing architectures have served so well in the past?'. There are in fact several good reasons why we should consider new architectures, and as always they stem from changes in the cost and performance characteristics of modern technology. Perhaps most importantly, the cost of *replicating* a piece of logic, as opposed to making it work faster, has fallen dramatically. This is due to advances in micro-fabrication technology. Thus it has become cheaper to build a system using a hundred microprocessors than to build a single-processor system that is one hundred times more powerful than a single microprocessor. This follows from two related facts: firstly, the cost of each transistor on a silicon die has fallen continuously since integrated circuits were developed, and secondly, the number of transistors that can be squeezed onto a single silicon die has also increased. This has now reached the point where complete processors, using many of the techniques found in volume I, can be fabricated as a single device. For

1

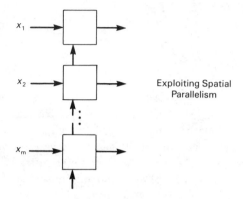

Figure 1.1 A spatially-parallel structure

example, the Motorola,M88100 microprocessor supports a number of parallel functional units and has a Scoreboard to deal with data dependencies as in the CDC 6600 and 7600 machines.

It is anticipated that as a result of the availability of high performance single-chip processors, and the ever-increasing demand for more powerful computing systems, the market for parallel processors will increase dramatically during the late 1980s. For example, one market prediction [JD86] states that the value of sales of parallel processors in the UK alone is likely to increase by 500% in the period 1988–89. The supercomputer market, traditionally the principal beneficiary of research into high performance computer systems, is expected to be eclipsed by the expanding market for parallel workstations and parallel symbolic processors as small-scale parallel systems become more widely available.

1.1 Parallel hardware structures

All computing systems are constructed from interconnected components, and depending on the level of abstraction at which a system is viewed, these components could be transistors, gates, registers, arithmetic units, memories, or even complete processors. At all levels of abstraction there are two fundamental ways in which components can be composed to create parallel computing structures.

Perhaps the simplest way to introduce parallelism into a computing structure is to replicate a component n times, as shown in figure 1.1. To exploit this form of parallelism, the units of information processed by the original (non-parallel) component must be partitionable. In other words the task *space* must be *parallelised*. For this reason this form of parallel-

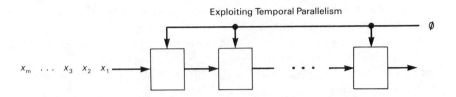

Figure 1.2 A temporally-parallel structure

ism is known as *spatial* parallelism. A typical example from the sphere of ordinary human activity is the familiar row of checkout desks one finds in supermarkets.

The other fundamental way of introducing parallelism into a processing activity is to partition the processing activity into a number of steps, as shown in figure 1.2, which when applied sequentially to each unit of information performs the original task. In other words, the task is partitioned in *time*, with each step of the task being applied to a separate unit of information. For this reason this form of parallelism is known as *temporal* parallelism. A typical example is 'assembly line' manufacturing. The application of temporal parallelism in computing produces pipelined structures (see volume I, chapter 4).

The amount of parallelism that can be exploited using temporal parallelism depends on the divisibility of the task being parallelised, whereas the amount that can be exploited using spatial parallelism depends only on the number of independent tasks.

1.2   Taxonomy of parallel architectures

There have been several attempts to devise classification schemes for computer architectures, particularly parallel architectures, none of which are entirely adequate. Probably the most widely accepted classification is that suggested by M. J. Flynn [Fly72]. Flynn's classification is based empirically on the multiplicity, or otherwise, of instruction and data streams. This leads to four classifications.

1. SISD — single instruction stream, single data stream.

2. SIMD — single instruction stream, multiple data stream.

3. MISD — multiple instruction stream, single data stream.

4. MIMD — multiple instruction stream, multiple data stream.

SISD machines employ no explicit parallelism, and within this classification fall machines such as the IBM System/360 and /370 and the CDC 6600 and 7600, even though these machines exploit small-scale parallelism. SIMD machines are those in which a single stream of instructions operates on a stream of data containing a large, and variable, number of data items. This normally includes array processors, such as those described in chapter 4, as well as vector machines such as the CRAY-1 and the CYBER 205 (see volume I, chapters 7 and 9 respectively). MISD machines are somewhat elusive, and the absence of machines in this category would seem to indicate that Flynn's classification is not particularly effective. MIMD machines are those machines in which there is more than one stream of independent instructions. This includes all multiprocessor systems, such as those described in chapters 7 and 8. Flynn's classification is used throughout this text.

Other classification schemes include PMS [SBN82] and Hockney and Jesshope's 'structural notation' [HJ81], both of which attempt to describe the physical structure of a machine in a similar style to a chemical formula. These classification schemes are little used, and at present Flynn's classification in the only widely accepted shorthand notation for distinguishing between broad classes of parallel machine.

1.3   Summary of the book

To study high performance parallel architectures requires a treatment of four primary aspects of system design; hardware structures, parallel language design, applications (algorithms), and performance (both analytical and empirical). In this book we attempt to address these issues in an integrated way for each major type of parallel architecture.

This book is concerned principally with two general types of architecture: SIMD-array processors and MIMD multiprocessors. Chapters 2, 4 and 5 deal with the former, and chapters 6 to 9 deal with the latter. Chapter 3 deals with interconnection structures for parallel machines, and is relevant to all forms of parallel machine.

In chapter 2 we examine issues in the design and performance of SIMD-array processors, and briefly trace the historical evolution of SIMD machines. Chapter 4 describes the the architecture of two example SIMD machines in detail: the ICL DAP and the TMC Connection Machine. Some of the principles and practice of programming languages for SIMD machines are outlined in chapter 5, and one example application for each of the machines described in chapter 4 is presented. Chapter 3 describes the principles of processor interconnection networks; their taxonomy, their structure, and their routing mechanisms. The material in chapter 3 should be consulted before studying the array machines described in chapter 4, and before considering the MIMD systems in chapters 7 and 8.

In chapter 6 the design principles of multiprocessor architecture, and their performance characteristics, are outlined. This chapter includes some material on general design issues, such as granularity, extensibility, reliability, and the basic ways in which processors can cooperate on a single task. We also describe a simple analytical model for the performance of multi-processor systems. Chapters 7 and 8 are each devoted to one of the two major types of multiprocessor architecture: shared-memory systems and message-passing systems. Within each of these chapters we characterise the respective architectural types in terms of the interconnection mechanism between processors. For example, in chapter 7 we divide shared-memory machines into those connected by cheap limited-bandwidth buses, expensive high-bandwidth cross-bar switches, and multi-stage networks — which are essentially a compromise between busses and cross-bars. Chapter 8 is divided into those systems which use small-degree static networks, typified by transputer-based systems, and those which rely on static networks of n-th degree, typified by hypercube-based multiprocessors.

It is hoped that through the analysis and discussion of the architectural examples in this book we are able to explain the need for, and the evolution of, the parallel architectures of today, as well as introduce some of the problems to be solved by the computer architects of tomorrow.

2 Array-processor Architecture

In his Turing Lecture entitled "Can Programming be Liberated from the von Neumann Style", Backus [Bac78] introduced the term *von Neumann bottleneck*. This refers to the fundamental speed limitation of machines which have physically separate processing and storage units. In such machines the link between the two parts creates a bottleneck, defining an upper-bound on performance. Furthermore, this two-part design produces extremely inefficient architectures when the metric of efficiency is the utilisation of individual switching elements.

Let us consider a conventional 'von Neumann' architecture consisting of a single processor and an associated memory. This processor-memory configuration is constructed from a technology which permits machine instructions to be executed at a frequency of f_I instructions per second. Let us assume that there are p switching devices (typically transistors) within the processor, and that every $t_I = 1/f_I$ seconds a proportion $r \{0 < r < 1\}$ of these devices switch, and thus perform some useful work. Let us also assume that the basic architecture of this machine does not alter as advances are made in device technology to increase the performance of the processor. Then of course r will remain constant. The memory contains m bits, and empirically the value of m is linearly dependent on the speed of the processor, f_I. Hence we can say that $m = k_1 f_I$, for some system constant k_1. This means that if each bit of memory requires k_2 switching devices (we ignore memory decode logic for simplicity), then the total number of devices in the machine is $p + k_2 m$. Since each instruction activates $O(1)$ bits of memory, then for some system constant k_3, the mean utilisation of devices, U_d, is

$$U_d = \frac{rp + k_2 k_3}{p + k_1 k_2 f_I} \qquad (2.1)$$

If we introduce constants $a = r + k_2 k_3/p$ and $b = k_1 k_2/p$ the above equation can be re-written as

$$U_d = a \left(\frac{1}{1 + bf_I} \right)$$

This is a familiar form for utilisation equations (see equations 4.3 and 10.3 in volume I, and equation 6.2 in this volume) and immediately indicates that utilisation decreases monotonically with increasing f_I. In other words, as the machine becomes more powerful the utilisation of individual switching devices falls towards an asymptotic value of zero; not exactly a favourable relationship. Some architects accept this as the price which must be paid for more powerful systems. Others see it as an argument in favour of alternative architectures, claiming that a more sensible organisation is one in which the ratio of processing power to memory size is fixed, and an increase in memory automatically produces an increase in processing performance. This is the approach adopted by SIMD-array architectures. In these architectures the units of processing are atomic processor-memory 'cells', and increments in performance are achieved by replicating complete cells rather than by simply using faster technology.

In volume I the use of pipelining and parallel functional units is discussed at length. Whilst these techniques are useful, and have their place in the standard repertoire of high performance techniques, the additional performance they offer is limited by the quantity of parallelism they can extract from a single stream of scalar instructions. For example, parallel functional units rely on the presence of independent operations within a single stream of scalar instructions in order to extract low-level parallelism automatically. Vector processors are able to exploit the parallelism in vector and matrix computations, but only to an extent determined by the degree of pipelining. In chapter 4 of volume I it was shown that there is an optimum degree of pipelining for every function, and hence the performance gained as a result of pipelining alone is fixed. These limitations are not present in array machines, since parallel operations within each computation are partitioned *spatially* rather than *temporally*. Therefore, the throughput of an array structure is only limited by the size of the array and the quantity of independent data.

In chapter 4 we examine two array machines in detail. In the remainder of this chapter we discuss some basic principles of array architectures, analyse their performance, and briefly review the historical development of a number of important array machines.

2.1 Design Issues

Empirical evidence suggests there are two basic ways in which an array of functional units (of whatever type) can be composed to form an array structure. These are known as *lockstep arrays* and *cyclic arrays*, and are illustrated in figure 2.1. The lockstep array comprises a number of array elements, each with an output register which is strobed by a common clock. Each element in the array requires a new set of input operands every clock period and produces a new result every clock period. To operate successfully, the computation in each element must be independent of all other elements, and all computations should take roughly the same amount of time. In a cyclic array the input operands are accepted in sequence and get *farmed-out* to the array elements on a first-come-first-served basis. Hence,

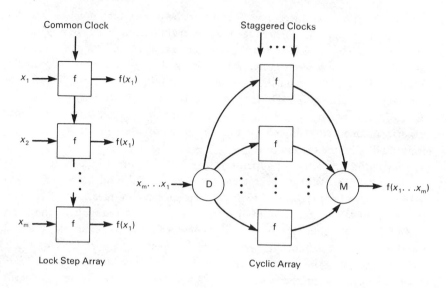

Figure 2.1 Lockstep and cyclic array organisations

if the latency of the array unit is t_f, and there are n of them in the array, the peak evaluation rate is n/t_f per second. Again, all computations must be independent, although they need not take the same amount of time. Interleaved memories, especially in vector machines, are often organised as cyclic arrays of memory modules.

Applying the concept of array-parallelism to processor design involves effort in three major areas. First of all the processing elements of the array must be replicated, secondly the memory must be partitioned in order that the aggregate processing and memory bandwidths are well-matched, and thirdly these components must be connected so that they form an integrated computing structure.

2.1.1   Array processor organisation

The classical structure of an SIMD-array architecture is conceptually simple, and is illustrated in figure 2.2. In such architectures a program consists of a mixture of scalar and array instructions. The scalar instructions are sent to the scalar processor and the array instructions are *broadcast* to all array elements in parallel. Array elements are incapable of operating autonomously, and must be driven by the control unit.

There are two important control mechanisms: a *local control* mechanism by which array elements use local state information to determine whether they should execute a broadcast instruction or ignore it, and a *global control*

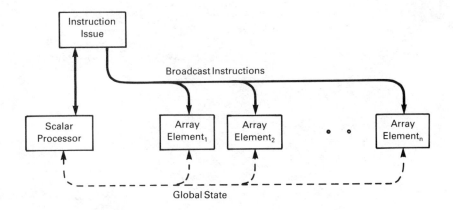

Figure 2.2 Classical SIMD-array architecture

mechanism by which the control unit extracts global information from the array elements to determine the outcome of a conditional control transfer within the user's program. Global information can be extracted in one of two ways. Either the control unit reads state information from one, or a group, of array elements, or it senses a boolean control line representing the logical OR (or possibly the logical AND) of a particular local state variable from *every* array element.

The three major components of an array structure are the array units, the memory they access, and the connections between the two. One can identify two ways in which these components can be organised. Figure 2.3 shows the basic structure of an array processor in which memory is shared between the array elements and figure 2.4 illustrates the basic structure of an array processor in which all memory is distributed amongst the array elements.

If all memory is shared then the switch network connecting the array units to the memory must be capable of sustaining a high rate of data transfer, since *every* instruction will require massive movement of data between these two components. Alternatively, if the memory is distributed then the majority of operands will hopefully reside within the local memory of each processing element (where processing element = arithmetic unit + memory module), and a much lower performance from the switch network can be tolerated. The design of the switch network is of central importance, and this topic is covered in chapter 3.

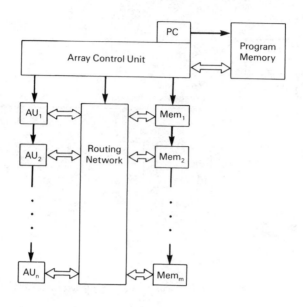

Figure 2.3 Array processor with global shared memory

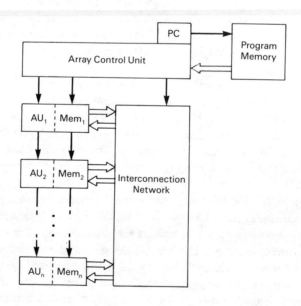

Figure 2.4 Array processor with distributed local memory

These two styles of array processor architecture are typified by the highly influential machine, which had a fully distributed memory, and the ill-fated Burroughs Scientific Processor (BSP), which had a shared memory.

2.1.2   ILLIAC IV — a distributed-memory machine

The ILLIAC IV system was the first real attempt to contruct a large-scale parallel machine, and in its time it was the most powerful computing machine in the world. It was designed and constructed by academics and scientists from the University of Illinois and the Burroughs Corporation. A significant amount of software, including sophisticated compilers, was developed for ILLIAC IV, and many researchers were able to develop parallel application software.

ILLIAC IV grew from a series of ILLIAC machines. The work on ILLIAC IV began in the 1960's, and the machine became operational in 1972. The original aim was to produce a 1 GFLOP machine using an SIMD array architecture comprising 256 processors partitioned into four quadrants, each controlled by an independent control unit. Unfortunately, as is often the case with such ambitious projects, escalating costs and unforeseen engineering problems resulted in just a single quadrant being built. The clock speed of the machine was intended to be 25 MHz but this too had to be reduced to 10 MHz, due partly to signal transmission delays resulting from the machine's large physical dimensions.

The processors in each quadrant were connected in the topology shown in figure 2.5. Although this looks superficially rather like a square-grid of connections it is in fact known as a *chordal ring* (see page 31), due to the shifted wrap-around of the boundary connections. Each inter-processor link consisted of a bi-directional 64-bit wide channel.

The control unit of ILLIAC IV, was responsible for performing scalar operations and issuing SIMD instructions to an array of 64 processing elements. These elements executed instructions in lockstep, although each processing element had the ability to execute instructions conditionally using *local* condition variables. This mechanism whereby processing elements selectively 'sit out' instructions makes the machine particularly flexible, and is a feature that has been included in all subsequent SIMD machines. It can even be seen in some vector machines in the form of control vectors (see volume I, section 9.2.5). Instructions for both the scalar section and the ILLIAC IV array were stored in the 2048×64-bit local memories associated with each processing element. These memories were constructed using thin-film storage devices and had access and cycle times of 120 and 240ns respectively. The control unit (CU) interface to these memories was a further example of array parallelism in operation; the data pathway between the CU and the memories was 512 bits wide permitting the CU to access

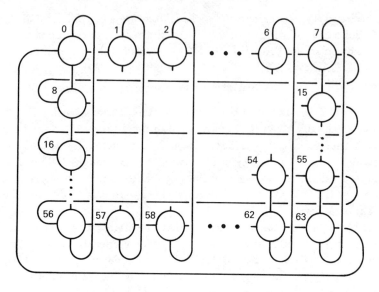

Figure 2.5 ILLIAC IV processor interconnection topology

one 64-bit word from each memory module in one *row* of processing elements concurrently (and at a common address), thus achieving an effective peak memory bandwidth of 1 word every 30 ns.

Although the actual performance of ILLIAC IV on real applications was only 2 to 4 times that of a CDC 7600, the machine is of significant historical value since it is arguably the origin of all subsequent parallel machines. Details of the architecture and of ILLIAC IV are given in Barnes *et al.* [BBK*68], and an account of the development of the machine is presented by Falk [Fal76].

2.1.3   BSP — a shared-memory machine

The Burroughs Scientific Processor (BSP) was effectively a successor to the ILLIAC IV machine, but with an architecture modified to reflect the fact that the BSP was intended to be a commercial product. It had fewer processing units than ILLIAC IV, just sixteen in the pre-production version, and most importantly these sixteen processors all enjoyed equal access to a common logical address space which was divided into a number of physically separate memory modules. The basic structure of the BSP is illustrated in figure 2.6. Each processing element was nothing more than an arithmetic unit with input and output registers, and these units were homogeneous and non-pipelined.

The BSP was a 48-bit machine, and each arithmetic unit (AU) per-

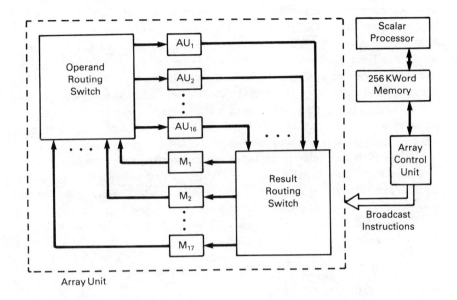

Figure 2.6 BSP array unit architecture

formed floating-point addition and multiplication in two 160 ns clock periods. The four units which constitute the array (the AUs, memories, result routing switch, and operand routing switch) formed a five-stage macro-pipeline, and by careful scheduling of micro-instructions the CU was able to overlap instructions in order to maximise the utilisation of the macro-pipeline. The BSP operated by partitioning multi-dimensional array operations between the AUs on an element-by-element basis. The CU received instructions from the scalar processor and decomposed them into micro-operations which were then scheduled using 'templates'. These were effectively pre-computed assignments of the five stages in the circular macro-pipeline to the micro-cycles within each instruction.

A typical sequence of micro-operations required to process each group of sixteen operands would be

1. read operands from memory
2. route operands to AUs
3. perform arithmetic operations
4. route results to their memory modules
5. write results to memory

The BSP provides equal access to all memory modules, from all arithmetic units, and as such is able to hide the array-like features of the machine from software. In practice the programming of the BSP, and the types of language structures most suitable for the form of parallelism it embodies, are reminiscent of vector processors. This is in fact true of all array processors with globally accessible operands, since parallel array units can be organised as simple cyclic arrays, and cyclic array structures have the same performance characteristics as pipeline structures. The BSP manages to achieve a high performance connection between an array of arithmetic units and an array of shared memory modules by a rather novel address interleaving mechanism, and this is worth considering in a little more detail.

In the BSP the unit of parallelism is the vector, and elements of these vectors are accessed at index locations which can vary by a fixed increment. This increment may be any integer value, and this allows rows, columns and diagonals of multi-dimensional arrays which are mapped on to a BSP vector to be extracted by the CU with ease. For example, a two-dimensional array X may be defined in Pascal notation as

```
X : array [1..column_length, 1..row_length] of real;
```

and in the BSP this would be laid out in memory in a column-wise manner. Therefore, to extract a column requires an inter-element *stride* equal to 1, and to extract a row requires a stride equal to column_length. Arbitrary diagonals can be extracted by using a stride equal to column_length + 1 or column_length - 1. High performance processing of these arrays is achieved by extracting sixteen elemental operand sets and presenting them to the sixteen arithmetic units in parallel, and naturally maximum throughput of the array can only occur if all elements are located in different memory modules. The interleaving scheme in the BSP therefore incorporates 17 memory modules, the lowest prime number greater than 16. For memory address a, the module number m containing that address is hence given by

$$m = \mid a \mid_{17}$$

and the offset within module m is given by i

$$i = \left\lfloor \frac{a}{17} \right\rfloor$$

This means that if we pick 16 values for a, separated by a constant value d, each will yield a different value for i provided d is not a multiple of 17. This results in a high probability of conflict-free access to many common array structures.

The movement of operands between memory modules and arithmetic modules was performed by two routing switches, one for input and one for output operands. Each routing switch comprised a full 16 × 17 cross-bar switch, moving data in units of 48 bits, plus error control bits. These switches had a maximum throughput of 16 words every 160nS, or 100 Mwords per second. The memory modules had a cycle time of 160nS, and most arithmetic functions required two clock cycles. This gave the BSP a peak operating speed of 50 MFLOPS.

Only a single pre-production version of the BSP was ever produced; by the time it had completed its development phase it had been superseded by the CRAY-1, and in 1979 Burroughs suspended the BSP project. One of the primary reasons for the demise of the BSP was arguably the decision to go for a slow clock speed and *non-pipelined* logic in the arithmetic units. This resulted in a lower peak performance than would otherwise have been possible from the ALUs, but made tractable the problem of connecting a small but significant numbers of ALUs to a physically common memory. The designers of the BSP believed that the ease with which its peak performance could be approached would counteract the slow clock speed argument, and as Austin observed [Aus79]

> "Simply put, the clock frequency does not indicate how fast a machine runs, just how often it stops !"

If the arithmetic units of the BSP had been pipelined internally the whole machine would have had a structure similar to a multiple-pipe vector machine, such as the CYBER 205 (see volume I, chapter 9) or the NEC SX Series machines [WKI86].

Despite the curtailment of its commercial career the BSP is often cited as an example of a global-memory array processor, and excellent accounts of its detailed architecture and engineering can be found in Kuck & Stokes [KS82] and Hockney & Jesshope [HJ81, pages 198–211]. The cost of providing full access to all memory modules in a shared-memory SIMD architecture has meant that to date no large-scale commercial systems have used this form of architecture.

2.2 Performance issues

To analyse the operational performance of processor arrays, on real problems, we need to model such systems at two levels, the *instruction* level and the *program* level. At the level of individual array instructions the mapping of application parallelism to the available hardware parallelism determines the net processing rate for the duration of a single operation, and this can be modelled fairly straightforwardly. At the level of a complete program the mix of highly parallel array instructions and sequential host-processor instructions determines the effective speedup bounds, and these depend ultimately on the structure of the application being processed.

Let us consider the evaluation of a single array instruction on a two-dimensional array of single-bit processing elements. Firstly, let us assume that the instruction in question defines a word-length operation over an $N \times M$ array of w-bit words. Secondly, let us also assume that the array processor consists of a grid of $x \times y$ bit-serial processing elements, each with a clock frequency of ϕ cycles per second. For example, in the ICL DAP (described in section 4.1), $x = y = 64$ and $\phi = 5 \times 10^6$.

Certain array processors[1] are capable of operating in one of two modes; *bit-parallel (word-serial)*, and *bit-serial (word-parallel)*. In bit-serial mode all word-length operations, for example 32-bit fixed-point addition, are implemented as loops of single-bit operations with each processing element operating on a unique pair of operands. In bit-parallel mode w single-bit processing elements operate in concert (rather like a w-bit ALU) to produce a w-bit result. In the best case xy/w word operations can take place concurrently. The organisation of bit-parallel and bit-serial operations is explained in more detail in section 4.1.3.

Hence, NM is the degree of parallelism within an array operation, xy is the degree of hardware parallelism when operating in a bit-serial fashion, and (assuming $w = y$) x is the degree of hardware parallelism when operating in bit-parallel mode.

To gauge the performance of a single array operation one must look at how an $N \times M$ problem can be folded onto an $x \times y$ array of processing elements. Without any sophisticated re-positioning of data values, the *array utilisation* in bit-serial mode, E_{bs}, is simply given by

$$E_{bs} = \frac{NM}{xy \left\lceil \frac{N}{x} \right\rceil \left\lceil \frac{M}{y} \right\rceil} \qquad (2.2)$$

The *throughput* in bit-serial mode depends on the chosen word length, and so to model the throughput we must include the number of clock periods required to complete a single-bit operation, β, and the number of single-bit operations required per word operation, α. In practice α will be a function of w. This gives an equation for throughput, W_{bs}, of

$$W_{bs} = \phi E_{bs} \frac{xy}{\alpha \beta} = \frac{\phi NM}{\alpha \beta \left\lceil \frac{N}{x} \right\rceil \left\lceil \frac{M}{y} \right\rceil} \qquad (2.3)$$

If we now examine how the same $N \times M$ problem can be folded on to an array of N rows of processing elements operating in a bit-parallel configuration we find that the array utilisation, E_{bp}, is now given by

$$E_{bp} = \frac{NM}{x \left\lceil \frac{NM}{x} \right\rceil} \qquad (2.4)$$

---

[1]Both the ICL DAP and the TMC Connection Machine are capable of operating in these two modes.

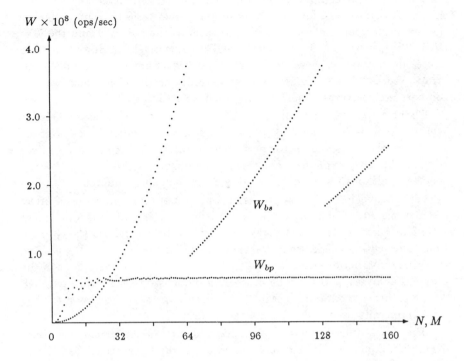

Figure 2.7 Raw performance curves for an SIMD-array processor

Here we get somewhat similar performance, but we are now folding in only *one* dimension. The throughput of the array, in this mode of operation, is now dependent upon ρ; the time to perform a single word operation using ripple-carry addition. For example, when the DAP (see section 4.1.5) is performing 32-bit integer arithmetic, and assuming 4 bit-positions of carry-propagate per clock period, we can expect a value of ρ in the range 8–10 clock periods. This produces a bit-parallel arithmetic throughput of W_{bp}.

$$W_{bp} = \phi E_{bp}\frac{x}{\rho} = \frac{\phi NM}{\rho\left\lceil\frac{NM}{x}\right\rceil} \tag{2.5}$$

To present a clearer picture of the performance of array processors, the equations for W_{bs} and W_{bp} vs. N (with $M = N$) are plotted in figure 2.7, for values of $x = y = 64$, $\alpha = 44$ (32-bit integer addition), $\beta = 2.5$, $\rho = 10$, and $\phi = 10^7$. It can be seen than for small values of N and M processing in bit-parallel mode gives greatest throughput, but for value of N and M greater than about 25 bit-serial mode is fastest.

These raw throughput equations are useful for characterising the machine architecture, and for permitting simple comparisons to be made against the raw performance of vector machines such as the CRAY-1 and the CYBER 205 (see volume I, chapters 7 and 9 respectively). However, these figures do not tell us how fast a particular algorithm will execute on an array processor, and this is the only sensible metric with which we can compare architectures of such widely differing structure.

Chapter 10 in volume I discussed some realistic performance models for vector machines incorporating the notions of vectorisation level, average vector length and scalar:vector performance ratios. The concept of a two-state machine was explained, and this applies equally well to an SIMD-array processor, although some of the equations are a slightly different.

Let us consider an array processor which supports a mixture of array instructions and scalar instructions. Furthermore, let the ratio of issued scalar instructions to issued array instructions be r, and let the average time to execute a single scalar instruction be S clock periods. We assume that array instructions operate on a matrix of $N \times M$ word values, as in the previous analyses, and that the processing mode is bit-serial word-parallel. Although other modes are possible, limiting the present discussion to that most commonly used simplifies matters greatly.

The space-time diagram of figure 2.8 illustrates the machine activity during a mix of r scalar instructions and one array instruction. Expressing the efficiency of the machine, on a mix of scalar and array instructions, is now a relatively trivial task.

$$\text{efficiency} = \frac{\text{active space-time}}{\text{total space-time}} = \frac{rS + \alpha\beta NM}{xy\left(rS + \alpha\beta\left\lceil\frac{N}{x}\right\rceil\left\lceil\frac{M}{y}\right\rceil\right)} \qquad (2.6)$$

Upper and lower bounds on efficiency

The efficiency of an SIMD system depends on two factors: the amount of scalar processing, and the effect of folding the processing of a data structure of arbitrary size onto an array of fixed dimensions.

From equation 2.6 we can see that in the limit, as the proportion of scalar operations increases (that is, as $r \to \infty$), the efficiency is defined by

$$\lim_{r\to\infty} \text{efficiency} = \frac{1}{xy}$$

This is a rather weak lower bound on efficiency since only very inappropriate applications will have values of r which are large in comparison with $\alpha\beta NM/S$.

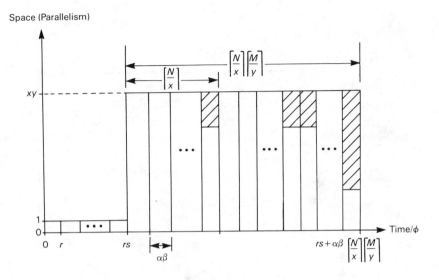

Figure 2.8 Space-time diagram for an SIMD-array processor

Conversely, as the proportion of scalar operations falls towards zero, the efficiency becomes

$$\lim_{r \to 0} \text{efficiency} = \frac{NM}{xy \left\lceil \frac{N}{x} \right\rceil \left\lceil \frac{M}{y} \right\rceil}$$

which is equivalent to equation 2.2. Therefore, we can consider the folding problem in isolation by assuming that $r = 0$.

Let us consider the best and worst case values for efficiency when the size of the data structure being processed is greater than the size of the physical array in both dimensions. The best case conditions for the folding problem occur when $N = k_1 x$ and $M = k_2 y$, where k_1 and k_2 are both integer constants. Under these circumstances the efficiency is unity. The worst case conditions, assuming $N \geq x$ and $M \geq y$, occur when $N = x + 1$ and $M = y + 1$. Then the efficiency is given by

$$\text{efficiency} = \frac{(x + 1)(y + 1)}{4}$$

This is always greater than 1/4, and hence the lower bound on efficiency when folding occurs cannot be less than 25%.

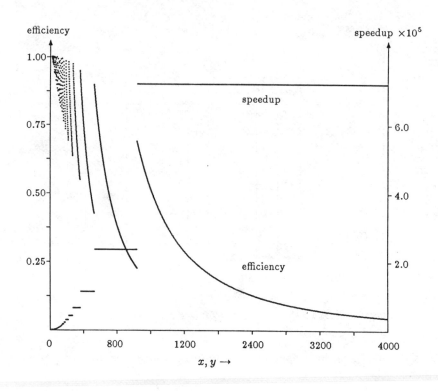

Figure 2.9 *Curves showing the relationship between computational effi-*
ciency, speedup and parallelism, in array processors

2.2.1   Scalability

One way of assessing the scalability of an architecture is to examine the performance of the system on a problem of constant complexity (fixed N and M) whilst varying the degree of hardware parallelism, x and y in the case of a two-dimensional array processor. Using the above models, it is possible to plot curves to show the relationship between computational efficiency, speedup and parallelism. Figure 2.9 illustrates these relationships, and it can be seen that as the size of the array increases the performance also increases, as one might reasonably expect, but that the efficiency falls away quite markedly. This is due to the *end-effects* becoming more noticeable as $x \to N$ and $y \to M$. It can be seen that speedup increases as a step function, as x and y increase. This continues until $x = N$ (and $y = M$), at which point all application parallelism is exploited optimally. Processor arrays larger than this do not exhibit any further speedup, and naturally their efficiency tends to an asymptotic value of zero.

One further point to note about the scalability of SIMD architectures is the problem of global synchronisation. If one assumes that all processing elements operate in lockstep, then the clock period of the array cannot be less than the time to propagate a broadcast instruction from the control unit to an arbitrary processing element. In a large array the propagation time of clock and control signals through fan-out logic will become noticeable. The fan-out delay will naturally grow logarithmically with the number of processing elements, but the transmission of signals takes $\Omega(n^{1/3})$ time, for an n-processor system. Proof of this is left as an exercise for the reader.

2.3 Summary

The evolution of array processors can be traced as far back as 1958, when Unger published a paper entitled "A Computer Oriented Towards Spatial Problems" [Ung58], from which the first array processor SOLOMON was developed [SBM62,GM63]. The SOLOMON design consisted of a two-dimensional array of 32×32 processing elements (PEs), each of which had 128 32-bit words of store and a bit-serial arithmetic unit. All PEs acted in unison, under the control of a single stream of broadcast instructions. The SOLOMON design had a major effect on the subsequent thinking of computer architects, and led to the development of several important high-performance architectures including the ILLIAC IV machine [BBK*68,Fal76], the Burroughs Scientific Processor [KS82], the Burroughs PEPE machine [CGH*72,VC78], the Goodyear Aerospace Massively Parallel Processor [Bat80], the Goodyear Aerospace STARAN [Bat74,Bat76] and [Bat77], and the ICL Distributed Array Processor (DAP) [Red73]. The advances in VLSI technology which led to the microprocessor revolution also had an impact on the design of SIMD array processors. The reduction in mimimum feature size, and the availability of high-density gate-arrays and full-custom VLSI as a means of realising a particular implementation contributed towards the construction of the Connection Machine [Hil85] by Thinking Machines Corporation in 1985. In chapter 4.1 we use the ICL DAP and the TMC Connection Machine as examples of practical array architectures and describe their operation in some detail.

3 Interconnection Networks

The first half of this book is concerned essentially with the ways in which massive data parallelism can be processed by large numbers of processing elements, acting in concert, under the control of a single sequence of common instructions. As outlined in chapter 2, these processing elements may either share a common memory or be provided with their own private memories. This leads to the two general array architectures shown in figure 2.3 and figure 2.4. In both cases an *interconnection structure* is required, either to provide all processors with equal access to a number of parallel memory modules, or to provide a data communication mechanism between processing elements. The second half of this book is concerned with parallelism of a different form; where large numbers of processors cooperate asynchronously on different parts of the same task, either through shared access to the data structures which define the problem or through a distribution of the problem coupled with the occasional exchange of messages between processors. Again, in both of these cases some form of interconnection structure is required; either to provide concurrent access to a shared memory structure, or to provide a message-routing facility.

The throughput of the interconnection structure, whether for use in SIMD array processors or in an MIMD system, should match the combined bandwidth of the processing elements, and must therefore be capable of supporting a large number of parallel connections. This chapter considers the design of such parallel interconnection structures, and most of the material is relevant to both the major forms of architecture discussed in subsequent chapters.

Conceptually, the simplest way to provide a full connectivity between m source units and n destination units is with a cross-bar switch, as shown in figure 3.7. The cross-bar switch is capable of realising any one-to-one, or one-to-many, set of connections. However, the hardware cost is proportional to $m.n$, and as m is normally similar in magnitude to n this equates to approximately n^2. This makes such interconnection structures impractical for highly parallel systems, where n and m are typically in the range 2^8 to 2^{16}. Designers must forgo the luxury of full connectivity, and accept more restricted, or slower, communication structures.

In an SIMD system the movement of data through the interconnection structure takes place under explicit program control. Therefore, data-movement instructions must define source-to-destination mappings, known as *routing functions*, from which network control signals can be generated. If the source-to-destination mapping defines a unique destination address for every possible source address, then the routing function is a *permutation* on the source address, and can be defined mathematically. This useful property of interconnection networks is explained in more detail in section 3.2.

3.1 Characteristics of interconnection structures

The design-space of interconnection structures can, according to Feng [Fen81], be represented as the Cartesian product of four primary design features: operating mode, control strategy, switching method and topology.

The operating mode of an interconnection structure refers to whether the transfer of data takes place *synchronously* or *asynchronously*. The operating mode of an SIMD interconnection structure is usually synchronous, since all processing elements will typically perform data-movement operations simultaneously. The operating mode of interconnection structures for multiprocessor systems is normally asynchronous, since the initiation of data movement is controlled by independent instructions in each processor.

Interconnection structures consist of *active* switching nodes connected by *passive* links. They can be represented as graph structures in which the active switching nodes form the vertices and the links between them form the edges. In order to implement specific routing functions a set of control signals must be generated for every active component. These control signals could be generated by a single control unit, using information about all the connections required; this is known as *centralised* control. Alternatively, the control signals may be generated locally, using only information about the input-output mappings required of a single switching node or a group of switching nodes; this is known as *distributed* control. Interconnection structures for SIMD systems normally use centralised control, whereas multiprocessor interconnection structures normally incorporate distributed control.

The switching method relates to the physical extent and duration of the switch settings for a particular routing function. There are two switching methods in common usage: circuit switching and packet switching. A third method which incorporates elements of packet and circuit switching, known as hybrid switching, has been suggested by Siegel and McMillan [SM81]. Circuit switching is normally used, in conjunction with a centralised control structure, for SIMD systems or bulk data transmissions. It has a relatively low control overhead, and requires relatively simple switching nodes. Packet switching is most commonly used in multiprocessor and other MIMD systems, or where short bursts of data transmission are required. The packets are normally self-routing, requiring complex switching nodes; often under distributed control. Routing conflicts are possible when self-routing packets are used, and this in turn requires a *conflict resolution strategy*. Examples of conflict resolution strategies are given in section 4.2.3 which describes an adaptive approach to conflict resolution for a large SIMD array processor, and in chapter 7 which describes several strategies used in a variety of shared-memory multiprocessor systems.

3.2   Network routing functions

A large number of network structures have evolved during the last few decades, with the early research in this area being conducted by telephone companies [Ben65,Wak68] that needed ever larger and more efficient circuit switching exchanges. More recently the application of interconnection networks to parallel computers has been investigated [MGN79,Fen81,Sie79] and [Law75].

The requirements of parallel computing structures are somewhat different from those of a telephone system. In a telephone network requests for the connection of a circuit-switched link between an originator and a respondent may occur at any time. The primary aim is to maximise the number of concurrent circuits. In a parallel architecture a network is required to support either processor-to-memory connections or processor-to-processor communication links. It is instructive to visualise an interconnection network in a parallel computer simply as a 'black box', with a number of input ports and a number of output ports, which performs a specified *routing function* to connect inputs to outputs.

In SIMD systems, where a single instruction operates on a multiplicity of data, the routing function may be completely defined within each data-movement instruction. Consequently all input-output connections will be distinct. Much of the remainder of this chapter discusses interconnection networks which fall into this category. In MIMD systems, where each connection is defined by individual processors operating independently, no assumptions can be made about the input-output connections requested by each processor. For example, two processors may both request data from the same shared memory bank simultaneously, resulting in network requests with distinct input ports but the same output port. Although this problem is not found exclusively in MIMD systems (for an example of routing conflicts in SIMD systems see section 4.2), most of the research into solving this problem had been on MIMD systems.

An idealised interconnection structure takes a set of labelled input ports and sets up a number of connections them to a similar set of output ports, as shown in figure 3.1. In order to simplify this discussion of interconnection networks it is assumed that the number of input and output ports in the network are equal. Hence if we define A to be an ordered set of N port

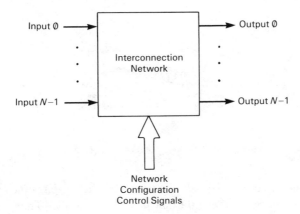

Figure 3.1 Idealised interconnection structures

labels

$$A = \{0, 1, 2, \ldots, N - 1\}$$

A routing function f is is a function from port labels to port labels, thus

$$f : A \rightarrow A$$

If f is an injection on A, then it can often be represented as a sequence of simple permutations of the labels in A. For example, if A represented a labelled deck of playing cards then a possible permutation to perform would be a perfect shuffle, and in fact this is a very useful permutation for interconnection networks.

Perfect-shuffle permutations

A perfect-shuffle permutation of port labels can be used to map from a set of source labels S to a set of destination labels D. The ordered set of input labels is divided into two subsets of equal size which are then interleaved. This can be represented by the bipartite graph of figure 3.2, from which it can be observed that this permutation can be produced by a simple manipulation of the binary representation of the source label. If we express a port label as an ordered set of binary digits, x, such that

$$x = \{a_n, a_{n-1}, \ldots, a_2, a_1\} = a_n.2^{n-1} + a_{n-1}.2^{n-2} + \cdots + a_1$$

then it is a relatively simple matter to define formally the perfect-shuffle permutation. Observing the source and destination port labels for $N = 4$,

$$
\begin{aligned}
S &= \{\{0,0\}, \ \{0,1\}, \ \{1,0\}, \ \{1,1\}\} \\
D &= \{\{0,0\}, \ \{1,0\}, \ \{0,1\}, \ \{1,1\}\}
\end{aligned}
$$

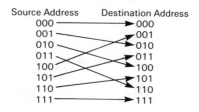

Figure 3.2 The shuffle permutation for $N = 8$

it can be seen that a perfect-shuffle permutation consists of a simple circular rotation of the port label bits one place to the left. Thus, we define the perfect shuffle permutation $\sigma(x)$ to be,

$$\sigma(x) = \{a_{n-1}, a_{n-2}, \ldots, a_1, a_n\}$$

It is also possible to rotate just a part of the binary representation of x, and this gives rise to the *super*-shuffle and *sub*-shuffle permutations. The kth super-shuffle, denoted σ^k, involves a rotation of the *most* significant k bits in x, thus

$$\sigma^k(a_n, a_{n-1}, \ldots, a_2, a_1) = \{a_{n-1}, \ldots, a_{n-1+1}, a_n, a_{n-k}, \ldots, a_1\}$$

The kth sub-shuffle, σ_k, involves a rotation of the *least* significant k bits in x, thus

$$\sigma_k(a_n, a_{n-1}, \ldots, a_2, a_1) = \{a_n, \ldots, a_{k+1}, a_{k-1}, \ldots, a_1, a_k\}$$

The main reason why the perfect shuffle alone is not sufficient to implement a full interconnection structure can be seen by observing figure 3.3, which depicts the perfect shuffle permutation in terms of all possible inter-nodal links. When the perfect shuffle permutation is repeatedly applied to x, effectively recirculating data through the network several times, we notice a number of unconnected groups of network ports. This is a consequence of the number of 1's and 0's in the binary representation of x remaining unaffected by the perfect-shuffle permutation.

The exchange permutation

Another useful permutation is the exchange permutation, $\epsilon_i(x)$, and this is defined as

$$\epsilon_i(a_n, a_{n-1}, \ldots, a_1) = \{a_n, a_{n-1}, \ldots, \overline{a}_i, \ldots, a_1\}$$

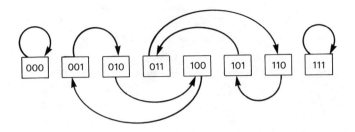

Figure 3.3 A recirculating shuffle network

Informally, the exchange routing function causes the movement of data to occur between pairs of network ports with labels whose binary representations differ only in the ith bit position. Therefore an eight-port ϵ_1 permutation yields the connectivity shown in figure 3.4. It may be noticed

Figure 3.4 Exchange permutations for $N = 8$

that the exchange permutation *does* alter the number of 1's and 0's in the destination label, compared with the source label, and consequently connects the disjoint groups of network ports produced by the perfect-shuffle permutation.

The butterfly permutation

The butterfly permutation, $\beta(x)$, is defined formally as

$$\beta(a_n, a_{n-1}, \ldots, a_2, a_1) = \{a_1, a_{n-1}, \ldots, a_2, a_n\}$$

Informally, the most and least significant bits in the binary representation of the network port label are interchanged, and this is illustrated in figure 3.5 which shows the bipartite graph for a butterfly permutation. Two variants of the straightforward butterfly permutation are possible, the kth sub-butterfly and the kth super-butterfly. The kth sub-butterfly permutation is

Figure 3.5 The butterfly permutation for $N = 8$

performed by interchanging bits one and k in the binary representation of x, thus

$$\beta_k(a_n, a_{n-1}, \ldots, a_1) = \{a_n, \ldots, a_{k+1}, a_1, a_{k-1}, \ldots, a_k\}$$

whereas the kth super-butterfly permutation is performed by interchanging bits n and k, thus

$$\beta^k(a_n, a_{n-1}, \ldots, a_1) = \{a_k, a_{n-1}, \ldots, a_{k+1}, a_n, a_{k-1}, \ldots, a_1\}$$

Visualising these permutations, as bipartite graphs, is left as an exercise for the reader.

The shift permutation

The shift permutation, $\alpha(x)$, is defined formally as

$$\alpha(x) = |x + 1|_N$$

Informally, the destination label is the numerical value of the source label plus one, modulo N. When represented as a bipartite graph the shift permutation looks like figure 3.6. The inverse of the shift permutation, $\alpha^{-1}(x)$, is also useful and can be observed by reading the bipartite graph for $\alpha(x)$ backwards. Hence

$$\alpha^{-1}(x) = |x - 1|_N$$

The shift permutation is an arithmetic permutation, rather than a logical permutation, as the label is permuted by a numerical function as opposed to a bit-manipulation function.

Permutations involving bit-manipulations, if capable of permuting any n-bit source label to an n-bit destination label, do so in a maximum of $n = \log_2(N)$ applications of the permutation. However, permutations involving incremental arithmetic functions on labels may require as many as N applications of the arithmetic function. As a consequence routing

Figure 3.6 The shift permutation for $N = 7$

functions constructed from shift permutations are not as powerful as those constructed from the exchange, shuffle and butterfly permutations unless the source and destination labels differ, on average, by less than $\log_2 N$.

The identity permutation

The identity permutation, $I(x)$, is defined formally as

$$I(x) = x$$

This permutation simply preserves the ordering of the input and is used to define inverse permutations such as $\epsilon^{-1}(x)$, the inverse exchange permutation, thus

$$\epsilon^{-1}(\epsilon(x)) = I(x)$$

or simply

$$\epsilon\epsilon^{-1} = I$$

3.3   Network topology

Having defined the characteristics of interconnection networks, and presented some formal routing functions, we now discuss their topology and physical implementation.

   An interconnection network can be depicted as a graph in which the nodes represent switching elements and arcs represent physical links. Such a graph is capable of describing the topology, but does not impart a great deal of knowledge about the network characteristics. Diagrammatic representations of network structures should not therefore be regarded as a comprehensive notation for the description of interconnection structures, although they are useful for the way in which they provide an immediate visual representation of the network topology.

In general, the input-output connections provided by a network may be either physical or virtual. If the links are dedicated, serving just two nodes, then the connections naturally represent a physical realisation of the network routing function. For example, the ring-structured topology depicted in figure 3.8 is a physical realisation of the shift permutation, $\alpha(x)$. Here there is a unique arc in the graph for every instance of the routing function. This type of network is known as a *static* network, and it can be characterised by the fixed routing between nodes, the dedicated links and the passive switching elements.

If the nodes between links are shared by several input-output connections, only one of which can be active at a time, then the network topology supports virtual connections. The cross-bar switch, shown in figure 3.7, is a good example of a network with virtual connections. The cross-bar realises

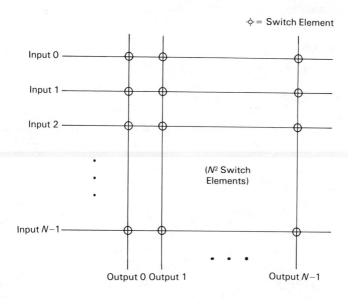

Figure 3.7 The cross-bar switch network

the routing function X, where

$$X(a) = b \;\equiv\; \neg\,(\exists c : X(c) = b)$$

Informally, X maps any a to any b if, and only if, it is not the case that there exists another input c which also maps to b. There is no longer a unique path through the network for every instance of the routing function, and hence there will be occasions when a cannot be routed to b. The routing function X is non-deterministic, in other words if a and c both want to map to b the routing function is not rich enough to decide which input maps to c and which does not. Nor does the routing function describe what happens to an input which cannot be mapped. These network characteristics are generally implementation dependent. This type of network is known as a *dynamic* network and can be characterised by the configurable routing structure, the shared links and the active switching elements.

3.3.1   Static networks

In a static network the connectivity between nodes is defined by the presence of physical links, and this makes the choice of network topology heavily dependent on the expected pattern of communication. The topology of static networks can be characterised very simply in terms of geometric dimensionality. Thus, we can define zero, one, two, three and even n dimensional networks, some examples of which are shown in figure 3.8.

Zero, one, two and three dimensional topology

The zero dimensional network is in fact a single network node, without any links to other nodes, and is shown here solely for the sake of completeness. It has a null routing function and no communication bandwidth. Increasing the dimensionality to 1 produces a chain of nodes; effectively a *bi-directional pipeline*. Linking the ends of the pipeline produces a simple two-dimensional *ring* topology. In a ring structure the throughput, the average path length between any two nodes, and the cost, are all proportional to N.

The topological 'dual' of the ring is the *star* network, and this has similar performance characteristics to a shared bus structure. The number of parallel connections is 1, the maximum distance between nodes is 1 and the cost is proportional to N.

Tree-structured networks have some useful properties, especially when the problems being solved can be decomposed into hierarchies of activity. The most important property is that the distance between any two nodes is always less than

$$2(\log_2(N+1) - 1)$$

The *rectangular mesh* network is another two-dimensional network, and is particularly suited to applications with highly localised inter-processor communications. It can be thought of as $2(n+m)$ inter-linked ring networks (where $N = nm$), and can therefore be expressed in terms of shift permutations. The number of possible data movement operations that can take place in parallel is proportional to N; however, the maximum distance between any two nodes is $\sqrt[2]{N}$.

If a network topology cannot be depicted without arcs crossing, then it is of three or more dimensions. Examples of three-dimensional static

0-dimensional

○ (Single Processing Element)

1-dimensional

─○─○─○─○─ (Chain)

2-dimensional

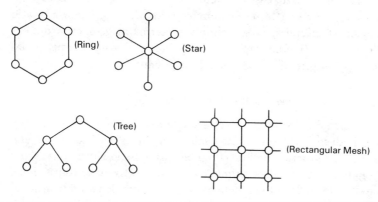

(Ring) (Star) (Tree) (Rectangular Mesh)

3-dimensional

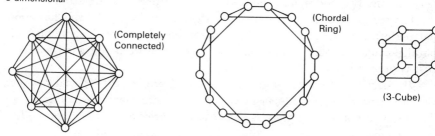

(Completely Connected) (Chordal Ring) (3-Cube)

Figure 3.8 Typical static networks

network topologies are the *chordal ring*, the *completely connected network* and the *3-cube*.

Variations on the chordal ring can be devised that are equivalent to square mesh networks with shifted wrap-around at the boundaries. This can be verified by a simple pencil and paper exercise, and in fact formed the basis for the ILLIAC IV interconnection network [BBK*68]. Such partially-connected chordal rings have a maximum distance between any two nodes of $\sqrt{N} - 1$.

The 3-cube consists of eight nodes connected in a three-dimensional cube structure, and is actually a particular instance of a more general network topology known as the *binary k-cube* [Pea77].

The binary k-cube

A binary k-cube, often referred to simply as a 'hypercube', connects $N = 2^k$ network nodes in the form of a cube constructed in k-dimensional space. The corners of this cube represent the nodes, and the edges represent the inter-nodal connections. More formally, if the nodes are numbered from 0 to $2^k - 1$, nodes whose binary numbering differs in exactly one position have connections between them. Figure 3.9 shows how binary k-cubes are constructed for k in the range 0 to 4.

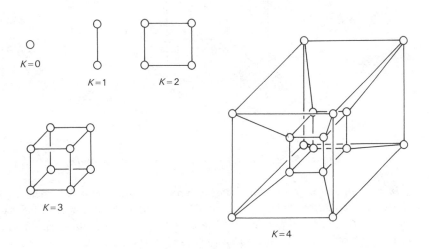

Figure 3.9 Constructing binary k-cubes

The binary k-cube therefore has k routing functions, $C_i \{0 \leq i \leq k-1\}$, one routing within each dimension, defined thus

$$C_i(x) = \{\epsilon_i \mid I\}(x)$$

Informally, for each dimension either an exchange permutation (ϵ_i) or an identity permutation (I) is applied to x in order to establish a route from any source to any destination node. A route from any source to any destination label can be found by starting at the source node and then comparing each bit in the source and destination labels in turn. If the bits are the

then the identity permutation is applied to the source label and the route
is not extended. If the bits are different, then the exchange permutation is
applied to the source label, and the route extends along the link connecting
the current node to a new node with a label equal to ϵ_i(current label).
Such a route is illustrated in figure 3.10. It is also apparent that since
the maximum number of bits required to identify n processors uniquely is
$k = \lceil \log_2 n \rceil$ the path length between an arbitrary pair of nodes is at most
k.

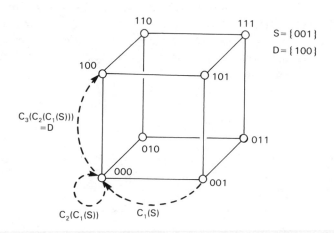

Figure 3.10 Routing in a binary k-cube network

It is immediately apparent that the binary k-cube has a very rich interconnection structure, with a total of $k2^{k-1}$ bidirectional connections, and
k communication links per node. One possible problem, which could limit
the number of nodes in an k-cube network, is the number of communication links required per node, and hence the physical complexity of the whole
network. In fact, it is the length of the interconnecting wires which poses
the most serious problem for networks with large values of k. This can be
shown by examining the rate of growth of the volume of the network.

The rate of growth of the inter-nodal distances in a binary k-cube depends on the length of one side of the machine. Since most machines are
~~b~~ ~~sically~~ in three-dimensional space, one side of a machine
is $\Theta(N^{1/3})$. Consequently, the time delay associ-
n of messages across the most significant dimension
be equal to $\Theta(N^{1/3})$. If the system is synchronous
he machine must decrease in proportion to this in-
vely, if each processor runs at $O(1)$ instructions per
between each communication event must increase in

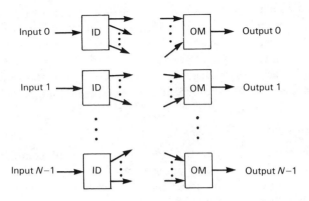

Figure 3.11 Single-stage dynamic network

proportion to the increased transmission delay. The net effect of increasing wire length is that the communication bandwidth per node decreases as the system becomes larger. This is essentially a problem of *physical scalability*, and is discussed with reference to multiprocessor systems in section 6.2.2.

The Cosmic Cube [Sei85] and Mosaic [Sei83] experiments carried out by Seitz at Caltech are typical of the kinds of architecture that can be constructed using binary k-cube topology, the commercial derivative of which is outlined in section 8.3.

3.3.2   Dynamic networks

A serious disadvantage of static networks is their lack of flexibility, and hence the need to provide physical links to match an *a priori* notion of the required pattern of communication. Dynamic network topologies normally support arbitrary communication patterns, and are therefore designed on the basis of their comparative throughput, cost and switching methodology rather than their physical structure.

Dynamic networks can be divided into two classes: single-stage and multi-stage. A single-stage dynamic network, depicted in figure 3.11, consists of a number of input demultiplexers (ID) and a number of output multiplexers (OM) connected according to a fixed permutation. A desired set of paths through the network is established by applying suitable control signals to the ID and OM switches. Under certain circumstances it may not be possible to establish a path to the desired destination in a single pass through the network, and the data being transmitted will be sent through the network two or more times. Such a network is known as a *recirculating network*.

The number of recirculations required to implement a particular routing depends upon the the connectivity of the network, and this leads to a trade-off between connectivity (cost) and routing time (1/bandwidth). At the extremes of this trade-off are the cross-bar switch, the most highly connected and costly single-stage dynamic network, and the shared bus, the least connected and cheapest form of single-stage dynamic network.

3.3.3 Multi-stage networks

When the required permutation for all input-output connections can be specified formally as a single homogeneous function a static network, such as a binary k-cube, can be used. However, when an *arbitrary* permutation of input-output connections is required a more flexible structure is required.

The Beneš network

As we have seen, the cross-bar switch is capable of connecting fully an arbitrary input-output permutation but at an impractically high hardware cost. In 1965 Beneš devised a method of reducing an $N \times N$ cross-bar switch to two $N/2 \times N/2$ cross-bar switches and two N-input exchange switches [Ben64], as illustrated in figure 3.12.

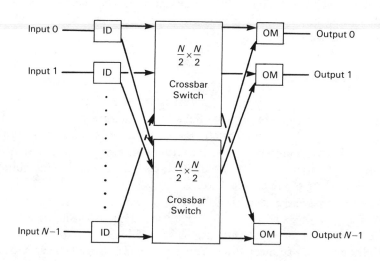

Figure 3.12 Beneš reduction of the cross-bar switch

The resulting $N/2 \times N/2$ cross-bar switches can be similarly reduced, and through this recursive trade-off between complexity and network latency a full connection network can be produced at a significantly lower cost than a full cross-bar switch. This network, illustrated in figure 3.13, is constructed entirely from 2-input 2-output switch-nodes, arranged as a sequence of stages connected by inverse shuffle permutations[1].

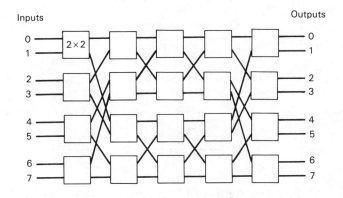

Figure 3.13 An 8-way Beneš network reduced to 2 × 2 cross-bar switches

The input-output mappings performed by the 2 × 2 switch-nodes may be either strict permutations of the inputs, or may include the upper and lower broadcast mappings $u_i(x)$ and $l_i(x)$, where

$$u_i(x) = a_n, \ldots, a_{i+1}, 0, a_{i-1}, \ldots, a_1$$

and

$$l_i(x) = a_n, \ldots, a_{i+1}, 1, a_{i-1}, \ldots, a_1$$

A general 2×2 switch-node routing function, E_i, can therefore be defined as a choice of one of the four switch settings illustrated in figure 3.14, expressed formally as

$$E_i(x) = \{\epsilon_i \mid I \mid u_i \mid l_i\}(x)$$

If only strict permutations are allowed, i.e. only $\epsilon_i(x)$ and $I(x)$, then a single control-bit per switch-node is all that is required to configure the network. If upper and lower broadcasts are allowed, then two control-bits per switch-node are needed. A Beneš network using strict permutation switches is capable of connecting all $N!$ permutations of N-inputs, and if upper and lower broadcasts are supported then all N^N well-defined input-to-output mappings can be connected. The Beneš network is known as a *rearrangeable* network since the switch settings can always be rearranged to accommodate any change of input-to-output mapping.

---

[1]The inverse shuffle, $\sigma^{-1}(x)$, is simply a right-circular rotation of the binary representation of x as opposed to a left-circular rotation for the ordinary shuffle permutation $\sigma(x)$.

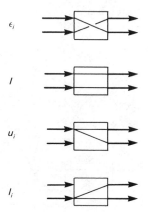

Figure 3.14 Generalised exchange switch mappings

Shuffle-exchange networks

In order to provide full connectivity the Beneš network requires $2\log_2(N)+1$ stages, each with $N/2$ switch-nodes. However, it is possible to reduce the cost of a multi-stage network still further by using a class of networks, which are not full connection networks, known as *shuffle-exchange* networks. In general, shuffle-exchange networks consist of a sequence of $\log_2(N)$ exchange permutations interspersed with shuffle or butterfly permutations.

On first inspection the following discussion on shuffle-exchange permutations may appear to be simply a notational convenience, but it is important to understand *how* a sequence of shuffle and exchange permutations can together form a useful network. The key to understanding multi-stage permutation networks is to consider the effect each successive permutation has on the label of an object in passage through the network. Assume that S is the label of an object entering the network, and D is the label of the destination of that object. We associate a temporary label L with the object, and this is initially set to S. If we can modify L by a sequence of permutations so that it becomes equal to D then the object will arrive at its destination.

Since the E_1 permutation provides us with the choice of inverting the least significant bit of the input label or leaving it intact, it is possible to use the E_1 permutation to make the least significant bit in L equal to the least significant bit in D. This is the basic step in converting from L to D, and the choice of ϵ_1 or I permutation determines the switch-node setting in the general exchange box of figure 3.14. The next step is to expose the next bit in L to the E_1 permutation, and this is done most simply by shifting L by one bit. This is directly equivalent to a perfect-shuffle permutation on all labels L in the range 0 to N, as shown for $N = 8$ in figure 3.2. After $n = \log_2 N$ applications of the shuffle and exchange permutations all bits in L will have been changed, and L will be equal to D. As a direct consequence of this, the object located at label L will have been routed to the output port identified by D, and the network will have performed its function.

A number of important multi-stage shuffle-exchange networks have been devised, and of these the *omega*, the *indirect binary n-cube* and the *banyan* networks are discussed briefly. The banyan network of Goke and Lipovski [GL73], denoted by the composite routing function Y_n, can be defined as a sequence of general exchange and butterfly permutations, thus

$$Y_n = E_1\beta_2 E_1\beta_3 \ldots \beta_n E_1$$

In this network there are $n = \log_2 N$ stages each consisting of $N/2$ active E_1 nodes, with successive stages connected by passive β_i permutations. This is illustrated in figure 3.15 which depicts a three-stage (8-input, 8-output) banyan network.

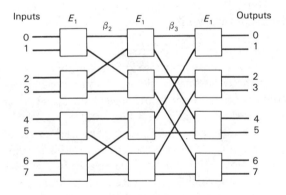

Figure 3.15 The banyan network

The n-stage Omega network of Lawrie [Law75], denoted by the composite routing function Ω_n, is defined as a sequence of shuffles and general exchange permutations, thus

$$\Omega_n = (\sigma_n E_1)^n$$

Lawrie's Ω-network uses switch-nodes with upper and lower broadcast capability, and it is worth noting that all stages in the network are identical. However, it can be seen from figure 3.16 that the Ω-network is incapable establishing connections from nodes 4 to 4 and 6 to 5 simultaneously. For this reason the Ω-network is a *blocking* network. In principle all multi-stage networks with log N stages are blocking networks, although techniques for overcoming blockages vary between implementations.

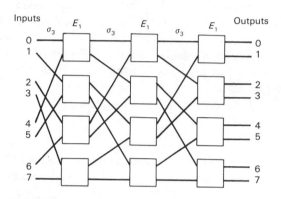

Figure 3.16 The omega network

The indirect binary n-cube suggested by Pease [Pea77], which we denote R_n, can be defined formally as

$$R_n = E_1 \beta_2 E_1 \beta_3 \ldots \beta_n E_1 \sigma_n^{-1}$$

The indirect binary n-cube, sometimes known simply as the *multistage cube*, is very similar to the Ω-network although the pairs of connections which it is unable to connect are different from those of the Ω-network. The indirect binary n-cube is illustrated in figure 3.17.

Although the shuffle-exchange class of networks are *blocking* networks they still have a rich interconnection structure, capable of supporting a large number of simultaneous connections, at a relatively low cost. Most high-performance computers which incorporate a multi-stage network use some form of shuffle-exchange switch, for example the Bolt Beranek & Newman Butterfly machine described in section 7.4.

Switch control mechanisms

A full connection network is one which is capable of realising every possible set of input-output connections. Blocking networks are not full connection

networks like the Beneš and the cross-bar *are* full connection
possible problem with these types of network is how one
trol signals for every possible permutation, since the ad-
nnection to an existing configuration of a Beneš network
ng connections to be re-routed.

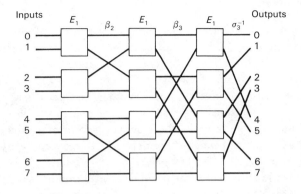

Figure 3.17 The indirect binary n-cube network

Given an arbitrary mapping and a full connection network, algorithms can be defined which analyse the mapping and factor it into a sequence of permutations [GS82], yielding as a result the control signals required to configure a set of switch-nodes. However, the best known algorithm for factoring an arbitrary permutation takes $O(\log^4 N)$ steps [OT68] compared with a total transmission latency through a typical multi-stage network of $O(\log N)$. Such techniques can therefore only be used to pre-analyse known network configurations in advance of their application, and this is the approach used in the IBM GF11 Array Processor [BDW85] which uses a modified Beneš network known as the 'Memphis Switch'.

The main difficulty with pre-analysis is that each permutation requires $\Omega(N \log N)$ bits of control information, and the network may be capable of configuring as many as $N!$ permutations. Needless to say, such quantities of control information could never be stored in full, and only a subset of the full set of permutations could be supported. This kind of switching is essentially static, and does not solve the problem of simultaneously moving large numbers of data items to unpredictable destination addresses.

The alternative to a centralised control strategy is a distributed control strategy in which each item of information is tagged with its destination address. Tags provide enough information to enable each switch node to compute its local switch setting dynamically, and hence then obviate the need to perform any pre-analysis. This introduces the problem of dealing with routing conflicts which can occur within a switch node, a topic which is discussed in more detail in section 7.4.4.

3.4   Summary

In this chapter we have introduced the theory behind interconnection networks without looking in any detail at how they are implemented in practice. This is covered in later sections which discuss individual machines incorporating these types of structure. There are two major categories of interconnection structure: static and dynamic, and each is appropriate for a different class of parallel system. We have seen how permutations are important in the design of multi-stage networks, and how they can be composed to create standard multi-stage networks like *omega*, *banyan*, and the *indirect binary n-cube*.

Interconnection structures are of fundamental importance in highly parallel systems. It is easy to replicate processing resources, and it is easy to replicate memory resources. However, to implement a high performance architecture through a replication of processing and memory resources an efficient method of connecting these components together *in parallel* is essential. This means providing an interconnection structure which supports a number of parallel input-output connections, preferably one where the number of input and output connections is not constrained by logical, electrical or physical limitations.

4   Practical Array Architectures

In each category of computer architecture, be it parallel or sequential, there are often one or two machines which embody a large majority of the principal techniques for that category of machine. In this text we have chosen to use the ICL Distributed Array Processor (DAP) and the TMC Connection Machine as examples of SIMD processor arrays, as they have particular significance, by virtue of their position in the chronology and taxonomy of these types of machine. The DAP, for example, was the first commercial exploitation of this style of architecture, a style which can be traced back many years. In particular, the design of the DAP owes much to the pioneering work carried out on the SOLOMON computer [SBM62], and later on the ILLIAC IV computer [BBK*68]. The Connection Machine represents a more recent evolutionary step embodying the integration of several processing elements on a single chip, and the consequent production of a massively parallel system. The target applications, and programming language, of the Connection Machine are also a departure from the conventional view of array processors as providers of high performance numerical facilities, and this is explored in more detail in the following chapter.

4.1   The ICL DAP

The DAP enjoyed moderate commercial success and extensive use by the scientific research community, particularly in the U.K. The success and architectural significance of this machine are due to a number of innovative features. For example, interactions between the array control unit and the two-dimensional array of processing elements can occur in either of the two dimensions. The architecture of the DAP also permits problems larger than the physical processor array to be processed without resorting to time-consuming overlay techniques.

The low cost of the DAP can be partially attributed to the use of conservative technology, although the method of connecting the DAP to its host processor certainly played an important part as well. The memories of the DAP processing elements are configured so that they appear, from the ICL 2900 host, to be simply an additional memory segment. The host therefore has full read/write access to the distributed memory within the processor array.

The architecture and technology of a machine should never be consid-

43

ered in isolation; more often than not technology is a limiting factor for the computer architect, effectively dictating what can or cannot be implemented at a reasonable cost. Occasionally, new technology gives rise to new architecture, rendering previously unimplementable structures feasible. Some of the most successful high-performance machines, particularly those designed by Seymour Cray, have been supported by such *technology-driven* advances. The DAP however is different, and is one of the most technology-independent of all high performance architectures covered in this book. This stems from the relatively low clock rate of 5 MHz, and the use of massive data-parallelism as a means of achieving high performance in preference to using very high speed logic and a pipelined architecture.

4.1.1   System architecture

The DAP, and its ICL 2900 host, together form a dual-processor system. The interconnections between the host, the array and their peripherals is illustrated in figure 4.1. It can be seen that the host has equal access to

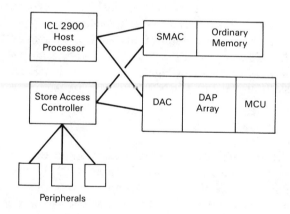

Figure 4.1 DAP system architecture

ordinary memory, via the Store Multiple Access Controller (SMAC), and the memory of the processor array, via the DAP Access Controller (DAC). The execution of array instructions takes place under the supervision of the Master Control Unit (MCU), and in parallel with execution of host instructions. The host steals unused DAP memory cycles when access is required.

The 2900 has a virtual memory architecture, enabling the physical DAP memory to be allocated anywhere within the virtual address space of a user of the host machine. The DAP memory then behaves as if it were a locked-in segment of virtual memory, and normal access permissions (read, write, execute) can be specified.

Input and output from the DAP are controlled by the host, and ordinary memory can be made available for the storing of incoming or outgoing DAP memory images in order to maximise the utilisation of the array.

4.1.2 Array architecture

The DAP unit as a whole, comprises five major functional parts, the Processor Array, the DAP Access Control Unit, the MCU Registers, the Instruction Issue Logic and the Array Control Unit. The relationships between these units are illustrated in figure 4.2.

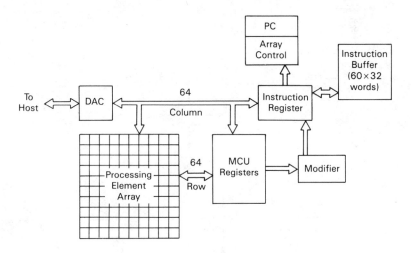

Figure 4.2 Organisation of the DAP

The primary route linking components within the DAP is the column highway. This 64-bit connection provides a mechanism for moving information between the host interface (DAC), or any of the DAP registers, and any row of Processing Elements (PEs) in the array. Each PE in the array is linked to one bit of the column highway and one bit of the row highway. This maps one 64-bit word, as seen by the host, into 64 single-bit entries in each row of processing element memories. The row highway enables 64-bit words to be transferred between the MCU registers and columns of PEs in the DAP array. Similarly, the row highway provides two-dimensional symmetry for data movements into and out of the array. The row and column highways, and the inter-PE connections are illustrated in figure 4.3.

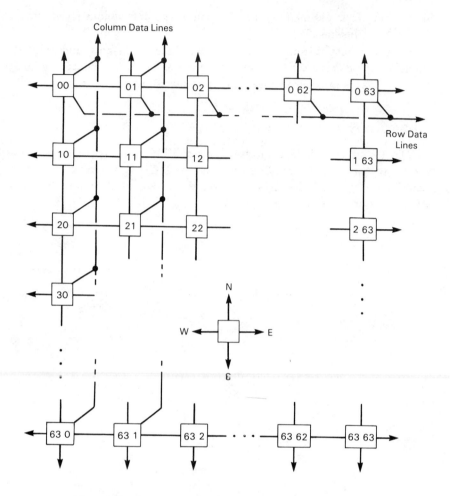

Figure 4.3 PE interconnections and MCU highways

Each PE has input connections from its four nearest neighbour processors in the North, South, East and West directions. The mechanism for dealing with the connections at the perimeter of the array is explained in section 4.1.4. An important feature of the DAP, from the manufacturing and construction point of view, is the simplicity and regularity of the array of PEs. The relatively low clock speed means that the layout of the processing elements is not critical and, by a careful mapping of the two-dimensional array on to printed circuit boards, connections between nearest neighbours can easily be kept short.

The DAP Access Control Unit interfaces the 2900 host to the column highway of the DAP array, allowing the host access to the memory of the processor array in units of 64 bits. The least significant 6 bits of the double word address from the host selects one row of PEs, and the memory associated with each one contributes a single data bit to the read or write cycle. Each processing element has 4096 bits of memory organised as a 4096 × 1-bit store. The mapping of bits in the array to bits in the host address space is illustrated in figure 4.4. Thus, a 64 × 64 DAP array has a total

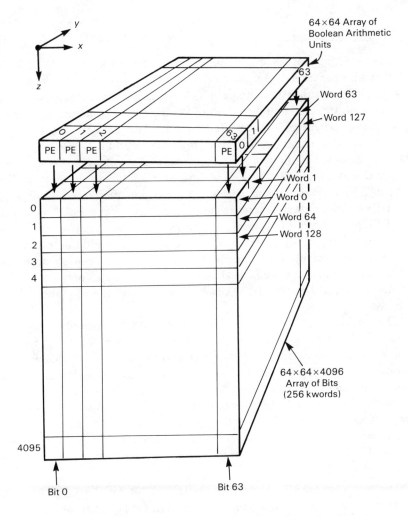

Figure 4.4 Three-dimensional structure of the DAP store

storage capacity of 256 K Words, or 16 M bits, with one PE assigned to each vertical segment of 4096 bits.

The instructions which make up a DAP program are stored in the array memory and, as each instruction is 32-bits wide, two instructions can be stored per row. This means that two instructions are fetched every time an instruction fetch cycle occurs. Within the instruction issue logic there is an Instruction Buffer, and this is capable of holding up to 60 instructions. It is used solely during the execution of loop instructions, when it is known that a group of contiguous instructions is going to be executed more than once.

4.1.3   PE architecture

The most striking feature about the processing elements in the DAP is the fact that all operations take place on single-bit operands. This leads to a very simple PE architecture and permits the construction of systems with as many as 4096 PEs. A simplified view of the internal architecture of a single PE is shown in figure 4.5. Each processing element consists of a single-bit adder, an input multiplexer, an output multiplexer and a 4096×1-bit store. The ALU consists of three one-bit registers, the accumulator Q, the carry register C and an *activity* bit A. The activity bit is used for local enabling or disabling of certain actions within the PEs, thus permitting a subset of the array to take part in whatever computation is in progress.

The input multiplexer selects data either from the output of one of the four nearest neighbours or from the local memory, depending on the instruction being executed (see section 4.1.4). The output multiplexer selects which source of information is used when writing to the local memory. The options include the output from the local adder and the row and column highways.

The single-bit adder performs full addition of the accumulator and the selected input, with an optional carry input. The selected input may be complemented before addition, enabling subtraction and logical inversion operations to be implemented. The carry-in to the single-bit adder may come from one of two sources, either the local carry register or the carry-out of the Eastern neighbour, depending on the operating mode of the array. This choice permits the DAP to perform word-arithmetic in two quite distinct ways, either *bit-serial (word-parallel)* or *bit-parallel (word-serial)*. These two modes of operation are illustrated diagrammatically in figures 4.6 and 4.7.

The normal mode of arithmetic in the DAP is bit-serial word-parallel. In this mode word values are assumed to be stored vertically as vectors of bits in the z dimension of figure 4.4. A full word operation is programmed out as a DO loop, consisting of n iterations, for n-bit words. Let us take as an example the addition of 64-bit integers, stored as the bit-vectors represented by $\underline{a}$, $\underline{b}$ and $\underline{c}$. To perform $\underline{a} + \underline{b} \rightarrow \underline{c}$ we must index through these three bit-

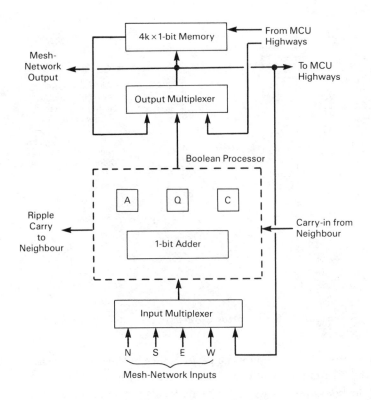

Figure 4.5 DAP processing element architecture

vectors, adding the two operands in bit-serial fashion, and storing the carry at each stage in the C register. This sequence of operations can take place in up to 4096 PEs simultaneously. Therefore, whilst the time to perform a single Integer Add takes many clock cycles, the massive parallelism can nevertheless produce very high overall processing rates.

An alternative method of performing word arithmetic, which is supported by the DAP system software, involves configuring each row of PEs as a 64-bit ripple-carry adder. This permits words stored in the x-dimension to be operated on directly with a guaranteed carry-propagate speed of at least four bit-positions per clock period. Under this scheme the three operand addresses are scalar values, addressing a single bit in each row memory. Although this method of processing is essentially word-serial within each row, the fact that there are 64 rows means that a moderate amount of word parallelism also occurs in this mode.

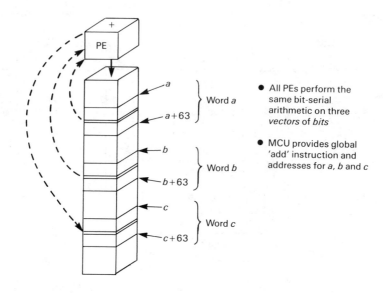

Figure 4.6 Bit-serial word-parallel mode of arithmetic

It is possible to compare the performance of these two processing modes, and the results for such a comparison are shown in table 4.1.   It is clear that the bit-serial word-parallel mode yields a much greater maximum performance level than the bit-parallel word-serial mode, and this is due to the relatively slow carry-propagate speed compared with the cycle time of the carry-save technique used in the bit-serial mode. However, the quoted performance figures are for *maximum* processing rates, and to achieve the maximum processing rate in bit-serial mode requires 4096 concurrent additions. Conversely, the bit-parallel mode of operation, whilst achieving a meagre 25 MOPS, requires only 64 concurrent additions to achieve this level of performance. Therefore, the final column in table 4.1 indicates how many concurrent integer additions are required to achieve 1 million integer

Table 4.1 Comparison of DAP processing modes

Word parallelism	Bit parallelism	Max. rate (MOPS)	Word parallelism per MOP
4096	1	213	19.2
64	32	25	2.56

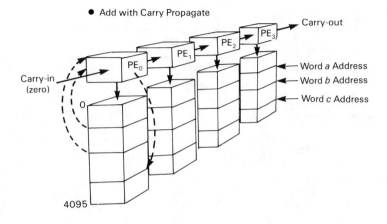

Figure 4.7 Bit-parallel word-serial mode of arithmetic

additions per second for these two main operating modes.

4.1.4 Instruction set

There are several important features of the DAP architecture which heavily influence the design of its instruction set. The most notable of these are

o Bit-serial arithmetic

o Two-dimensional array topology

o The MCU registers and the row/column highways

Coupled with these hardware features is the predominance of FORTRAN within the scientific computing community. In FORTRAN the primary control construct for coding iterative algorithms is the DO loop, and in order to eliminate loop-control overheads the DAP instruction set provides a special DO loop instruction.

Normally, the instruction issue logic fetches instructions from consecutive DAP locations, two at a time, and executes them. Both the fetch and execute cycles take 200 ns (for a 5 MHz clock) and therefore each sequential instruction takes on average 1.5 cycles. When a DO loop instruction is encountered, a field in the instruction format identifies how many instructions there are within the loop and these instructions are assumed to follow. When these instructions are fetched on the first iteration through the loop they are placed in consecutive locations within the Instruction Buffer, as

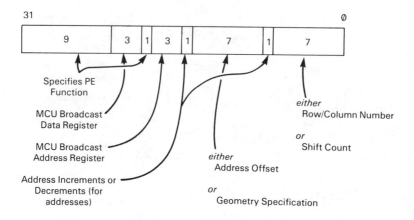

Figure 4.8 DAP instruction format

well as being placed in the Instruction Register. On the second and subsequent iterations through the loop, no instruction fetch cycles are needed,
thus saving an average of 1 cycle for every two instructions inside the loop.
The size of the Instruction Buffer limits the length of buffered DO loops
to 60 instructions. The DO loop format also contains a Count field, which
may be modified by the contents of an MCU register identified in the Modifier Register field. This Count value determines the number of iterations
through the loop.

The memory addresses used to access operands for instructions inside
DO loops may be auto-incremented or auto-decremented, by one, on each
iteration. This makes for relatively easy indexing through a vertical bit-
vector, and simplifies the implemention of bit-serial word arithmetic. The
fine control which the programmer has over the bit-level realisation of word
arithmetic is seen by many as a positive feature of the DAP instruction set.
It means that highly optimised macro sequences can be generated, for example to implement variable word-length arithmetic or very high precision
floating-point operations.

The DAP instruction format, illustrated in figure 4.8, contains a 9-bit
Operation-Code field and this, together with an Inversion bit for selecting
either a true or inverted input operand, identifies the instruction to be
executed. The MCU Register field identifies any data register which may
be required by the instruction, and the Modifier Register selects one of the
MCU registers to be used either as a modifier for memory addressing or as
a source of shift instruction parameters. The movement of data between

DAP memory and the MCU registers is also supported in the instruction set, and for these instructions one row or column must be specified as well as an address within the 4096-bit memory space. This is achieved by providing a 7-bit row/column identifier field and a 7-bit address field within the 32-bit instruction format. Both of these fields can be optionally modified by the contents of an MCU Modifier register, as illustrated in figure 4.9.

Another group of very useful instructions are those which perform data movement operations between processing elements. These operations make use of the two-dimensional square grid of inter-processor links to transfer data between the Q registers of adjacent PEs. The shift instructions move 64×64 bits of information in parallel, in any one of four directions, and through relative distances of up to 64 grid positions. Shift instructions also specify what happens at the boundary elements of the array, and here two options are available in each dimension. Either the boundary inputs are set to zero and boundary outputs are discarded, or else the boundary inputs are taken from the boundary outputs within the same dimension. Hence, East may be connected to West and North may be connected to South. These four geometries and their relationship to the instruction format are illustrated in figure 4.10.

The DAP approach to scientific software bears some similarity to the approach taken by Texas Instruments in their Advanced Scientific Computer (TI-ASC), described in volume I section 4.3. Both machines support the FORTRAN DO loop in their respective instruction sets to varying degrees of sophistication. The TI ASC provides support for triple-nested loops which are iterated sequentially. In comparison the DAP has a single-nested loop which evaluates all iterations of a double-nested 64×64 loop (in the x and y dimensions) in parallel.

4.1.5 Performance

In this section we look at the performance of the DAP in several ways. At the simplest level we examine the raw speed of its component parts and compare them briefly with other high performance scientific machines. This produces a set of *peak* performance figures, but does not advance any insight into how well the machine will perform on a real problem. This is remedied by using the simple analytical performance model introduced in section 2.2 to predict the performance, firstly of isolated array operations, and secondly of programs in general.

It is possible to characterise the raw performance of the DAP in terms of the bandwidth of the distributed memory, the serial arithmetic rate and the rate of data manipulation through the processing element network. The clock period of the production DAP is 200 ns, and in this time it is capable of performing one memory cycle in each processing element memory.

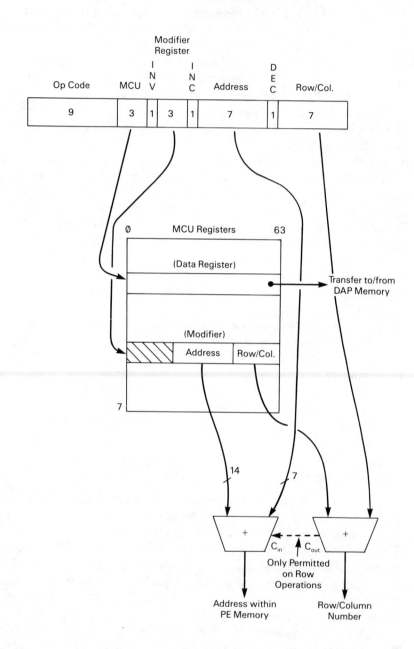

Figure 4.9 Word address modification in the DAP array

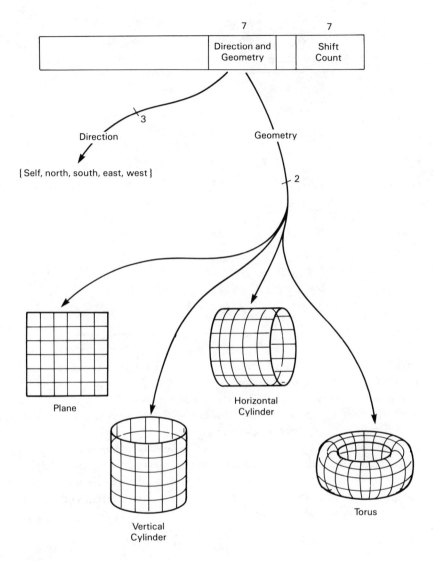

Figure 4.10 Configuration options for DAP shift instructions

Each memory operation involves one bit, and therefore the raw memory bandwidth is

$$\frac{4096}{2 \times 10^{-7}} = 20.48 \, \text{Gbits/s}$$

This is four times the 80 MWord/s effective memory bandwidth of the CRAY-1, although in fairness the CRAY-1 also has a very fast set of vector

Table 4.2 Instruction timings for the DAP

Operation	Time (μS)	Processing rate (MOPS)
$Z \leftarrow X$	17	241
$Z \leftarrow X * S$	40–130	32-102
$Z \leftarrow X^2$	125	33
$Z \leftarrow X + Y$	150	27
$Z \leftarrow \sqrt{X}$	170	24
$Z \leftarrow X * Y$	250	16
$Z \leftarrow X/Y$	330	12
$Z \leftarrow \mid Z \mid$	1	4096
$S \leftarrow \sum_{i=1}^{4096}$	280	175
$I \leftarrow J + K$	22	186

registers which provide all the operands for the computational units. The CYBER 205 has a memory bandwidth of 200 M Word/s per Pipe, and hence a 2-Pipe CYBER 205 has 25% more memory bandwidth than the DAP. This is a fair comparison since the CYBER 205 architecture implements memory-to-memory vector operations.

Arithmetic performance in the DAP is heavily dependent on the chosen word length, w; addition and subtraction requiring $O(w)$, and multiplication requiring $O(w^2)$ micro-cycles respectively. According to Reddaway [Red73], integer addition takes $3w + \Delta$ cycles, where Δ is a small constant value, and fractional integer multiplication takes

$$\frac{w \left(3w + 13\right)}{2}$$

cycles. Floating-point operations require extra cycles due to the exponent arithmetic, mantissae alignment and result normalisation. Table 4.2 shows the timing, and resulting processing rates for a representative sample of fixed and floating point operations, taken from [Red79]. All operations are in 32-bit precision and are hand-crafted, assembler-coded system routines. The X, Y and Z values are real arrays containing 4096 elements, S is a real scalar value and I, J, and K are integer arrays containing 4096 elements.

Several points are worth noting from these figures. Firstly, because bit-serial algorithms for transcendental functions are very different from their equivalent algorithms on bit-parallel machines we find that, for example, the time to compute the square root of a real number is less than the time to compute the product of two real numbers. The implementation of certain functions is trivial; for example, computing the absolute value of 4096 real numbers takes only 1 μs thus yielding a burst processing rate of 4096 MOPS. The technique of optimising at the bit level is exemplified by the $\sum$ operation which, instead of taking $\log_2(4096) \times 150$ (i.e. 1650) cycles, takes only 280 cycles.

These figures are all based on bit-serial arithmetic. As we have outlined earlier, bit-parallel arithmetic is also possible on the DAP, although the peak processing rates are much lower and the array is much less flexible in this mode.

A major feature of the DAP architecture is the two-dimensional PE interconnection structure. This structure is capable of shifting an array of 64 $\times$ 64 bits, held in the Q registers at a rate of one shift per clock period, excluding instruction startup overheads. Hence, to move a bit of information from one memory to another takes

$$x + y + \Delta$$

clock cycles, where x and y are the relative displacements of the source and destination memories within the array and Δ is a small overhead for instruction fetch and memory read/write cycles. The grid of interconnections and the Q registers together form a parallel switch with a peak throughput of 4096 bit position transfers per clock period, or 20.48 G bit-positions/s. It is also possible to use the row and column highways to move any single row or column of 64-bits into an MCU register, or to move the contents of an MCU register into one or all of the rows or columns of the array. These data transfer operations can be carried out at a rate of one every 2.5 clock periods. This is an extremely powerful mechanism, as it permits the rows and columns to be selected, exchanged or broadcast to the whole array very rapidly.

The performance of the DAP on real programs can be gauged by modelling the instruction execution rate as a function of the parallelism within the application. This was done in chapter 2 for a generic SIMD array processor, and the parameters of the model were chosen to be the same as the parameters of the DAP. Consequently the throughput and efficiency curves in figures 2.7 and 2.9 refer to the DAP.

4.1.6 The DAP-3

The DAP architecture was revived recently, when a company called Active Memory Technology (AMT) designed a new version of the DAP using VLSI.

This machine, known as the DAP-3, consists of a 32 × 32 array of processing elements similar to the processing elements in the original DAP. The clock speed of the DAP-3 is expected to be between 80–100 ns. This machine is physically much smaller than the original DAP, being housed in a relatively small desk-height enclosure, and is hosted either by a MicroVAX or a Sun workstation.

4.2   The Connection Machine

The designers of most of the major and influential high performance architectures each had a particular motivating philosophy which underpinned their design. For example, the philosophy of IBM S/360 is one of software compatibility across a wide performance range. This resulted in designs at the top-end of the performance spectrum which incorporated features that were transparent to software (pipelining and data-forwarding). Cray machines, on the other hand, have a design philosophy centred around intensive numeric calculations. Consequently, their machines all use vector pipelines coupled closely to a set of very fast vector registers in order to minimise startup times. The design teams for these machines made decisions based on their collective understanding of what constitutes an 'efficient' computing machine. Roughly speaking this means getting as many instructions as possible past the control point per second for as low a cost as possible, whilst satisfying numerous secondary design criteria such as physical size, power consumption, product-line compatibility, and so on.

Connection Machine design philosophy

The design philosophy of the Connection Machine [Hil85] sets out to challenge the conventional view of what constitutes an efficient computing machine, by shifting the emphasis from an obsession with instruction cycle times to a more realistic consideration processor-memory bandwidth requirements. In order to process information *decisions* must be made. In effect each decision produces one bit of information. If one analyses a complete computation at the macro-level it is obvious that to make faster computers one must either make the time for each decision shorter or make a number of decisions at the same time. Conventional machines generally take the first option, not by choice but because the programming model they are pledged to support requires a certain type of machine. The Connection Machine, in common with all SIMD-array machines, takes the second option and couples a novel parallel hardware structure with a new programming style.

The philosophy of the Connection Machine philosophy is one of removing the division between processor and memory by placing the processor *in* the memory to create a *cell* which is then replicated as a unit to create large and highly parallel systems. This form of logic-in-memory machine is no different in principle to the ICL DAP, or SOLOMON for that matter. What the Connection Machine emphasises is the *programmability* of the connections between processing cells. In this section we describe the hardware structure of the Connection Machine, and in section 5.1.2 we describe a parallel version of Lisp for the Connection Machine and look at a typical application.

4.2.1   System architecture

The prototype connection machine, known as CM-1, is manufactured by Thinking Machines Corporation (TMC), and its primary design goals are to test out the principles of connection machine architecture, and the CM-1 is only one of many possible implementations of a connection machine[1].

The system level architecture of CM-1 is illustrated in figure 4.11, wherein the similarity with the DAP (and most other SIMD array processors) is clearly visible. The array of processing elements, comprising a simple boolean processor and some local memory, is seen by the host machine simply as an extended region of memory. The host computer directs the connection machine to implement parallel portions of code, and in this respect it differs from the DAP which has an instruction processor built into the array unit. The CM-1 host broadcasts a sequence of instructions to the array micro-controller, which interprets the instructions and broadcasts an appropriate sequence of micro-instructions to the array of PEs, for each received host instruction.

The processor-memory cells, like those of the DAP, are so small and slow that individually they cannot perform meaningful computations. In CM-1, running CM-Lisp, these cells are linked together in data-dependent patterns called *active data structures*. Low-level operations on active data structures can be evaluated in parallel by the low-level boolean processors acting in concert on their local segments of those structures. This is how Connection Machines exploit parallelism and sustain high processing rates.

Network structure

An important feature of a connection machine is its support for programmable links between PEs. In the DAP, when one processor communicates with its Northern neighbour all processors must communicate with their Northern neighbour, or not at all. This is because the DAP has a static square-mesh communication network, which only supports eight routing functions. Communication in CM-1 is significantly more powerful than this,

---

[1]It could be argued that the DAP is also a connection machine.

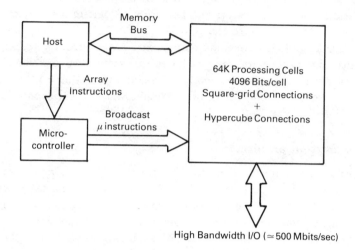

Figure 4.11 Architecture of the Connection Machine

since each group of sixteen processing elements share a link into a packet-switched binary 12-cube network, as well as having individual connections to a DAP-like grid (known as the North-East-West-South, or NEWS grid). Essentially this means that all PEs can compute the address of a PE to which they want to send a message, and then use the 12-cube network to route the message in logarithmic time. A two-dimensional grid routes messages in $O(\sqrt{N})$ time, where N is the number of PEs. A full set of N^N permutations are supported by a dynamic binary k-cube network, where $k = \log N$, and in the case of CM-1 this produces a quoted worst-case bandwidth of $\approx 3.2 \times 10^7$ bits/s and a best-case bandwidth of $\approx 1.0 \times 10^9$ bits/s. The operation of the CM-1 communication network is described in section 4.2.3.

Technology

The implementation of CM-1 relies on a single custom VLSI component which contains a group of sixteen boolean processors, a local controller, and a message-routing interface to the cube network. This chip is fabricated in CMOS technology, and contains approximately 50,000 active devices in an area of about 1 cm^2. It dissipates around 1 Watt when operated at 4 MHz. The local memory for each group of sixteen processors is supplied by four 4K×4-bit static RAM chips.

Each printed circuit board in the CM-1 processor array contains 32 sets of processor/memory chips, corresponding to 512 individual cells. This also represents the lowest five dimensions within the 12-cube network of a 65536-cell system. The PCB modules slot into backplanes containing up to 16 such modules, representing the next four dimensions of the cube. Two backplanes constitute a single rack, and each rack contains its own micro-controller. Four racks together make up a complete system, packaged a cube measuring approximately 1.3m on each side. The entire system is air-cooled and dissipates about 12 kW.

Implementing the higher-dimension network connections, between backplanes and between racks, requires a significant amount of wiring. In CM-1 this is constructed using controlled-impedance flat cables. All lower-dimension connections are routed on the module and backplane PCBs.

4.2.2 Processing elements

The processing element of CM-1 is a completely general-purpose single-bit processor with a private $4K \times 1$-bit memory. Whereas in machines like the MPP and STARAN special architectural features, such as shift registers, are introduced to support integer multiplication, in CM-1 the processor cell is kept as simple as possible. It is also highly programmable.

Figure 4.12 shows the logical structure of a CM-1 processing element. It consists of a single-bit arithmetic and logic unit, a file of sixteen single-bit registers (called flags) and connections from the local memory to the ALU and from the flags to the message router. The ALU is capable of realising all 256 possible boolean functions of three inputs (two memory operands and one flag), and it does this for both the value to be written back to memory and the value to be written back to one of the flag registers. This requires a total of sixteen bits of control input to the ALUs. In addition, the PE microcontroller must also specify the following parameters for each operation.

1. A-address and B-address. The two memory operand bits are read from the A and B addresses and the memory output from the ALU is written back to the A address location.

2. Read and write flag addresses. These specify one input flag for the ALU, and one flag register to which the flag output from the ALU is written.

3. Condition flag address. Specifies which of the sixteen flags is to be used to determine whether a conditional operation will take place locally.

4. Condition sense. Selects either active-high or active-low state for the condition flag selected.

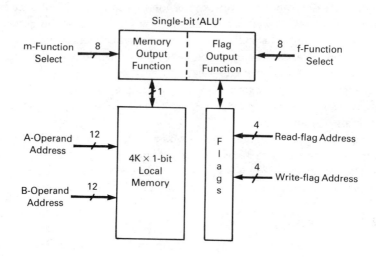

Figure 4.12 Structure of a CM-1 processing element

5. NEWS direction. Specifies which of the four 2D mesh permutations is selected for operations involving the NEWS grid.

The flag register file contains eight general purpose flags and eight special purpose flags. The special purpose flags provide links between the ALU (and hence memory) and the interconnection networks (that is, the NEWS grid and the router). For example, one read-only flag contains information written from the flag output of the neighbouring ALU in the direction specified by the NEWS direction controls. The sixteen PEs in each CM-1 processor chip can also be linked to form a chain of processors, as well as a square mesh, and this permits (rather slow) carry propagation across 16-bit slices of processing elements. So, whilst the design of the processing elements is not highly optimised for speed, the flexibility of the ALU and the flags together compensate somewhat, and the massive replication of the PEs puts their combined power of about 10^9 integer 32-bit additions per second, well into the supercomputer category.

4.2.3 The router

Each group of sixteen PEs shares a single message router, which itself constitutes one node in a binary k-cube network. In CM-1 $k = 12$, and so there can be a maximum of 4096 routers, with each router being connected directly to twelve other routers. For a formal description of the binary k-cube network topology and routing functions see section 3.3.1. The main

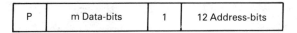

Figure 4.13 CM-1 message format

point to note here is that processors whose node addresses differ in only
the ith bit-position have a direct connection in the ith dimension of the
cube network. Since any two addresses can only differ in a maximum of
twelve bit-positions (that is, one is the inverse of the other) there can be at
most twelve unique links forming a path between them. Hence, in a k-cube,
no pair of nodes is separated by more than k links. We now describe the
operation of the packet-switched CM-1 network.

Routing algorithm

The routing algorithm used in CM-1 is based loosely on the standard routing
functions for binary k-cubes described in section 3.3.1. The message format,
shown in figure 4.13, consists of an address and a data field, with a one-
bit separator and a single trailing parity bit. The address of a message
comprises a *relative* router address field (12 bits), a PE address within a
group of sixteen (4 bits), and an address in the memory of the destination
processor where the message is to be deposited on delivery (12 bits). Router
addresses are said to be *relative* because they specify the distance to be
moved in order to get from the source to the destination processor. Hence,
a 1 in bit position i indicates that the message must be routed through
dimension i before it can arrive at its destination. Conversely, a 0 in bit
position i means that no routing through dimension i is required. Therefore,
when an address is all zeros the message must be at its destination. Also,
when a message is routed through dimension i *towards* its destination, bit i
must be *cleared*; and when routed away from its destination, bit i must be
set.

In the terminology of the designers of CM-1, each parallel message delivery cycle consists of a sequence of repeated *petit cycles*. In a single petit
cycle all messages which do not encounter routing delays (caused typically
by contention in the network) will be delivered. These petit cycles are repeated until all messages within a 'burst' of messages have been delivered.

Message bursts are normally associated with 'beta reduction' operations (see section 5.1.2). Each petit cycle consists of a sequence of twelve *dimension* cycles, and during the ith dimension cycle messages are routed (where required and where possible) through the ith dimension.

The injection of messages into each router occurs at the beginning of each petit cycle, but no more than four messages can be injected into each router on each cycle. This number may be reduced if insufficient buffering space is available in the router, since routers operate on a store-and-forward principle. This all means that each router must make decisions on which messages are accepted for injection, and on which messages are to be given priority for forwarding along connected links. The router does this by searching its buffers of pending messages during the ith dimension cycle to discover which messages have bit $i = 1$ in their relative node address field. An ith-bit set indicates that the message needs to be routed on the ith output link. The router chooses the 'oldest' such message, essentially implementing a first-come, first-served, policy. It is worth noting that whilst twelve routing functions must be applied to a message (some of which may be null) before it can be delivered, there is no *ordering* on the evaluation of these functions. Therefore, if a message is blocked during the first dimension cycle it can still be routed on the remaining eleven dimension cycles, subject of course to further blockages. However, it cannot be delivered until the first dimension cycle has been repeated successfully, and this takes at least one whole petit cycle.

Since routers can accept injected messages regardless of the blockages they may cause further on in the routing cycle, there is no obvious upper bound on the degree of store-and-forward buffering required at each node to cope with network congestion. The router is clearly hardware limited, so an occasional overflow mechanism must be provided. The mechanism used in CM-1 is called referral, and entail sending overflowed messages along 'unused' but incorrect links, effectively taking them further away from their destination. To do this the router simply selects an unused output dimension and *sets* the corresponding bit in the relative node address field for that message.

Referral also provides a means of supporting fault-tolerant networks. Failure of one node in the 12-cube network simply results in a permanent blockage of the 12 links to which it is attached. The adaptive routing policy then causes messages to be routed around the offending node, with some time penalty of course, but in a manner transparent to the software.

Network performance

The performance of the interprocessor communication network in the DAP is easy to analyse since all permutations are homogeneous[2]. However, in the Connection Machine routing functions are not homogeneous, and hence the distribution of message addresses can have a major effect on the net communication bandwidth.

It follows from the routing algorithm that the number of inter-nodal hops that a message must make is equal to the number of 1's in the destination address. Uniformly distributed message addresses will have a mean of $n/2$ 1's, where n is the number of bits in the address. Only one message can occupy each link during a single petit cycle, and during each dimension cycle only one twelfth of all communication links can be active. This is not a particularly efficient use of wire, the component which most severely limits the extensibility of cube-connected architectures. From the assumptions above we can predict the sustainable bandwidth of the network. A cube network with $N = 2^n$ nodes has $nN = n2^n$ wires in total. Since the number of 1's in all message addresses can only be changed to 0's at a rate of one per wire per petit cycle, in its steady-state the network cannot accept more than $n2^n$ injected address bits which are 1. This means it cannot accept more than twice this number of uniformly distributed messages. Thus there can only be $2N$ injected messages, or two injected messages per node, in each petit cycle.

The network does however contain some message buffering, and so at the beginning of a burst of messages the message-injection rate can be higher than two per node in each petit cycle. Higher levels of message injection can also be sustained when message addresses are localised. This must be considered when allocating elements of an active data structure to processing cells. Some operations naturally require local communications only. For example, steps in each beta-reduction operation specify near-neighbouring processors, and hence the number of 1's in each message address is just 1.

Another important consideration for message delivery in an SIMD system is that each burst of messages only terminates when *all* messages have been delivered. Where routing conflicts occur, additional petit cycles must be provided during the latter stages of the burst. Since all messages destined for the same node must be delivered *sequentially*, the maximum number of messages going to any one node during a burst of messages defines the number of additional petit cycles that will be required. Fortunately for the Connection Machine there are only a moderate number of destination processors per network node (sixteen in CM-1), and during most operations only one or two messages are destined for the same processor.

---

[2]In other words, all processors communicate using the same routing function.

4.3   Summary

In this chapter we have examined the architecture and operational characteristics of two SIMD array processors: the ICL DAP, and the TMC Connection Machine. The DAP uses a significantly more conservative technology in its implementation than the Connection Machine, has considerably fewer processing elements, and occupies a much greater physical space, than the Connection Machine. However, this is to be expected since the DAP predates the Connection Machine by about ten years. So, what advances in the architecture of SIMD array processors during those ten years have been assimilated into the Connection Machine? The answer is, not very many. The major difference of course is the binary 12-cube interconnection network and its associated adaptive message-routing algorithm. However, this could be emulated by the square-grid connections of the DAP. The major advance is purely technological, in the form of a higher level of integration.

The architects of the Connection Machine claim than logic-in-memory (LIM) machines such as CM-1 overcome the von Neumann bottleneck by replicating the processor-memory interconnection many times. However, this is only true for operations which are massively parallel, and all operations executed by the host computer are still limited by this problem. Furthermore, SIMD array processors have high values for $n_{1/2}$ (for a definition see volume I, chapter 10), which are typically $N/2$ for N processing elements. Some would say that this does not matter since each PE in an SIMD array machine is so much smaller than the unit of parallel hardware in other SIMD architectures. In effect, the utilisation of processing elements in a LIM machine should be compared with the utilisation of the *memory* of other parallel machines rather than the utilisation of the processing parts. This produces a far more favourable comparison, since as we observed at the beginning of chapter 2, the memory utilisation of SISD machines and vector machines falls as these machines become more powerful — but remains constant in LIM machines.

These sentiments must be tempered with a little objectivity, however, and it is clear that applications with only moderate quantities of data-level parallelism are better suited to vector machines with low values of $n_{1/2}$ rather than massively parallel array machines. As we shall see in the next chapter, massively parallel applications can gain a great deal from the use of the types of machine described in this chapter.

5   Array Processor Software

An appreciation of SIMD-array architectures is not complete without at least an overview of the types of languages and algorithms that have been developed for these machines. One of the most striking features of almost all SIMD-array machines is the way in which moderate to large amounts of *data-level* parallelism need to be explicitly described by the applications programmer, and this impacts on the design of both languages and algorithms. For the language designer these machines present a problem; how should the parallelism in the architecture be made visible to the programmer? Should the structure of the architecture be reflected in the langauge to give the programmer complete control of the hardware, or should the language provide a machine-independent interface to improve software structure and portability, albeit at some reduction in absolute performance? Some languages do attempt to provide a high level of abstraction, CM-Lisp for example, whereas others constitute what can only be described as augmented assembler language, for example DAP Fortran. Between these two extremes exist languages such as Actus, a language based around Pascal but with extensions for defining and operating on parallel data objects. In this chapter we examine the facilities within both CM-Lisp and DAP Fortran for defining parallel data objects and for performing parallel operations on them, and then go on to consider representative algorithms for each machine and look at how they can be expressed in their respective languages.

5.1   Array processing languages

Distributed processor arrays support a particular type of parallelism which is often referred to as *data-level* parallelism. In this type of parallelism individual instructions are executed strictly in sequence, but each instruction can be applied to a large number of data objects in parallel. To exploit this kind of architecture from a high-level language requires features for declaring data structures upon which such operations can take place, and for expressing parallel operations on these data structures. The features provided may reflect the architecture of a particular machine very closely, as in the case of DAP Fortran, or may provide a more abstract interface to the parallel machine architecture, as in the case of CM-Lisp. In general, an abstract interface is desirable since it masks the hardware details from the programmer and this encourages the production of portable software.

In DAP Fortran, the data structures upon which array operations take place are conventional Fortran vectors and matrices. The operations available correspond directly with the functions provided by the instruction set of the DAP; such a language is little more than an extended assembler. Conversely, in CM-Lisp, a special data type is introduced to represent collections of Lisp objects upon which parallel operations can take place, and special notations for applying functions to these collections of objects are defined.

The aim of the following sub-sections is to impart something of the flavour of these two languages without attempting to provide complete descriptions of the many features in these languages which are not directly relevant to the design of array processor architectures. The interested reader is encouraged to follow up the references cited for each language.

5.1.1   DAP Fortran

In DAP Fortran the primary data types are *scalars*, *vectors* and *matrices*, and these relate directly to the physical storage layout of the DAP (see section 4.1). The size of the DAP array is fixed at 64 × 64 processing elements[1] and, to permit a trivial mapping of vector and matrix elements to the DAP array, the language assumes that all vectors are 64 elements long and that all matrices contain 64 such vectors. Consequently, array bounds do not need to be specified in variable declarations. For example:

```
DIMENSION W(), X(,), Y(,21), Z(,,7)
```

This statement declares W to be a vector of 64 elements and X to be a 64 × 64-element matrix. In addition, Y defines 21 64-element vectors and Z defines 7 64 × 64-element matrices. Note, this convention makes the mapping of large matrices and vectors to the store of the DAP the explicit responsibility of the programmer.

Within vectors and matrices individual sub-structures can be specified by including or omitting subscripts as follows.

X()	the whole of X
X(2,)	the second row vector of X
X(,6)	the sixth column vector of X
X(4,1)	the scalar value X(4,1)

This extends naturally to include structures with more than two dimensions. Another useful method of selecting elements of a vector or matrix is to define a boolean control vector, and use it to index the vector or matrix, thus:

---

[1] With the exception of the recent AMT DAP-3, which has a 32 × 32 array of processing elements.

```
REAL   DVEC(), DMAT(,)
LOGICAL  CVEC(), CMAT(,)
```

It is possible to select a subset of the elements of vectors and matrices by writing DVEC(CVEC) and DMAT(CMAT). Only elements of DVEC and DMAT at index positions coinciding with *true* values in the control vector or matrix will be selected. The implementation of this relies on the conditional form of array instructions described in section 4.1.4.

A major feature of the DAP is the way in which processing elements (PEs) are connected in form of a square mesh. If each PE holds one element of a 64 × 64-element matrix then an obvious feature for the language to support is the *alignment* of data by means of the near-neighbour connections. In terms of vector and matrix data types this means applying a simple linear transformation to the index of every element, effectively either adding or subtracting one from all row or column indices simultaneously. This can be expressed in DAP Fortran as:

DMAT(+,)	≡	shift all elements upward
DMAT(-,)	≡	shift all elements downward
DMAT(,+)	≡	shift all elements to the right
DMAT(,-)	≡	shift all elements to the left

What happens at the boundary of the array during alignment operations depends on the currently selected *geometry*. The columns running from North to South, and the rows running from West to East, can each be connected either in a PLANAR or a CYCLIC geometry, corresponding to the geometry specification of DAP shift instructions (see figure 4.8 on page 52). Alignment by more than one position can be specified by the SHIFT statements. There are eight of these, one for every combination of direction and geometry. Hence to shift a matrix DMAT along the positive diagonal by I places can be done using SHift South Planar and SHift East Planar alignments, thus:

```
SHSP(SHEP(DMAT,I),I)
```

One of the most useful features of the CYBER 205 and CRAY vector architectures is the way in which conditional expressions within loops can be vectorised by using *control vectors* (see volume I, chapters 7 and 9). This permits statements of the form

```
DO 10 I = 1, 1000
IF A(I).GT.THRESHOLD THEN
    B(I) = S * C(I)
10 CONTINUE
```

to be compiled to a sequence of two instructions; one to evaluate the control vector, and one to compute S*C(I), storing the result in B if and only if the

Ith element of the control vector contains a 'true' value. A similar feature is available in DAP Fortran whereby an array of LOGICAL values can be used to index an array of data values on the *left-hand* side of an assignment, thus:

```
LOGICAL GTHAN(,)
REAL AMAT(,), BMAT(,), CMAT(,), S
 :
GTHAN = AMAT .GT. 0.0
BMAT(GTHAN) = S * CMAT(,)
```

These mechanisms are fine for manipulating arrays explicitly, but when the application task does not decompose naturally into arrays, and array-like operations, a more general solution must be found.

5.1.2   CM-Lisp

In the same way that DAP Fortran comprises standard Fortran with extensions to handle SIMD data structures and operations, the version of Lisp designed for the Connection Machine uses Common Lisp as a base language and augments this with several novel features. CM-Lisp introduces a new data type known as the *Xector*, and Xectors constitute the operands of all parallel operations. A Xector can be thought of as a set of values, with each value stored in a unique processing element. Each element of a Xector is identified by a unique label, which in practice would be either the address of the home processing element or a unique tag to be associated with the value in the home processing element. A Xector therefore defines a *mapping* in which the domain and range are both elements of the powerset of Lisp objects. For example, the following is a Xector.

$$\{\text{sky} \to \text{blue grass} \to \text{green apple} \to \text{red}\}$$

Note, the humble vector can now be seen as a special case of the Xector in which the domain is simply a set of contiguous integers, for example:

$$\{0 \to 1.3 \ 1 \to 4.7 \ 2 \to 6.8\}$$

Vectors such as this can also be written in a shortened form which omits the domain values.

$$\{0 \to 1.3 \ 1 \to 4.7 \ 2 \to 6.8\} \equiv [1.3, \ 4.7, \ 6.8]$$

Xectors can also be interrogated, given a definition of a Xector called colour-of as the following:

$$(\text{SETQ colour-of '}\{\text{sky} \to \text{blue apple} \to \text{red grass} \to \text{green}\}$$

it is possible to extract the 'colour' of an apple, using the XREF function, thus.

$$(\text{XREF colour-of 'apple}) \Rightarrow \text{red}$$

Alpha notation

When a Lisp expression is preceded by α, it is interpreted as a Xector in which the range consists of only the constant value produced by the expression. So, for example,

$$\alpha 3 \quad \Rightarrow \quad \{\rightarrow 3\} \quad \text{produces a Xector where all domain values map to 3}$$
$$\alpha + \quad \Rightarrow \quad \{\rightarrow +\} \quad \text{produces a Xector of 'plus' functions}$$

Parallel operations as we know them in SIMD machines can be specified by applying a Xector of functions to a pair of Xector operands. For example, the add function can be applied in parallel to a pair of Xectors where the range type are either fixed or floating-point numbers as shown below.

$$(\alpha + \text{'}\{a \rightarrow 1\ b \rightarrow 2\}\ \text{'}\{a \rightarrow 3\ b \rightarrow 3\}) \Rightarrow \{a \rightarrow 4\ b \rightarrow 5\}$$

It is possible to factor out the alphas to make expressions more readable, for example:

$$(\alpha + \alpha 1\ \alpha 2) \quad \equiv \quad \alpha(+\ 1\ 2)$$

However, if X and Y are Xectors, then $\bullet$ can be used to nullify the effect of an alpha, thus:

$$(\alpha +\ X\ Y) \quad \equiv \quad \alpha(+\ \bullet X\ \bullet Y)$$

This form of notation is comparable with the () and (,) notation in DAP Fortran, but is slightly more powerful since the size of each parallel data object is not restricted. Expressions involving alpha notation create objects on demand, and so the effect of writing $\alpha +$ is to create as many scalar plus functions as there are parallel data operands.

Beta reduction

Alpha notation is useful for specifying functions on independent data objects that can be executed in parallel. Conceptually, both the operands and the results are distributed throughout the array of processing elements. Therefore Alpha notation is only capable of expressing parallel functions of the form:

$$\text{Xector} \times \text{Xector} \times \ldots \times \text{Xector} \longmapsto \text{Xector}$$

Some other mechanism is therefore required to permit elements of a Xector to be *combined* if the full range of operations on Xectors is to be supported. Consider for example the vector dot-product operation used extensively in numerical algorithms. If vectors are represented as Xectors, then performing the multiplication step is trivial.

$$\alpha(* \bullet A \bullet B) \quad \equiv \quad \texttt{Forall i do A[i] * B[i]}$$

However, alpha notation is not capable of expressing the *cumulative reduction* phase, in which elements of the result Xector from the above operation need to be combined using the 'plus' function to produce a single scalar result. This is where β-reduction becomes important.

Beta-reduction expressions require three arguments; a combining function and two Xector operands. They return a third Xector in which the domain consists of the set of values in the range of the second Xector operand. The range includes those values in the range of the first Xector operand for which the domain values are in the range of the second Xector operand. Where two or more values in the range of the second Xector operand are identical the combining function is applied to reduce the corresponding values in the range of the first Xector operand to a single value. This all sounds rather tortuous, but can be readily understood with the aid of a simple example.

$$(\beta \ '\{1 \to 1 \ 2 \to 3 \ 3 \to 5\} \ '\{1 \to A \ 2 \to B \ 3 \to B\}) \Rightarrow \{A \to 1 \ B \to 8\}$$

If the second Xector is null (or not specified) then *all* values in the range of the first Xector are combined, and the result is a scalar Lisp object. Now the vector dot-product can be expressed as:

$$(\beta+ (\alpha* \ X \ Y))$$

The theoretical minimum number of parallel applications of any dyadic cumulative reduction function is $\lceil \log_2 n \rceil$, where n is the number of values which must be combined. Given appropriate parallel hardware, where the depth of the inter-processor connection network is $O(\log n)$, this lower bound on computation time can be approached by β-reduction expressions.

The production version of Lisp for the Connection Machine is known as *Lisp, and uses slightly different syntactic marks to identify the special features of Connection Machine Lisp. The interested reader is referred to Hillis 1985 [Hil85] or [TMC86].

5.2 Algorithms for array processors

The purpose of this section is to consider the types of application algorithm that are suitable for efficient implementation on distributed SIMD processor arrays, and introduce some general principles for the design of algorithms for such systems.

In general, for an algorithm to be suitable for a large-scale distributed processor array, it must contain a significant quantity of data-level parallelism. Often there will exist sequential algorithms for a problem under consideration, and a simple inspection may reveal extensive data structures and extensive, independent operations. Such sequential algorithms are useful starting points from which to begin the design of a parallel (SIMD) algorithm.

One of the most important design considerations with distributed array algorithms is *data decomposition*. Since processing elements only have direct access to data stored locally, a sensible distribution of data between processors is essential for efficient processing. But what is a sensible distribution of data?

Although the answer to this question is highly dependent on the problem being considered, a few general rules can be observed. Firstly, when designing an algorithm which requires the distribution of data, the overriding consideration must be in maximising the independence of data stored in distinct processors. An examination of the granularity which results from each candidate distribution will provide an indication of how much data alignment (the SIMD equivalent of inter-processor communication, as discussed in section 6.1.2) is required in proportion to parallel array operations. In general, the granularity should be maximised.

Another important design criterion is the topology of the inter-processor communications network, since this determines the types of data alignment which can be performed efficiently. More often than not the primary language used on each machine will restrict the user to those operations which are supported directly in hardware, making the choice of system somewhat dependent on the intended applications.

The performance distinctions between different SIMD network topologies can be observed readily by considering the implementation of Beta reduction operations on two different network topologies; the square mesh and the binary k-cube.

The type of β-reduction in which we are interested is similar to the vector sum-of-products function shown below.

```
s := 0;
Forall i do
    s := s + a[i] * b[i]
```

On a square mesh topology, with North, South, East and West data alignments, and with $\sqrt{n} \times \sqrt{n}$ processing elements, a suitable reduction scheme could be as follows.

Assume that the values of a[i] and b[i] are distributed such that each processing element has at most one element of each vector, and that the individual products can be formed in a single step. The algorithm outlined below will enable the sum of these products to be computed using only the orthogonal alignments provided by the hardware; notably single place planar shifts in the North, South, East and West directions.

1. Define $\sqrt{n}$ partial sum variables, one located in each processing element of the left-most column. Initialise them with the product of a[i] * b[i] produced locally.

2. Shift the column of partial sums one place to the right and add in the products found in the new local processing element.

3. Repeat step 2 until the partial sums are in the right-most column.

4. Shift the partial sum located in the top-right processing element down by one place and add in the partial sum from the processing element into which it moves.

5. Repeat step 4 until the partial sum is in the bottom-right processing element.

6. The partial sum in the bottom-right processing element contains the sum-of-products.

A simple analysis of this algorithm indicates that it takes $2(\sqrt{n}-1)$ alignment steps, and that the array operates in parallel during only half of the steps. Furthermore, when the array is operating in parallel the parallelism is only $\sqrt{n}$. However, this is asymptotically optimal for a two-dimensional square mesh topology. This fact can be verified intuitively by observing that all products, or partial sums in which they are included, must be combined at some point in the algorithm, and the maximum separation of any two products is $2(\sqrt{n} - 1)$ inter-processor links. Hence, the execution time of this algorithm is bounded below by the restricted communication bandwidth provided by a square mesh network.

On a binary k-cube topology, with $n = 2^k$ processing elements (where k is an integer) and a one-to-one correspondence between products and processing elements, the sum-of-products can be formed in the following way.

1. Let processing elements be identified by binary labels (addresses) of the form $a_k \ldots a_1$, and let there be two label variables in each PE called *mask* and *dimension*.

2. In each PE set $mask = 1 \ldots 1$ and $dimension = 10 \ldots 0$

3. For all PEs with labels (interpreted as unsigned integers) that are less than or equal to $mask$ perform steps 4 and 5.

4. If the local label logically ANDed with $dimension$ is equal to $dimension$ then transmit the local partial product to its nearest neighbour in dimension i else receive a partial product from dimension i and add it to the local partial product, where $i = \log_2(dimension)$.

5. Shift arithmetically the $mask$ and $dimension$ variables one place to the right in each PE.

6. Repeat steps 3, 4 and 5 until $mask$ is zero.

Again, an analysis of this simple algorithm is relatively straightforward. Each of steps 3, 4 and 5 can be assumed to take constant time, and are all repeated $k = \log_2 n$ times. The parallelism at each stage is equal to $mask + 1$, and this halves after each iteration. The computational power of binary k-cubes in SIMD architectures should be apparent from this elementary example, for as well as having an ability to process independent data items in parallel they can *combine* distributed data items in logarithmic time, and this is known to be asymptotically optimal.

5.2.1 Partial differential equations

In this section an indirect algorithm to find a solution to a set of partial differential equations (PDEs) is used as an example of how a highly structured problem can be mapped to a mesh-connected SIMD array, such as the DAP, using a primitive parallel language such as DAP Fortran. Whilst it is not the purpose of this book to discuss algorithms for parallel machines in any great detail, some background to the techniques for solving PDEs is required in order to appreciate the choice of algorithm.

A linear second-order PDE in two independent variables has the general form

$$A\frac{\delta^2 \phi}{\delta x^2} + B\frac{\delta^2 \phi}{\delta x \delta y} + C\frac{\delta^2 \phi}{\delta y^2} + D\frac{\delta \phi}{\delta x} + E\frac{\delta \phi}{\delta y} + F\phi = G$$

where the coefficients A through G can be dependent on x and y, but must be independent of ϕ. This general form covers a number of important equations which characterise problems in engineering and physics, such as diffusion, gravitational and electrical potential, Schrödinger's Equation, and many more.

Numerical solutions to PDEs can be found by using finite difference methods [FW60], and since these involve large numbers of computational steps they are likely candidates for parallel processing. For equations in two independent variables (x and y) the solution-space is represented by an $n \times n$ array of points (representing values for ϕ), spaced equally in the x and y dimensions. There are two general methods for arriving at a solution; *direct* and *indirect* (often referred to as *iterative*). Direct methods involve a fixed number of computational steps, and are certainly faster than indirect methods. However, when the number of points in the solution-space becomes large the computational errors for direct methods become unmanageable. The amount of parallelism in direct methods is therefore somewhat restricted. With indirect methods an initial estimate to the solution is made, from which successive refinements are computed iteratively. Various techniques for computing the refined values for $\phi_{x,y}$ are possible, and the choice of which one to use depends heavily on the resultant rate of convergence.

In the finite difference method a set of algebraic difference equations relates the value of a single point in the solution-space to its nearest neighbours in the x and y dimensions according to the values of local coefficients derived from the coefficients of the PDE. A simplification of the general case, known as the *model problem*, relates the refined values for the solution-space to the old values according to the following recurrence.

$$\phi'_{x,y} = \frac{\phi_{x-1,y} + \phi_{x+1,y} + \phi_{x,y-1} + \phi_{x,y+1}}{4} \qquad (5.1)$$

Jacobi's method for producing a converged solution involves computing all values of ϕ' simultaneously, and consequently contains a large amount of parallelism. However, it has been shown [Var62] that this method converges very slowly. The convergence rate can be improved by using a technique known as *successive over-relaxation* (SOR), whereby the new value at a point in the solution-space is defined as the weighted sum of the old value and the new estimate. In addition, new values are used in the calculation of other new values, within the same iteration, as soon as they have been computed. This produces a rapidly converging solution, but unfortunately the recurrence relation between ϕ values within the same iteration makes this method essentially sequential.

Several ways of partitioning the points to weaken the recurrence relation exist, for example one could compute all even-numbered lines in the x-y plane in parallel, followed by all odd-numbered lines (SOR by lines). One could compute all rows of points in parallel and then all columns of points in parallel, and this is known as the *alternating direction implicit* (ADI) method. However, a method which is particularly well-suited to the DAP architecture, where communication takes place with near-neighbouring elements only, is *odd-even ordering with Chebychev acceleration*. This is also known variously as the *chequer board algorithm* or the *red-black algorithm*.

The odd-even algorithm operates by partitioning the points into two disjoint sets; those for which $x + y$ is odd, and those for which $x + y$ is even. It then operates by calculating all odd points in parallel, followed by all even points in parallel. This is equivalent to visualising the points in the solution-space as squares on a chequer board, and processing all the red squares in parallel, followed by all the black squares. Chebychev acceleration is simply a method for adjusting the over-relaxation weight after each set of odd or even points have been updated.

It is now possible to consider a concrete algorithm for computing the PDE solution using odd-even ordering with Chebychev acceleration. This is first expressed using an informal step-wise notation, and secondly as a sub-program unit in DAP Fortran.

1. Define two distributed matrices of LOGICAL values to enable the *odd* and *even* locations in the solution-space to be selected independently.

2. Generate an initial approximation to the solution, and calculate the number of iterations that are required for a given level of accuracy in the final solution.

3. For all *odd* points in the solution-space calculate the new estimate and the new over-relaxed value, and update each point using a weighted sum of these values.

4. Re-calculate the over-relaxation weight.

5. Perform step 3 again, but this time operate on the *even* points only.

6. Re-calculate the over-relaxation weight.

7. Repeat steps 3 to 6 for the required number of iterations.

Let us now analyse this algorithm to ascertain the degree of parallelism it contains. Steps 1 and 2 are initialisation steps and can be ignored. Steps 3 to 6 comprise the main iterative loop, and contain two parallel calculations and two scalar calculations. The parallel calculations (steps 3 and 5) involve the computation of new estimates for ϕ_{xy} in half of the 64×64 array of processing elements (assuming the size of the problem is exactly 64×64) and therefore has a parallelism of 2048.

The calculation of each new value involves what is sometimes described as a *cross-point* calculation corresponding to equation 5.1, and this can be expressed quite concisely in DAP Fortran using data alignment notation as follows.

```
0.25 * (U(-,) + U(+,) + U(,-) + U(,+))
```

This requires four shift operations which must be performed sequentially, four floating-point Add operations, and a floating-point multiply operation. In addition to this, the new estimate must be weighted and added to a weighted version of the old solution. Again, these weighting and addition operations can be performed in all odd (or even) PEs concurrently. The scalar operations consist of the re-calculation and distribution of the new weight after each half-iteration. There are two ways in which these could be implemented. Either the scalar part of the machine calculates the new value for W once only and distributes it serially via the row (or column) highway, or each processing element calculates its own private copy of W. The second method involves a large number of 'redundant' computations, but avoids the distribution phase, and for some tasks this approach may actually be faster.

A skeleton of a DAP Fortran routine to compute this algorithm is presented below. To aid readability the initialisation parts and the weight calculations are commented out.

```
INTEGER I, ITERATIONS
REAL U(,), W
LOGICAL ODD(,), EVEN(,)
- initialise the ODD and EVEN mask variables
- initialise the weight W
- calculate the number of iterations required
DO 10 I = 1,ITERATIONS
    U(ODD) = (1-W)*U(,) + W*0.25*(U(-,)+U(+,)+U(,-)+U(,+))
    - calculate new value for W
    U(EVEN) = (1-W)*U(,) + W*0.25*(U(-,)+U(+,)+U(,-)+U(,+))
    - calculate new value for W
10 CONTINUE
```

The main points to note about this algorithm, and its implementation on a machine like the DAP, are that its structure fits the architecture very well and that DAP Fortran simply provides a means of expressing it succinctly.

This is an example of an algorithm which is well-suited to the machine on which it is implemented, but there are many parallel algorithms for which the mapping to a square mesh architecture in not quite so obvious. Nevertheless, techniques for implementing more sophisticated data alignments on a square mesh exist, although these encounter a *simulation slow-down* factor which in some cases can be significant.

The Connection Machine (section 4.2) supports hypercubic connections between groups of processing elements, as well as a square mesh network (known as the NEWS grid), and together these make the Connection Machine a very flexible SIMD architecture. In order to appreciate this we now examine how the Connection Machine, and CM-Lisp, can be used to implement an elementary graph algorithm in parallel.

5.2.2 Minimum path length

Numerical applications, such as partial differential equations, are not the only types of application with significant amounts of data-level parallelism. There are a great many *manipulative* algorithms involving sorting, searching and dictionary operations which are also inherently parallel. Many important problems can be modelled in terms of graph structures, for which there are mature sequential graph algorithms as well as an increasing number of parallel algorithms. Such non-numerical applications are known collectively as *symbolic algorithms*, since their prime concern is in the arrangement of symbolic objects rather than the arithmetic combination of floating-point values. In this section we discuss the implementation of an SIMD algorithm for finding the shortest path between any two vertices of an arbitrarily connected graph. The language chosen to express this parallel algorithm is CM-Lisp, and this is chosen in order to emphasise that with a reasonably high level of data abstraction it is possible to describe parallel activities in a succinct and machine-independent manner.

Let us first consider how one might compute sequentially the minimum path length between a single source and a single destination vertex in a graph $G = (V, E)$, where V is a finite set of vertices and E is a finite set of edges. Let us assume that G is an unweighted connected graph, since this simplifies the solution without significant loss in generality. Moore's algorithm [Moo59] for finding the shortest path from a single source vertex to all other vertices is a suitable sequential algorithm, and thus forms the basis for the parallel SIMD algorithm presented here as an example.

Moore's algorithm

Let *length(u,v)* represent the length of the edge from vertex u to vertex v, and let this be ∞ if u and v are not connected directly. Let *distance(v)* hold the best (shortest) path length from the source vertex s to vertex v, and for all $v \in V - \{s\}$ this is set initially to ∞. The value of *distance(s)* is initially set to zero. Moore's algorithm operates by expanding outwards from the source vertex, along all possible edges, maintaining a queue of all vertices connected to parts of the graph which have been reached by the algorithm, but which have not yet been expanded. Initially this queue contains only the source vertex, and for as long as the queue contains unexamined vertices the algorithm continues by removing a vertex u from the head of the queue and performing the following sequence of actions.

1. For all edges $(u, v) \in E$, if $distance(u) + length(u, v)$ is less than $distance(v)$ then set $distance(v) = distance(u) + length(u, v)$, and add vertex v to the queue if it is not already present.

2. repeat step 1 until the queue is empty.

The parallel version

To parallelise this algorithm, and modify it for a single destination and an unweighted graph (unit length edges), it is modified as follows. Firstly, the calculation of distances to the vertices held in the queue is performed in parallel for all queued vertices. Secondly, the algorithm iterates until the distance to a specified destination vertex d is finite. Hence, if there is no path from s to d this parallel version of Moore's algorithm will not terminate. An outline of this algorithm is given below.

1. Let $distance(s) = 0$

2. $\forall u \in V - \{s\}$, let $distance(u) = \infty$

3. $\forall u \in V - \{s\}$, assign $MIN(distance(k)) + 1$ to $distance(u)$, $\forall k \in neighbours(u)$.

4. Repeat step 3 until $distance(d) \neq \infty$

5. Return $distance(d)$.

The algorithm defines an additional set of vertices for each vertex u, called $neighbours(u)$, which contains all vertices v such that $(u, v) \in E$. Let us now examine where parallelism can be exploited in this algorithm.

The iterations, defined by steps 3 and 4, cannot be processed concurrently since there is a recurrence relationship from one iteration to the next. The parallelism is instead found within the $\forall u$ of step 3, and here two forms of parallelism are possible. Firstly, at the outer-most level of step 3, calculation of the new distance for all vertices from the source can take place concurrently. Unfortunately many of these calculations will be redundant, simply attempting to assign $\infty + 1$ to a *distance* which is already ∞, or re-calculating a known minimum path length. Secondly, the evaluation of the MIN function is an example of a *cumulative reduction* operation, and can therefore be performed with exponentially decreasing parallelism in logarithmic time (given suitable hardware of course).

In CM-Lisp the vertices and edges of G can be represented by the following structure definition.

```
(DEFSTRUCT (VERTEX:CM) Label Neighbours)
```

This CM-Lisp expression defines indirectly three functions; make-vertex, Label and Neighbours. The Label and Neighbours functions perform field selection on VERTEX objects, and make-vertex is the constructor function for vertices, in much the same way that CONS is the constructor function for lists. The :CM suffix means that vertices are to be stored in the Connection Machine memory and distributed amongst the processing elements, rather than being stored in the Host processor.

Thus, it is possible to write down a CM-Lisp function (due to Hillis), which takes three arguments s, d and G, corresponding to the source and destination vertices and a Xector of vertices (the graph) respectively. The complete function is given below.

```
1.    (DEFUN path-length (s d G)
2.        α(SETF (Label •G) +INF)
3.        (SETF (Label s) 0)
4.(a)     (LOOP UNTIL (< (Label d) +INF)
4.(b)         DO α(SETF (Label •(REMOVE s G))
4.(c)             1+ (βMIN α(Label •(Neighbours •G)))))
5.        (Label d))
```

This piece of program requires some explanation. The second line sets the Label fields of all vertices of G to $+\infty$, and does so in parallel (assuming each CM processing element holds a single vertex). The third line sets the Label field of the source vertex s to zero. Line 4 defines an iteration construct which repeats until the destination label (Label d) is less than +INF. Within this loop, lines 4.(b) and 4.(c) perform the business of calculating intermediate minimum path lengths by setting the labels of all vertices in G to be one plus the mimimum of the labels of their neighbouring vertices. Within this expression, (REMOVE s G) is effectively a set-difference operation, yielding a Xector of vertices containing $G - \{s\}$.

The parallelism in this elementary example is clearly evident, and the expression of parallelism is explicit. However, the code is remarkably conventional and machine independent. The degree of parallelism is determined by the connectivity of the graph, and in the worst case (where G defines a *chain* of vertices) there is no parallelism at all. The parallelism in this example becomes significant when the real-world problem that is being modelled produces a large, highly connected graph. Typical examples of such a real-world problem are finding the shortest route between two buildings in a large city, and finding the optimum route for a either a copper track on a printed circuit board or track within a VLSI circuit.

5.3   Summary

In this chapter we have looked briefly at the topic of software for large distributed arrays of processing elements, such as one finds in machines like the ICL DAP and the TMC Connection Machine. Within the languages that have been designed for such machines we find features which permit parallel data objects to be declared explicitly and operated upon in parallel. The functions made available to the programmer often reflect the specific features of the underlying architecture, for example the data alignment operations in DAP Fortran, but there is evidence that more general-purpose and flexible languages such as CM-Lisp could be used in conjunction with any distributed SIMD machine.

Generating and understanding parallel programs for SIMD machines is often no more difficult than it is for sequential machines, particularly if the language and the machine both match the application. Two of the most important considerations for producing efficient software for these types of architecture are discovering which computational steps can be performed in parallel, and distributing the data so that the number of data alignment operations is minimised.

6   Multiprocessor Architecture

In the first volume we examined the range of techniques which are employed in high-performance architectures to improve the throughput within a single processor. These techniques included pipelining, multiple function units and a variety of mechanisms designed to meet the necessary memory throughput and latency requirements. However, the so-called 'von Neumann bottleneck', which is the fundamental limit imposed on sequential processing by the rate at which information can be moved across the boundary between processor and memory, limits both the rate at which instructions can be issued and the rate at which operands can be supplied.

In the first half of this book we saw how data-level parallelism can be exploited to some effect by SIMD architectures, through the array-like hardware structures and specialised languages. In these types of architecture a single instruction causes a large amount of data to be operated on by a common instruction. Also, the predictability of memory reference patterns can be used both to maintain a high flow-rate of operands from memory or to arrange for a large number of identical operations to occur simultaneously in an array of arithmetic units. Using this model of computation the arithmetic throughput on suitable applications can be very high indeed.

In chapter 10 of volume I, we saw how the 'Flynn limit' defines an upper bound on the speed of instruction issue in SISD and SIMD machines, and in many cases the single-instruction stream model can become a serious limitation for these classes of architecture. At this point Amdahl's law, stating that there is a diminishing return on the investment in parallel hardware, itself provides some clue as to how we might progress beyond this limitation imposed on us by those parts of an application which are not regular, and which cannot be vectorised.

Recall from section 10.2.3 in volume I, that the performance of a two-state machine is defined in terms of the relative speeds of the parallel and sequential computations and the ratio of parallel to sequential activity in a particular application, and that from this the upper bound on speedup can be defined as

$$S \leq \frac{1}{(1 - \alpha) + \alpha/f}$$

In this equation the proportion of work that can be performed using parallel processing, α, is speeded up f times (where f is the ratio of parallel to sequential processing rates), whereas the proportion of work which cannot be performed in parallel (using SIMD technique) is not affected by the introduction of parallelism. What needs to be done, clearly, is to somehow reduce the $(1 - \alpha)$ term in the denominator by some factor p which can be increased through the introduction of hardware capable of executing scalar instructions in parallel. Hopefully, the speedup might then be determined by

$$S_p \leq \frac{p}{(1 - \alpha) + \alpha/f}$$

This requires a different model of program execution in which there are a multiplicity of instruction streams, and whilst this may not seem to be such a radical step to take, the implications for software and hardware design are wide ranging and occasionally problematic.

The most obvious implication arising from the change to an MIMD style of architecture is that there must be several active *loci of control* (involving a multiplicity of program counters) within the machine, with duplicated instruction issue logic. This seems to be the direction in which existing manufacturers of SIMD machines have been moving, for example, with the introduction of M-SIMD machines machines such as the CRAY X-MP, the CRAY-2, the CRAY-3 and the ETA[10]. As we have seen, these machines use parallel memory structures to overcome the von Neumann bottleneck, and multiple processors to attack the problems of scalar processing and the speed-of-light limitation on clock frequency.

Most computer scientists, and users of MIMD machines, draw a distinction between *multiprocessor* and *multicomputer* systems. If one considers a processor as simply a component of a computer system, then the distinction becomes clearer. A multiprocessor is then a system in which there is a simple replication of processors within a framework which does not alter the relationship between the processor(s) and other components (such as memory). Conversely, a multicomputer is a system in which the whole computer (processor and memory together) are replicated, and some form of communication network added, to allow them to exchange information.

The use of MIMD machines is still in its infancy, and the long-term performance potential of multiprocessor and multicomputer systems is still unclear. One might reasonably ask whether MIMD architectures are really needed, since with hindsight it can be seen that the speed of conventional SISD and SIMD machines increases by an approximately ten-fold factor every five or so years. This has encouraged some users of computers to conjecture that one should simply 'wait a few years' for improved technology to provide the required performance. Furthermore, they might argue, by the time a new and novel architecture has been developed it may well be superseded by a faster sequential machine. The problem with this argument is that the development of implementation technologies, sequential processor architectures and MIMD architectures complement each other. Thus, faster sequential processors mean faster processing elements within MIMD machines, and higher performance overall. Ideally, MIMD machines with n processors should simply be n-times faster than SISD machines constructed from equivalent technology, although as we shall see later this is rarely the case.

An interesting empirical 'law', attributed to Grosch [Gro75], states that the performance of a computer is proportional to the square of its cost. In other words, if one had twice the purchasing power, it would be possible to purchase a machine roughly four times as fast. Alternatively, it is more cost-effective to buy a single large computer than a number of smaller, interconnected computers. The problem with this counter-argument to MIMD architectures is that whilst it is true within a particular class of architectures, such as main-frames or mini-computers, it is not true between different classes of architecture. Consequently, the cost per MIPS (or per MFLOPS) in a multi-microprocessor system is significantly less than the cost per MIPS in a typical ERDA[1] Class VI supercomputer (such as the CRAY-1). For example, the ratio of cost (in thousands of dollars) to performance (in MFLOPS) for a CRAY-1S is 105.3, compared with an equivalent ratio of just 8.6 for a 128-processor BBN Butterfly machine [JD86].

Examining currently available supercomputers, it becomes apparent that the majority are pipelined vector processors, of the CRAY-1 or CYBER 205 variety. Furthermore, a large proportion of the applications which require very high performance can be processed relatively efficiently on such architectures, and this begs the question of whether anything other than very high performance vector processors is required. The answer to this question has already been provided by the manufacturers of vector machines, who are now developing and marketing M-SIMD machines such as the CRAY X-MP and the ETA[10]. The problem of scalar processing, mentioned earlier, simply cannot be solved by using faster, or longer pipelines.

In 1971, Minsky and Papert conjectured that the speedup achievable by a parallel computer is proportional to the logarithm of the number of processors, therefore rendering very-large-scale MIMD processing ineffective. However, in recent years, the development of practical MIMD systems (some of which are described in the following two chapters) has provided substantial evidence to disprove this theory. For example, systems containing several hundred processors have been shown to yield a speedup which is almost linearly proportional to the number of processors.

Perhaps the most serious problem limiting the speedup of MIMD systems is the existence of inherently sequential segments of code in every application. These pieces of sequential code, together with fundamental

---

[1]A machine satisfying the ERDA Class VI requirement has a floating-point performance from 20 to 60 MFLOPS [Rus78].

limitations in machine design, determine a maximum speedup for any application. Thankfully, most of the applications which need the power of a large MIMD system contain so much potential parallelism, that this constraint will only become apparent when very large numbers of processors are used. Section 6.2.1 contains a detailed discussion of the performance of MIMD systems, and attempts to quantify the effect of certain fundamental algorithm and machine limitations on their speedup.

6.1 Design issues

In order to understand how various MIMD machines operate, and what level of performance it is reasonable to expect from them, one must examine the design-space of MIMD machines a little closer. For example, the two most fundamental design decisions which must be taken very early on in the design process are, firstly how powerful each processing element should be, and secondly how many processing elements should be supported. For a system performance of P, and an ideal architecture containing n processors, each with an individual processing capability of p, the hyperbolic relationship between n and p (shown in figure 6.1) defines a span of possible architectures satisfying $P = pn$. Therefore, one could use a small number of very powerful (and expensive) processors, or a large number of relatively slow (and cheap) processors. The use of large numbers of cheap and simple processors is made attractive by the development of VLSI. However, this technological 'push' may provide the architect of a high performance system with large quantities of small and powerful processing elements, but does not in itself provide a complete solution to the problem of providing high performance through massive parallelism.

From the computer architect's point of view, the central problem posed by the requirement for very high processing rates, assuming the availability of cheap VLSI computing elements, is how to match the parallelism in the computation with the parallelism-potential in the hardware. This means putting together a highly parallel assemblage of computing elements in such a way that the performance of each individual element is made available to the application. In turn, the application programmer requires new ways of expressing the problem, in order that the available parallelism can be exploited successfully. In the simplest sense, therefore, this is a problem of connecting processing elements together and providing a means of programming them sensibly.

This raises a number of fundamental design issues, which the architect of a high performance MIMD system must consider. For example, suppose a designer is given an unlimited supply of small, but powerful computing elements, how should they be connected together? Since the number of connections that can be made to each element is finite (and probably quite

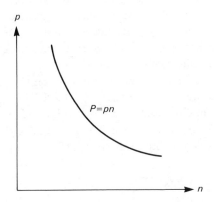

Figure 6.1 Processor performance v. number of processors

small), it is impossible connect every element to every other element. Is there then an interconnection strategy which is sufficiently universal that it provides adequate connectivity for the majority of applications?

If it were possible to construct such a system, which languages would be appropriate for expressing highly parallel applications, and should the identification and expression of parallelism in the application be the responsibility of the programmer? This is an issue which influences heavily the design of parallel programming languages as well as MIMD architectures. If we assume that a highly parallel MIMD architecture and a suitable programming language exist, the next question to ask is what algorithms are available to exploit the parallelism provided by the machine ? Algorithms for sequential machines have been studied at great length, and classical sorting, searching and numerical algorithms for such machines have been documented [Knu73]. The availability of high-performance parallel computers has stimulated much research on the design of parallel algorithms, and this is now becoming an increasingly important area of study.

In the next chapter a number of software issues for multiprocessors are discussed, and this includes an overview of some languages and algorithms for such architectures. A full treatment of parallel programming languages and algorithms in, however, beyond the scope of this book. The interested reader is referred in the first instance to Perrott [Per87] who describes several parallel programming languages and the ways in which they may be used, and to Quinn [Qui87] who describes numerous algorithms for MIMD and SIMD architectures.

Some would claim that the sequence of design decisions outlined above, namely *architecture*, then *language* and finally *application*, is entirely the wrong way to go about designing an MIMD system. The design of architectures is always heavily influenced by the needs of the users, by the characteristics of the intended applications, and by the languages through which they are to be programmed. In short, machines can never be designed without a thorough understanding of their intended use.

An equally important issue, which impinges on the architectural design, the languages used, and the applications, is the resulting performance of the system as a whole. In this respect, a predictable model of the performance of a system is vital, and in section 6.2.1 we consider the performance of a generalised MIMD machine in order to illustrate this point.

6.1.1   Categories of MIMD architecture

Research into the design of parallel systems has led to the emergence of a number of distict categories of MIMD architecture, each with its own advantages and disadvantages. For example, at the beginning of this chapter, the difference between a multicomputer and a multiprocessor was explained, and this very coarse distinction effectively defines two broad categories of MIMD architecture.

The relatively simple technique of replicating processors, and providing them all with access to a common store, produces *shared-memory multiprocessors*, and the design of machines of this type is considered in chapter 7. In common with SIMD array processors (section 2.1.1), the possibilities for the placement of the interconnect yield two styles of shared-memory multiprocessors; those with *distributed* memory, and those without. Distributed-memory architectures operate on the principle that data that is local to a processor will be placed in the local memory of that processor, thereby reducing the load on the interconnection network. In situations where locality is absent, or in which a uniform access cost is prefered, centralised-memory architectures can be used. For many applications, not all processors *need* access to all memory locations, and then a partitioning of the memory is clearly sensible.

If the sharing of data is not permitted, processors will need to exchange information in some other way. When exchanging information through a shared memory location, the processors involved must become synchronised before the transfer can be completed. The writing processor must ensure that valid data is not being overwritten, and the reading processor must ensure that the location is read *after* the writing processor has placed a value there. This is analogous to passing a message from one processor to another. Ensuring that processes are synchronised can be done using standard operating system techniques, such as semaphores, but an alternative technique is to forgo the shared-memory and simply provide dedicated communication channels between processors. This leads to the *message-passing* category of

MIMD machines, and these are explained in more detail in chapter 8.

Shared-memory systems are often thought of as *closely-coupled*, since the interconnection mechanism binds processors together (via the shared memory) in what must be a physically compact design. Message-passing architectures, however, are often considered to be *loosely-coupled* systems, since processors can tolerate a greater physical separation, and normally interact relatively infrequently.

The shared-memory versus message-passing dichotomy therefore defines two classes of machines that are distinquished by the way in which the cooperation between processors is *implemented*. However, both message-passing and shared-memory implementation techniques are equally capable of supporting programming models with message-based process communications or shared-variables. One must always be aware of the difference between the *architecture* of a machine (the characteristics of the machine as seen by the lowest level of software) and its *implementation* (the logical structures used to support the architecture), and this is particularly important in the field of multiprocessor systems.

The performance attainable by each mechanism for processor cooperation depends, as we shall see, on the time-penalty associated with its invocation and the relative frequency with which the language model and application requires its use.

6.1.2 Granularity

The relative frequency with which processors interact (and hence, synchronise with each other) is another important design issue. The frequency of interaction can be quantified as simply the ratio of the amount of computation to the number of communication events. This ratio is known as the *granularity* of the process, with a small ratio corresponding to a *fine-grained* process, and a large ratio corresponding to a *coarse-grained* process. Fine-grained processes synchronise with each other relatively frequently, whereas coarse-grained processes perform significant amounts of computation between synchronisation events. The granularity says nothing about the amount of code, or the expected lifetime of a process, since the relative frequency of communication is not necessarily related to these other factors. In order to get a specific measure of granularity one might count the average number of basic machine instructions each process executes between each synchronisation event. Coarse-grained processes could be expected to execute several thousand instructions between each synchronisation event, whereas fine-grained processes could execute just one. Throughout the remainder of this chapter we denote the granularity by g, and this is then equal to the number of useful instructions executed during each grain of activity.

The architecture of a multiprocessor system, and the performance of the communication medium, together determine a minimum level of process granularity that can be supported with reasonable efficiency. This constraint on the exploitation of parallelism is discussed in greater detail in section 6.2.1.

6.1.3   Load balancing

Consider a multiprocessor architecture in which a workload consisting of m independent parallel processes is distributed between n processors. The efficiency of the system depends critically on the work being shared out equally between the processors, and this can be illustrated quite simply. If all the work is allocated to a single processor, the system will perform no better than a single processor. Conversely, if the work is divided exactly between the n processors, the performance could be up to n-times that of a single processor.

In fact the problem of load balancing is more complex than this suggests, since the workload presented by each process is not necessarily the same, and furthermore it is not generally known how much processor time will be consumed by a process before it is started. This problem is further complicated by the multiprogramming of a single processor, which is likely to be responsible for m/n processes.

This leads to a consideration of several design issues related to load balancing. First of all, should individual processors divide their time between a number of multiprogrammed processes? Secondly, should a process be statically bound to one processor, or should it be able to migrate from processor to processor depending on the availability of processing resources? Thirdly, should the dynamic creation of processes be permitted, or should the extent of parallelism be fixed at compile-time?

There is no single set of correct answers to these questions, since in practice each MIMD system is optimised for a particular type of computation. However, a few basic rules can be defined. For example, a process should only migrate between processors if the performance gained as a result of the move is greater than the performance lost due to organisational overheads. In a tightly-coupled shared-memory architecture, the context information for all processes will be available to all processors, and therefore the cost of scheduling a process will be independent of the identity of the processor on which it is scheduled. However, in a loosely-coupled message-passing architecture, there is a high cost associated with moving a process, since the entire memory image for the process must be moved physically from one processor to another. Hence, in a loosely-coupled system, it is generally more difficult at run-time to arrange the load across the system to ensure optimal throughput of the system.

If processors do not share their time between a number of processes, the utilisation of the system is likely to be relatively poor. This is because interacting processes occasionally need to synchronise, at which point a process must wait for another to catch up. If a processor has no other work to perform during this waiting period, it will stand idle. However, when a waiting process is eventually freed, there may be a significant delay before it regains control of the processor. If the real-time response of the system (to external events for example) is critical, then the designer may trade off occasional idle periods for a fast response time.

An issue which affects both the architecture and programming language of an MIMD system is whether processes can be created *dynamically* during program execution, or whether the number of parallel processes is determined *statically* at compile-time. Static systems have the advantage that a compile-time allocation of processes to processors can be performed (possibly under programmer control), and hence the utilisation of computing resources can be optimised. The disadvantage of static systems is that certain types of parallel algorithm, which create processes *on demand*, cannot be expressed naturally. Furthermore, the actual number of parallel processors must be known to the programmer, and a change in the number of processors will necessitate the re-compilation of programs. Dynamic systems can be highly flexible, permitting programmers to remain ignorant of the available parallelism. However, every machine has finite resources, and parallel algorithms which generate very large numbers of processes may execute with relatively poor efficiency. This is due to the fact that each process requires a certain amount of memory space in order to run efficiently, and is especially true in virtual memory systems, where the working-set model applies [Den68]. This results in there being an optimum level of multiprogramming, above which performance falls away due to virtual store interrupts, and below which performance falls away due to unused processor time.

6.2 Performance issues

There are many ways to measure the performance of a system. For example, the metric of performance commonly assumed is *speed*, but reliability, cost, and programmability are just as important. For the architect of MIMD systems, however, speed is usually the primary concern. One of the major problems in discussing performance, and comparing the performance of different MIMD systems, is that it is extremely difficult to compare quantitively two systems with radically different structures. There are simply too many variable factors involved in the equations of performance for scientific deductions to be made. Consequently, architects develop *models* which *characterise* performance in terms of the most important parameters of a system. These models are necessarily crude, but often yield useful and un-expected results. In this section we present a general model of an MIMD system, and characterise this system in terms of the most important features of the architecture and the algorithm being executed.

Characterising the Application

There are essentially just two ways in which the transition to multiple in-struction stream processing can improve performance: either by providing a number of independent users with a superior time-sharing service, or by providing one or more users with a parallel programming environment in which process-parallelism is translated into application speedup through the cooperation of a number of processors on a single task. To provide the first category of service is relatively easy, since without interaction between processors, very low inter-processor communication bandwidths can be tol-erated. This is the philosophy behind distributed workstation networks, and it can work very well. To provide the second category of service re-quires both a logical and a physical mechanism for permitting a number of distinct processes to exchange information during the course of their co-operative effort. It is hence the provision of a communication mechanism (whether through shared-memory or via message-passing) which is central to the design and performance of MIMD systems. A corollary to this is that the performance of an MIMD system depends not only on the efficiency of the cooperation mechanism, but also on the relative frequency with which cooperating processes interact.

The pattern of behaviour of a number of processes can be characterised crudely, in terms of the amount of time each process spends computing in relation to the amount of time it spends communicating. This corresponds to our dimensionless ratio *granularity*, and this is therefore one of the most important parameters of a parallel algorithm.

Now, regardless of the programming language used in an MIMD sys-tem, the computation at the physical level consists of a number of parallel grains of activity. If we assume for a moment that the finest possible level of granularity is used, then the computation consists solely of atomic opera-tions whose inputs operands are the output results of preceding operations. Such a sequence of dependent operations is illustrated in figure 6.2. Since it takes a finite amount of time to process these atomic operations there will be, at any instant, a certain number of atomic operations which have their input values available. In theory, all such operations could be processed in parallel, if there were enough processors. If all atomic operations take an identical time to compute (this is a slight simplification), then the com-putation can be divided into a sequence of *stages*. Within each stage, all atomic operations can be evaluated in parallel, and every atomic operation

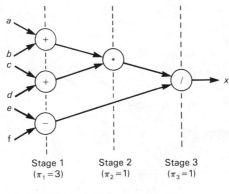

Figure 6.2 Parallelism and dependencies

at stage i requires at least one operand that is computed at stage $i - 1$. Therefore, if there are π_i atomic operations at stage i, then we say that π_i is the *instantaneous parallelism at stage i*.

The variation of π_i over all stages in a computation can be plotted graphically for any potentially parallel algorithm. The resulting *parallelism profile* illustrates very clearly the parallel behaviour of a particular algorithm. A sample profile is shown in figure 6.3, and by inspection it is obvious that the area under the profile is equal to the total number of atomic operations performed, and that the horizontal distance over which the profile extends equals the absolute minimum number of computational steps. In figure 6.3 a vertical slice has been taken out of the profile, and this represents the instantaneous parallelism, π_i, at stage i. The vertical slices are time-ordered in their execution such that

$$\forall i, j \left(\pi_i \text{ executes before } \pi_j \rightarrow i < j \right)$$

When we consider algorithms in which granularity is not minimal, the parallelism at stage i is generally reduced. However, this is not always the case. A totally sequential algorithm may have $\pi_i = 1$ for all i, and then π_i is always the same, irrespective of granularity. For most multiprocessor systems it is too time-consuming to treat each instruction as an individual process. Instructions are therefore composed into sequences, with communication events defining the start and end of each grain.

Some novel architectures do attempt to treat each instruction as an individual process. Since the program counter for each process can then take

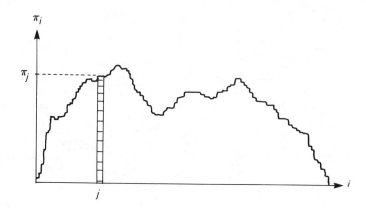

Figure 6.3 Maximal-parallelism profile

on only one value it is totally redundant and then the issuing of each instruction is determined solely by the availability of its input operands. Such
architectures are known as *dataflow architectures*. A significant amount of
research has been done in the area of dataflow architectures, but to date
their early promise has failed to be realised commercially. A treatment of
dataflow architectures is beyond the scope of this book, but interested read-
ers should consult Hwang and Briggs[HB84], or the February 1982 issue of
the *IEEE Computer* journal.

When granularity is not minimal, each stage in the computation consists
of more than one atomic operation. The atomic operations within a single
grain are assumed to be executed sequentially, and may therefore have sequential dependencies between them without adversely affecting the time
taken to execute the grain. Note, if all atomic operations within a grain of
activity are dependent on results computed in preceding grains, then moving to a finer level of granularity will not raise the parallelism profile. In
effect, the inherent sequentiality of the algorithm enforces an upper bound
on the instantaneous parallelism that can be extracted. Hence, any algorithm can be characterised in terms of its maximal-parallelism profile and
its granularity, and both of these are measures which are independent of
the architecture on which an algorithm runs. Granularity, when not equal
to unity, would normally be expected to vary considerably from grain to
grain. However, for the purposes of this simple analytical model we assume
it is constant.

Characterising the architecture

In order to complete the specification of a parallel processing system, the parameters of the architecture which define the performance of the system need to be determined. In the same way that certain general assumptions are made about the application in order to simplify the application model, the overall model of an architecture also relies on a few basic assumptions.

The first assumption is that each processor has an internal clock, with a period of t_c seconds, and that each instruction executes in one clock period. In a practical architecture instructions often have variable execution times, and so t_c may be looked upon as the *average* instruction execution time. The second assumption is that the system contains n processing elements, and is both homogeneous and orthogonal. This means that all processing elements are identical, and have equal access to whatever mechanism is used to connect the processors. The third assumption concerns the unavoidable cost of communicating values between concurrent processes, particularly when they reside within distinct processors. Consider the sequence of events which occurs when a process initiates a communication event. This event may be the synchronised access of a shared variable, or it may be the sending of a message from one processor to another. In a dataflow machine communication occurs at the completion of every instruction, and typically consists of moving a result packet from an execution unit to a matching store. In addition, the input of data in a dataflow architecture is implicit, since all 'instructions' which are not in a state of execution are normally waiting for input. Therefore, whatever the model of execution, the time taken to communicate can be modelled in terms of the time taken to decide whether the current process must wait, plus the time taken to de-schedule the current process if indeed it needed to wait. We therefore define D to be the *decision time*, and X to be the *context-switching time*.

In practice, the time taken to decide whether the communication event can proceed immediately will depend on the mechanism for access to shared variables, or on the method for examining the status of a communication channel. The context-switching time will depend on the amount of context information to be preserved during a process-change, and on the speed with which this can be achieved. However, suppose for a moment that each processor is capable of performing both of these tasks in zero time, the results it produces are still required by another processor. The laws of physics state that the transfer of information takes a finite time, and therefore each machine must have a characteristic *latency* associated with the movement of information from one processor to another. In practice the latency, denoted here by L, will be determined by the interconnection architecture. The latency can be expressed as a multiple of the instruction cycle time t_c, and hence we introduce the *latency factor* $l = L/t_c$.

Consider, therefore, what happens during the execution of a single grain of activity. If we assume that a grain of activity is scheduled as a result of the previously scheduled process becoming suspended, then the processor must exchange process contexts before the scheduled grain can begin. As we have mentioned already, this takes a time of X seconds or $x = X/t_c$ atomic time intervals. This change of variable simply converts X into multiples of the instruction execution time. Following the context switch, g instructions are executed, and these take a time of $g\,t_c$. Finally, the grain terminates when the current process decides that it must synchronise with another process, and this incurs a time D. Again, we would prefer to measure the decision time D relative to t_c, and so we introduce the decision time factor $d = D/t_c$. Therefore, the total time required to process a grain of activity is t_g

$$t_g = t_c\,(g + x + d) \tag{6.1}$$

Clearly different machines will have different values for x and d, and these can be used to further classify multiprocessor systems. For example, there are some multiprocessor architectures which are able to overlap the time to access a decision variable with other useful processing. Furthermore, some machines are able to change context instantaneously, effectively multiplexing their time between different processes at the hardware level. Hence, using d and x, it is possible to define some simple and yet useful classes of architecture.

The class of *latency tolerant* (LT) architectures is the class of all architectures for which $d = 0$. Those architectures for which $d \neq 0$ are termed *latency sensitive* (LS). The class of *state multiplexed* (SM) architectures is the class of all architectures for which $x = 0$. Conversely those architectures for which $x \neq 0$ are termed *static state* (SS) architectures.

Within the class of LS architectures, the decision time is normally an increasing function of n (the number of processors in the system), and such architectures can be further classified according to the order of this function. For example, in binary k-cube architectures $d = O(\log n)$ whereas in 2-D mesh architectures $d = O(n^{1/2})$.

To summarise this architectural model, we have a system in which there are n processors and an intrinsic machine latency factor l. Each processor takes a time $d\,t_c$ to effect a proceed/wait decision based on some shared state information, and takes a time $x\,t_c$ to exchange the context of a suspended process for the context of a runnable process.

6.2.1 Speed-up and efficiency

In the design of multiprocessor systems we are concerned primarily with the performance that can be gained through the use of parallelism. It is therefore instructive to develop a theory for the expected speedup from the model described above. First let us consider the processing efficiency in our model. Since we define efficiency as the amount of useful computing performed in unit time, such overheads as context switching (x) and decision-making latency (d) can have an adverse affect.

The true effect of x and d on performance depends critically on the granularity of processing, g, and to model the degradation in performance due to multiprocessing overheads we define the *granular efficiency* η_g to be

$$\eta_g = \frac{g\,t_c}{t_g} = \frac{g}{g+x+d} = \frac{1}{1+\left(\frac{x+d}{g}\right)} \tag{6.2}$$

Note the similarity to the equation for *vector efficiency* (equation 10.3) presented in chapter 10 of volume I, which exhibits the same form. Here granularity is analogous to vector length and $x+d$ is analogous to $n_{1/2}$. We can therefore correctly surmise that a granular efficiency of 0.5 results from a granularity of $x+d$.

Furthermore, it is clear that architectures which are both latency tolerant *and* state multiplexed *must* have a fixed granular efficiency of 1.0, such architectures are therefore 100% efficient.

Let us now consider the parallelism profile of figure 6.3, and how the arbitrary level of parallelism, at each stage during execution of the application algorithm, could be scheduled on a fixed number of processors. At stage i in our model of computation there are π_i parallel processes[2] and these are to be evaluated by at most n processors. We will assume that each process can be scheduled on any processor with equal ease. In cases where this is not so, some reduction in performance may result due to imbalances in the loading across the system.

In order to describe the behaviour of the whole system over time, we use a simple graphical notation known variously as a *space-time diagram*, or *Gantt chart*. These diagrams indicate what the machine resources of interest (in our case processors) are doing at a particular instant in time, and hence map out the utilisation of machine resources over time. The space-time graph for the model system is shown in figure 6.4, and this plots space vertically with time proceeding from left to right. Here it can be seen that the degree of concurrency has been restricted by the available hardware (since in many cases π_i will be greater than n). This is achieved by scheduling the parallel processes sequentially, in groups of n, during each stage of the computation. Since all processes within each stage are

---

[2]The term *process* is used to denote any activity which can occur in parallel with activities of the same (or other) type. It therefore encompasses coarse-grained processes in the Operating System sense, as well as fine-grained dataflow processes.

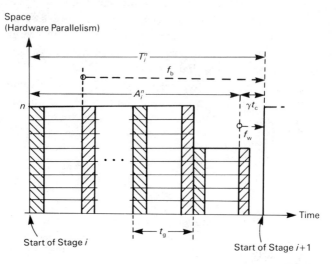

Figure 6.4 Space-time diagram for an n-processor system

independent, the actual order in which they are evaluated does not alter the result of the computation[3].

The dotted area in figure 6.4 represents the processor time used during the execution of a single grain of activity, and the areas shaded with oblique lines represent the processor time spent switching context and accessing non-local status information in order to synchronise with other processes. Figure 6.4 shows a snap-shot of the activity from the beginning of stage i to the beginning of stage $i+1$, under the assumption that the average level of granularity throughout stage i is g_i $\{g_i \geq 1\}$ and that the parallelism at stage i is π_i. Therefore, the average number of process grains that must be allocated to each processor in stage i is π_i/n, and the number of time-slices in stage i must be $\lceil \pi_i/n \rceil$. Hence, the time within stage i during which processors are busy, in an n-processor system, will be

$$A_i^n = \left\lceil \frac{\pi_i}{n} \right\rceil t_g \tag{6.3}$$

If we consider the worst-case and best-case analysis of the total time, for stage i on n processors, then we will get a lower bound and an upper bound on speedup (and processor utilisation) for n processors.

---

[3]The outcome may be different for different schedules if the computation as a whole is not determinate.

Worst-case analysis of speedup

The reason why grains of activity are processed in stage $i + 1$, rather than stage i, is that they need at least one value which is computed at stage i. The grains of activity in stage $i + 1$ cannot be evaluated until the values they require have not only been computed, but also transmitted (perhaps through an inter-processor communication network) to the receiving processor. In the worst case, the first grain of activity for every processor at stage $i + 1$ requires a value computed during the last time-slice of stage i. The worst-case critical path for the *flow-dependence* between stages i and $i + 1$ therefore extends across the interval labelled f_w in figure 6.4. Hence, stage $i + 1$ cannot begin until a time γt_c seconds after the completion of stage i, where γ is defined as

$$\gamma = max(d, l)$$

Therefore γ represents the minimum separation of two successive stages in the computation. In a latency sensitive architecture γ will be equal to d, the decision time factor, since in deciding that one process must suspend due to a flow-dependence with stage $i + 1$ enough information is exchanged to enable the first grain in stage $i + 1$ to begin execution. In a latency tolerant architecture ($d = 0$) the latency of information transfer at the end of stage i cannot be overlapped with any useful processing, and so γ must be equal to l. Therefore, the total machine time (active and inactive), consumed during the execution of stage i on n processors, is given by T_i^n

$$T_i^n \leq A_i^n t_g + (\gamma - d)t_c$$

However, $\lceil \pi_i/n \rceil$ can be simplified, since it is a fact that for any x and y,

$$\left\lceil \frac{x}{y} \right\rceil = \frac{x}{y} + \epsilon \quad \{0 \leq \epsilon < 1\} \tag{6.4}$$

Hence,

$$T_i^n < \left(\frac{\pi_i}{n} + 1 \right) t_g + (\gamma - d)t_c \tag{6.5}$$

This can be compared with the time required to process stage i, without modification to the granular structure of the application, on a single processor in order to discover the speedup resulting from the use of n processors. The time on a single processor is denoted T_i^1 and is given by

$$T_i^1 = \pi_i t_g \tag{6.6}$$

Therefore, combining equations 6.5 and 6.6, the lower bound on speedup at an arbitrary stage in the computation, $S(n)$, can be defined as

$$S(n) \stackrel{\text{def}}{=} \frac{T^1}{T^n} \geq \frac{n\pi(g + x + d)}{(n + \pi)(g + x + d) + n(\gamma - d)}$$

At this point it is useful to define λ, such that

$$\lambda = \frac{\text{grain time}}{\text{minimum stage time}} = \frac{g + x + d}{g + x + \gamma} \tag{6.7}$$

Hence, the equation for $S(n)$ can be rearranged, thus

$$S(n) \geq n \left[\frac{1}{1 + \frac{n}{\lambda \pi}} \right] \tag{6.8}$$

This analysis produces a lower bound which is independent of the clock speed of the machine and dependent only on the number of processors, the amount of parallelism in the application, the granularity of processing, the cost of processor communications and an inherent machine latency factor.

Best-case analysis of speedup

Consider now the best case arrangement of activity within stages i and $i + 1$, where the values required during the first time-slice within stage $i + 1$ (on all processors) are produced during the very first time-slice of stage i. Under this condition one might reasonably expect the latency of transmitting these values to be overlapped with the processing of the remaining grains of activity in stage i. The best-case critical path for the flow-dependence between stages i and $i + 1$ therefore extends across the time interval f_b, again illustrated in figure 6.4.

An analysis of the time required to compute stage i, in an n-processor system, requires us to consider two cases. The first case to consider occurs when *all* transmission latency can be overlapped by parallel activity within stage i, whereas the second case occurs when there is some latency which cannot be overlapped within stage i.

The case where all latency is overlapped with other processing can be written as

$$\text{Case 1} \quad \stackrel{\text{def}}{=} \quad A_i^n - (g_i + x)t_c > \gamma t_c \tag{6.9}$$

From equations 6.3 and 6.4, we know that

$$A_i^n = \left(\frac{\pi_i}{n} + \epsilon \right) t_g \quad \{0 \leq \epsilon < 1\}$$

Clearly in the best case we must set $\epsilon = 0$, since this leads to the lowest possible execution time on n processors and hence the greatest speedup. Therefore, let

$$A_i^n = \frac{\pi_i}{n} t_g \tag{6.10}$$

The condition under which case 1 holds can be derived from equations 6.9 and 6.10, resulting in

$$\text{Case 1} \quad \stackrel{\text{def}}{=} \quad \frac{\pi_i}{n}(g_i + x + d) > (g_i + x + \gamma)$$

which can be rearranged, and applied to an arbitrary stage of the computation, to define Condition 1 thus

$$\text{Condition 1} \quad \overset{\text{def}}{=} \quad n < \pi \left(\frac{g + x + d}{g + x + \gamma} \right) \quad \text{or} \quad n < \lambda \pi \qquad (6.11)$$

Since we know that under Case 1 all flow-dependence latency from stage i to stage $i + 1$ can be overlapped with other processing in stage i, the time for T_i^n will be simply

$$T_i^n \geq A_i^n$$

and hence, using equation 6.10

$$T_i^n \geq \frac{\pi_i}{n} t_g$$

Since we know what the time for stage i on one processor is, from equation 6.6, we can write down an equation for the best-case speedup (at any stage of the computation) under Condition 1, and this turns out to be exactly n, thus

$$S(n) \quad \overset{\text{def}}{=} \quad \frac{T_i^1}{T_i^n} \leq n \qquad (6.12)$$

Under the second case to be considered, not all of the latency involved in the transfer of information from stage i to stage $i + 1$ can be overlapped with other activity in stage i, and therefore the second case can be defined as

$$\text{Case 2} \quad \overset{\text{def}}{=} \quad A_i^n - (g_i + x)t_c < \gamma t_c \qquad (6.13)$$

Again, using equation 6.10, we can rearrange equation 6.13 and apply it to any stage of the computation. This defines Condition 2 as

$$\text{Condition 2} \quad \overset{\text{def}}{=} \quad n > \pi \left(\frac{g + x + d}{g + x + \gamma} \right) \qquad (6.14)$$

It can be seen from figure 6.4 that the time between the start of stage i and the start of stage $i + 1$, under Condition 2, is determined by the inherent machine latency and the time for the first time-slice. Therefore

$$T_i^n \geq (g_i + x + \gamma)t_c$$

Again we know the time to process stage i on a single processor, from equation 6.6, and hence we can express the best-case speedup under Condition 2 (at an arbitrary stage in the computation) as

$$S(n) \quad \overset{\text{def}}{=} \quad \frac{T^1}{T^n} \leq \pi \left(\frac{g + x + d}{g + x + \gamma} \right) \quad \text{or} \quad S(n) \leq \lambda \pi \qquad (6.15)$$

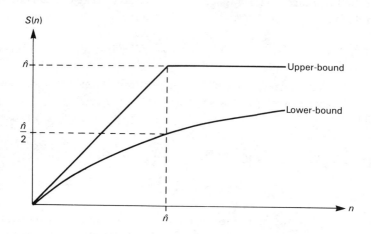

Figure 6.5 Upper and lower bounds on speedup in a multiprocessor

The upper and lower bounds on speedup can be plotted graphically to indicate the rate of growth in performance in relation to the number of processors engaged in processing the parallel activities. Figure 6.5 illustrates these bounds, with the shaded area defining the operating region of the combined algorithm and architecture. It is not possible for any parallel system to operate above the shaded region, and this is as one might reasonably expect. The upper-bound on speedup states that linear speedup is the best that is achievable, and again this appears reasonable. A poor algorithm (low value for π) or a bad architecture (high value for l and/or high value for d) will move both the upper and lower bounds downwards.

It is worth noting that the asymptotic upper-bound on speedup (equation 6.15) is equal to the value of n (the number of processors) at which the latency just begins to dominate the computation time. This value of n therefore has a special significance, and defines an *inflexion point* in the speedup curves. The inflexion point is denoted by $\hat{n}$, and is defined by

$$\hat{n} = \lambda \pi \qquad (6.16)$$

The upper and lower bounds on speedup can now be combined to give a general equation for speedup, thus

$$n \left[\frac{1}{1 + \frac{n}{\hat{n}}} \right] < S(n) \leq \begin{cases} n & \text{for } n \leq \hat{n} \\ \hat{n} & \text{for } n > \hat{n} \end{cases} \qquad (6.17)$$

Another interesting point to note is that the maximum difference between the upper and lower bounds actually occurs at the inflexion point
$(n = \hat{n})$. This can be seen quite clearly, since for $n < \hat{n}$ the difference
between the upper-bound and the lower-bound increases with n, whereas
for $n > \hat{n}$ the difference decreases with n. As $n \to \infty$ the upper and lower
bounds both approach the asymptotic maximum speedup of $S(\infty) = \hat{n}$.
Furthermore, if we substitute $n = \hat{n}$ into the lower-bound equation (equation 6.8) we find that the lower-bound on speedup at the inflexion point is
exactly $\hat{n}/2$. This means therefore, that for a given set of parameters the
actual speedup can never be worse than half the maximum speedup.

The variations in speedup, between the upper and lower bounds, are
caused by random scheduling of parallel activities. If it were possible to
optimise the scheduling of operations, so that the latency associated with
actual dependencies between successive stages in the computation could be
overlapped as much as possible with normal processing, then the machine
would operate as close to the upper-bound as the dependencies permitted.
It is unlikely that such scheduling could be performed during program execution, since the scheduling would almost certainly take longer to perform
than the computation itself. However, there may well be certain static op-
timisations that can be performed at compile-time, although in practice a
factor of two improvement is not a significant goal.

Naturally, the sales literature for commercial parallel machines normally
contains speedup curves showing the first (almost linear) section of the $S(n)$
curve, and the applications are likely to have been conveniently chosen so
that $\hat{n}$ is much greater than the actual number of processors provided.
Clearly, with realistic figures for l, d and x, machine users could construct
their own speedup curves, and then of course the results might be somewhat
different.

If the speedup for latency-sensitive static state architectures is examined
more closely it can be observed that since $d \neq 0$, γ will be equal to d (since
d can not be less than l). This produces a value for λ of exactly 1, and a
simplified speedup relationship of

$$n \left[\frac{1}{1 + \frac{n}{\pi}} \right] < S(n) \leq \begin{cases} n & \text{for } n < \pi \\ \pi & \text{for } n \geq \pi \end{cases} \tag{6.18}$$

In this relationship the level of granularity appears to be immaterial,
and indeed this is the case. Surely, however, something is missing in this
equation, since the realistic performance of machines with a large context
switching time on fine-grained applications *must* be low. The truth of the
matter is that $S(n)$ measures only the *relative* variations in performance
as n is changed and does not take into account the processing overheads
associated with multiprocessing each processor. To complete the model,

we define $G_\parallel$ to be the *parallel processing gain*, and this is essentially the net speedup of a parallel system compared with an equivalent sequential system. This is equal to the granular efficiency multiplied by the speedup, hence

$$G_\parallel = \eta_g S(n) \tag{6.19}$$

Using this measure of gain we can compare particular instances of parallel systems, as opposed to simply comparing the *rates* at which performance increases with the size of the system.

6.2.2　Extensibility

The high performance potential of multiprocessor systems derives directly from the replication of processing elements within those systems, and the concurrent operation of those processors on one or more tasks involving one or more processes. A fundamental consideration for the designer of multiprocessor systems is therefore the effect on the system of altering the degree of replication, usually upward.

There are several aspects of the design which must be considered. Firstly, as the number of processing elements in increased the total cost of the system must also increase. It is obviously desirable to minimise this increase in cost, and if the degree of replication is to be very large then a careful analysis of the rate of growth in hardware complexity (and hence cost) must be performed. For example, we know that the cost (measured as a gate-count) of a cross-bar switch grows in proportion to n^2 (for an $n \times n$ switch). Therefore, any multiprocessor which uses such a switch to connect the component processors will be limited in the degree to which they can be replicated by the cost of the interconnecting switch. We can therefore say that a cross-bar switch is not *extensible*, since an n^2 cost function yields diminishing returns on the investment in hardware. We might choose to alleviate this problem by connecting the processors together in the form of a ring. The rate of growth in hardware complexity for such a ring is clearly proportional to n (with a small constant of proportionality). However, whilst the cost of a ring structure is more than acceptable, the average processor-processor latency is proportional to the circumference of the ring, n. Therefore the latency factor, l, for a ring-structured multiprocessor will be proportional to n (unless all processors only communicate with processors which are a constant distance away). Since a low value for l is a desirable attribute for a multiprocessor system, having a value for l which is linearly related to n is counter-productive.

It is clear that one must consider two independent aspects of design when assessing the extensibility of a particular multiprocessor machine. Firstly, how close to linear is the growth in hardware cost? And secondly, how do the basic machine parameters, such as l, vary as the processing elements are replicated?

A further important consideration, particularly for very large-scale multiprocessors, is the *space* occupied by the system as a whole and more particularly by the inter-processor wiring. For example, consider n processors densely packed in a 3-dimensional volume. If each processor occupies a constant volume c, then the space occupied by the whole system must be at least nc. If the system is contained in a regular cube, then each side will have length which is at most $O(n^{1/3})$.

Assume these processors are connected in the form of a binary k-cube ($k = \log_2 n$), where a k-cube is defined recursively as two ($k-1$)-cubes, with corresponding processors in each sub-cube having a direct connection (see section 3.3.1). It should be possible to partition the volume containing the k-cube into two equal-sized volumes containing $n/2$ processors. To satisfy the interconnection requirements of the binary k-cube topology these two sub-volumes must have $\Omega(n)$ wires passing between them. However, the plane which bisects the n-processor system into two ($k - 1$)-cubes has an area which is at most $O(n^{2/3})$, and it is therefore clear that $\Omega(n)$ wires cannot pass through such a bisection. As a result, either the total volume occupied by the k-cube must be a super-linear function of n, or the communication bandwidth across each dimension of a binary k-cube must decrease as k increases. In order to reduce the communication bandwidth some wires crossing the dimension boundaries must be shared between a number of processors on either side of the division, and this requires multiplexing logic. In practice architectures with large binary k-cube routing networks have yet to suffer significantly from this problem, although in machines such as the Connection Machine [Hil85] and the NCUBE/10 [JRW86] (where each circuit board accommodates a relatively large sub-cube) pin-boundedness is certainly in evidence. The ability to extend a particular multiprocessor architecture is clearly only important within a given range, since commercial systems have a finite lifetime and the buyers of these systems have finite budgets. However, in the longer term, as configurations become larger, the effects of scaling will become more inportant and architectures which exhibit super-linear growth in volume will become less attractive. The extensibility of multiprocessor architectures is still a subject which is of much research interest, and the interested reader will find further information in Lipovski and Malek [LM87].

6.2.3 Reliability and fault-tolerance

The reliability of high performance computer systems is often considered to be an issue which is secondary to the most important task of designing for maximum throughput. However, the operating efficiency of a high performance system is the product of its throughput and its availability, and the availability of a machine depends on both the *mean time between failures* (MTBF) and the *average down time* (ADT). This is nowhere more important than in multiprocessor architectures since, as we shall see, the MTBF of very highly parallel MIMD systems can be extremely poor.

It is a commonly held belief that multiprocessor architectures are inherently tolerant of faults since the replication of processing elements leads to the natural availability of *spares* which can be *switched in* when the occasional processor fails. Designing machines which are fault-tolerant (and hence reliable) involves a great deal more than simply providing spares, however. For example, each fault must be located before any hardware reconfiguration can be performed, and when the fault has been rectified the state of the computation prior to the occurrence of the fault must be reinstated if fault processing is to be transparent.

Consider a hypothetical multiprocessor system containing 1000 processing elements, each consisting of just 100 components. If it is assumed that the failure rate for each component is 10^{-7} failures per hour $(\lambda = 10^{-7})$ then the MTBF for each component is $1/\lambda = 10$ million hours. The MTBF for the whole system can be calculated as the MTBF for each component divided by the number of components. Therefore, since there are 1000×100 components, the MTBF for the multiprocessor system will be just 100 hours, or approximately 4 days. This calculation includes only failures caused by faulty components. In addition there are *transient* faults caused by environmental factors such as changes in ambient temperature, or even cosmic radiation, and *intermittent* faults caused by poor production quality, and these normally occur more often than component faults. In addition to the problems of hardware reliability there are further problems associated with *software reliability*, and these are compounded in multiprocessor systems by the added software complexity of process synchronisation and communication. Diagnosing software faults in a multi-process environment can be a particularly difficult task.

Improvements in technology could, in the future, reduce the failure rate per gate within multiprocessor systems through the use of higher levels of integration. However, higher levels of integration will also result in systems with larger numbers of processors, and hence the problem of reliability will remain. Since faults cannot be avoided, and prolonged unavailability of high performance systems is unacceptable, the only alternative is to design high performance multiprocessors for maximum resilience and fault-tolerance.

Designing for maximum resilience means discovering which components are least reliable, and either minimising their use or making them more reliable. Designing for fault-tolerance means two things: firstly, designing systems with the ability to *detect* the occurrence of an error, and secondly imbuing those systems with the ability to correct and recover from an error. There are many ways in which the detection and recovery from faults can be implemented, for example one well-known method involves replicating sensitive components (usually thrice) and accepting the behaviour exhibited by the majority (this is known as triple-modular-redundancy, or TMR). This level of redundancy can be very costly, and of course the logic which compares the behaviour of the replicated modules may also be faulty.

The techniques that are applied to uni-processor architectures to detect faults, such as error-detecting codes (SECDED and parity checks), can be applied within each processing element of a multiprocessor system. However, in a multiprocessor system there is a further problem caused by the reliability of the network logic which connects processors to memories, or processor-memory pairs with each other. It is well known that the most unreliable elements in a computer system are the electrical connections between physically distinct component parts, and this is particularly true of intermittent faults. Hence, in a large multiprocessor system it is reasonable to expect interruptions in the interconnection network, since these normally contain large numbers of wires and connectors. Therefore the protocol for data-movement through the network should be robust, and capable of detecting and correcting transient errors. More permanent errors in the network logic will result in one or more paths becoming unusable. This may in turn reduce the connectivity of the network, and result in one or more processors being unable to communicate with the rest of the system. This can be overcome by designing networks with multiple paths between every pair of connectable components, so that if one path becomes inoperable another can be used.

Large high performance computers are sometimes designed with a particularly time-consuming application in mind. For example, the IBM GF11 project[4] [BDW85] was designed primarily for the solution of numerical problems in quantum chromodynamics. A calculation of particular interest has been estimated to take approximately one year on the GF11 machine, and under these circumstances reliability is a very important consideration. Since it is highly unlikely that a year-long computation could ever proceed to completion without encountering a system failure, such lengthy calculations must be partitioned into a sequence of computational segments which each occupy a time-span somewhat shorter than the system MTBF. At the end of each segment the state of the computation must be saved, allowing the computation to be *rolled back* to a previously known correct position and re-started in the event of failure. This ensures that the amount of time wasted as a result of each system failure is limited to the time for one

---

[4]The component count for the GF11 machine is approximately 4×10^5, 1296 of which are located in the network.

segment of the computation.

6.3 Summary

In conclusion, we have seen that in order to achieve significantly greater performance than has been possible with uni-processor machines the next generation of high performance computers must use multiprocessor or multicomputer architectures, and these are likely to incorporate large numbers of processing elements. The design issues which are important for these types of system have been discussed, and the expected performance has been modelled. This model emphasises the difference between granular efficiency and speedup; granular efficiency defines the slow-down which occurs when a single processor emulates a number of virtual processors, whereas speedup is simply the ratio of execution times for the same algorithm on one processor compared with n processors. This can never be greater than unity. Measured execution times, however, can sometimes yield parallel processing gains which are greater than n. This apparent 'super-linear' speedup is caused by side-effects, such as reduced working-set sizes, or the improper comparison of a sequential program and its parallelised version.

We have also seen why the reliability of multiprocessor architectures cannot be ignored, and briefly mentioned the issues to be considered when designing fault-tolerant multiprocessor systems.

The following two chapters discuss the two major categories of multiprocessor architecture; those which use shared-memory to enable their processors to interact, and those in which processors communicate through message-passing.

7 Shared-memory Multiprocessors

Architectures which incorporate a number of tightly-coupled processors often seem a natural choice for the computer designer in search of very high performance. For some applications SIMD vector or array processors are just not suitable, and a number of distinct instruction streams are required. However, multiprocessor architectures all face the fundamental problem of *data sharing* and *process synchronisation*, problems which can be illustrated by an analogy drawn from the experience of human organisation.

For a group of people to cooperate closely on a complex task, the task must be partitioned into a number of simpler sub-tasks that are of roughly equivalent complexity. During the course of their work the cooperating parties may need to exchange information in order to coordinate their activities. In some instances the results of one person's endeavours might have to be made available at all times to everybody else who is involved. Consider, for example, a man calculating prices in a financial market; these prices must be displayed and continuously updated throughout the course of a day's trading. In a similar way, cooperating processors in a multiprocessor system share the computational workload and occasionally communicate with each other. If a number of processors require access to the same piece of information then each must have Read and Write access to a shared area of physical memory. In this chapter we look at how this can be achieved, what problems arise and, for three important categories of shared-memory multiprocessor, we describe example machines in detail.

7.1 Shared-memory architecture

Probably the most attractive feature of shared-memory multiprocessors, seen particularly from within the existing programming community, is the flexibility and relative ease with which many different programming styles can be accommodated. This stems from the availability of a 'global state' which, together with elementary process synchronisation primitives, permits a full range of parallel programming paradigms to be supported. All shared-memory multiprocessor systems, although implemented in many different ways, are logically equivalent to one of the two abstract models illustrated in figure 7.1. These differ only in repect of their implementation; in case (a) the cost of accessing each memory location in the machine is the same, wherever the request emanates, and in case (b) access to non-local

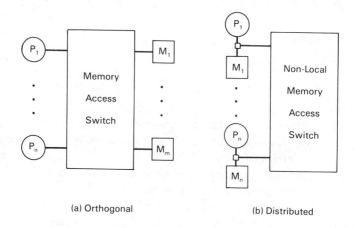

(a) Orthogonal   (b) Distributed

Figure 7.1 Basic shared-memory architectures

incurs an additional time penalty for all processors. The programmer's model of this abstract machine is extremely simple, and in most cases the programmer is unaware of any physical distribution of memory. This type of multiprocessor architecture is therefore particularly flexible, lending itself well to the porting of parallel algorithms between different shared-memory architectures.

The options open to the implementor of a shared-memory multiprocessor revolve around the mechanism for providing a path between each processor and each memory location, and the mechanism for ensuring temporary exclusive access to regions of memory when critical data-structures are being processed. Secondary issues include the balancing of computational load between the processors, deciding on whether each processor should timeshare its activity between more than one process, and the allocation and mapping of the global address space. These secondary issues present themselves in the design of any MIMD architecture, and were discussed in chapter 6.

Shared-memory multiprocessor systems can be classified in many ways. For example, it is possible to classify them according to whether they have strictly pub''   ry or some public memory and some private memory,
language model used. However, since the performance
multiprocessor is so closely linked to the architecture
ory interconnect, this will be the basis of the broad
his chapter. The range of possible interconnection
ctrum of generic shared-memory multiprocessor ar-
ost, *connectivity* and *maximum size*. At the low-cost
find multiprocessor systems constructed with lit-

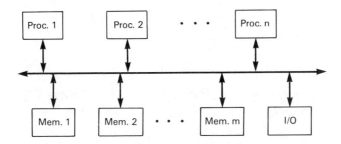

Figure 7.2 Shared-memory architecture using a common bus

tle or no parallelism in the interconnect. In such a system the memory requests of all processors must be serviced sequentially, and this places an upper bound on the number of processors that can be supported by this type of interconnect. At the highly-connected end of the spectrum there we find multiprocessor systems with interconnection mechanisms capable of servicing all memory requests in parallel (assuming distinct addresses). Unfortunately, the interconnection hardware in these architectures becomes extremely costly as the number of processors increases, and again this effectively places a vague upper bound on the number of processors that can be supported. Somewhere between these two extremes of cost and connectivity there are a class of architectures with interconnection schemes that are not *full* connection networks and where the size (and hence the cost) remains manageable for large numbers of processors. In the following sections of this chapter we look at these three categories of shared-memory multiprocessor, and for each category we discuss one example machine.

7.1.1 Sequential-access shared-memory systems

Conceptually, a sequential-access shared-memory architecture is one in which a number of processors share a common route to gain access to a global memory space. This is illustrated in figure 7.2, which shows a number of processors connected to a number of memory modules via a common bus. This is a natural extension of conventional single-processor buses, which were designed originally for their low-cost and high degree of flexibility. The major shortcoming of a common bus, in a shared-memory multiprocessor, is self evident; the data transfer capacity between processors and memories is determined by the bandwidth of the bus, and is therefore constant. This limits the number of processors that can be usefully incorporated into such a system, and hence fixes an upper limit on performance.

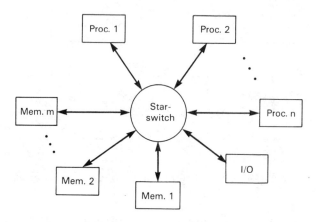

Figure 7.3 Multiprocessor system connected by a star-point network

The low cost of bus-structured multiprocessors has however proved to be advantageous for a number of small-scale parallel systems, yielding high performance/cost ratios without any pretensions of scalability. For configurations of between 1 and 20 processors, a bus-structured architecture can be a most effective interconnection mechanism, as witnessed by the evolution of commercial systems such as the Sequent Balance 8000 and the Encore Multimax, to name but two.

A sequential memory architecture can also be implemented with a star-point network, as illustrated in figure 7.3, although the cost is generally higher than a bus. An example of a star-point network is the MU5 Exchange [MI79], in which the MU5 and PDP-11 computers shared memory, I/O and Block-Transfer devices through a 100ns cycle-time packet-switched network.

With any shared resource, access conflicts can occur, and some mechanism for arbitrating between contenders for these resources is required. Two options are open to the designer; either a centralised mechanism or a distributed mechanism. In both cases a conflict resolution strategy is required. System costs can often be minimised by having a central arbitrator, although this adversely affects reliability since the system then becomes reliant on a single component. A distributed arbitration mechanism increases the cost of each processor, but promotes reliable or fault-tolerant behaviour. The performance of the arbitration strategy may also be improved by distributing the mechanism for performing arbitration amongst the contenders for the resources.

Conflict resolution strategies

In order that utilisation of the available bus bandwidth be maximised, the resolution of simultaneous requests for the bus must be performed in a time which is less than the bus cycle time. This means that the algorithm for assigning priority to bus devices must be implemented in hardware.

Many algorithms for assigning priorities have been devised, and their characteristics are well-known. Probably the simplest algorithm is the *fixed-priority* algorithm. As its name suggests, the fixed-priority algorithm assigns a fixed priority to each contender for the shared resource and allocates cycles accordingly. This algorithm is useful in single-processor bussed architectures for assigning permanent priorities to time-critical devices, such as disks, but its lack of 'fairness' makes it particularly unsuitable for multiprocessor systems. Fairness can be defined in terms of the standard deviation of average wait-times perceived by contending devices, with a low standard deviation indicating a fair arbitration algorithm. For example, an algorithm which always gives rapid attention to some devices and always gives poor attention to others, will have a significant spread of average wait-times. Conversely, an algorithm which does not favour any particular device, or group of devices, when allocating bus cycles, will have approximately equal wait-times on all devices.

A much fairer method of sharing the limited resources of the bus is the *fixed time-slice* algorithm, in which bus cycle x is allocated to processor $\mid x \mid_n$ regardless of whether that processor is requesting a cycle. Hence, each device gets one cycle in n, and may have to wait up to $n - 1$ cycles before receiving attention. The relatively poor bandwidth available to individual processors makes this scheme inefficient when devices are operating sporadically, or in bursts.

The fixed priority and fixed time-slice algorithms are essentially static algorithms; more sophisticated algorithms resort to using dynamic device priorities in order to combine the throughput of static priority with the fairness of time slicing. Two important algorithms of this type are the *least recently used* (LRU) and the *cyclic priority* (CP) algorithms. The LRU algorithm is a well-known algorithm from Operating Systems [Lis88] which, as its name suggests, assigns the lowest priority to the processor which used the bus most recently and assigns the highest priority to the processor which used the bus the least recently. The usual way to implement this is with a central arbitrator containing an ordered list of bus devices. Whenever a bus device is allocated a bus cycle, the device given the cycle is placed at the bottom of the list. Then arbitration is performed by selecting the highest requesting device in the list. Conversely, the CP algorithm can be implemented as a distributed arbitration algorithm through the use of a closed *daisy chain* mechanism. The modification of priority occurs by assigning the highest priority to the device whose position in the chain is immediately after the device which last used the bus.

Finally, the algorithm with the minimum average wait-time (and also the smallest spread of wait-times) is the *first-come-first-served* algorithm. However, this requires the order of occurrence of requests to be known in order to operate correctly, and this is difficult to discern when multiple requests can occur with very little time interval between them. In practice this algorithm is not used for bus arbitration, even though it is optimal.

Effects of scaling

One can assess the usefulness of sequential access shared-memory multiprocessor systems by analysing how the *cost* and *throughput* vary in response to changes in the number of processors in the system. The cost, C, can be defined quite simply in terms of the basic cost of the bus backplane, b, plus the cost of n processors. The cost of each processor is equal to the cost of the processing hardware p, plus the cost of the bus interface logic l. Hence, for an upper bound of N processors;

$$C = b + n(p + l) \quad \{0 \leq n \leq N\}$$

If p and l are genuinely constant then C represents a linear cost function, within the specified bounds. The upper bound N is determined by three factors; the bus bandwidth, physical constraints on the length of the bus, and electrical fan-out limitations. The bandwidth available on the bus depends on the technology used in the bus interface logic of each bus device, and on the protocol used to implement global read and write cycles. The bandwidth required by each processor depends on the frequency with which requests are generated. The propagation time of signals on the bus limit the length of each bus signal to around 1 metre, and this limits the size of a bus-connected system to a single card-frame. The fan-out of the devices used in the bus interface circuitry will also place a limit on the maximum number of bus devices which can shared the same electrical signals. In practice, this will be on the order of twenty devices.

In theory the throughput of a sequential access device, such as a common bus, is equal to t_c^{-1}, where t_c is the bus cycle time. However, in practice this is reduced by a utilisation factor ϵ $\{0 \leq \epsilon \leq 1\}$. This reduction in throughput is caused by occasional requests failing after being allocated a bus cycle. In a multiprocessor system this occurs when memory modules are 'busy' when they receive requests. A memory module is considered 'busy' if it is performing a cycle on behalf of another processor, or if the location requested is 'locked-out' on behalf of another processor in order to ensure exclusive access to a shared data structure. This occurs during spin-lock operations (see section 7.3.2), and can result in a serious degradation of bus performance.

Bus utilisation can be improved by providing larger numbers of memory modules, hence reducing the probability of modules being busy, and by increasing the re-try intervals for locked-out memory requests exponentially.

The main points to note about bus-connected multiprocessor systems are that, however well engineered they may be, the maximum configuration is limited to around 20 processors with current technology, and the prospects for improving this with future technology are not good. In addition to the problem of scalability, synchronising processes through flags held in memory can seriously degrade system performance. In spite of these difficulties several commercial systems have emerged, and the innovative techniques used to circumvent the above-mentioned problems are explained with reference to one particular machine, the Sequent Balance 8000, in section 7.2.

7.1.2 Highly-connected shared-memory systems

A natural method of alleviating the bottleneck of a single bus in a shared-memory multiprocessor is through the provision of *multiple* buses, and this technique has the added advantage of introducing some degree of fault-tolerance to the interconnection mechanism (often the most error-prone component in any system). The multiple-bus technique was used in the Pluribus system [KEM*78], a multiprocessor architecture in which small numbers of Lockheed SUE processors were connected to independent *processor, memory* and *I/O* buses. Although Pluribus used multiple buses primarily to improve system reliability, an important consideration in high-performance architectures, the possible application of this technique for increasing the processor-memory bandwidth is obvious.

The number of buses in a multiple-bus architecture could be extended until there are as many buses as there are shared memory modules, at which point the interconnection between processors and memories effectively would become a cross-bar switch. This is the other extreme of connectivity from the sequential-access mechanism considered earlier, and one which has been used in several small and medium sized systems. This approach to processor-memory interconnect is really only suitable for a 'herd of elephants' configuration (as opposed to an 'army of ants' configuration) in which a relatively small number of powerful processors are used (as opposed to a very large number of low-powered processors). Probably the most influential multiprocessor system to use this form of interconnection between processors and memories was the C.mmp system, although subsequent machines such as the Stanford S-1 [Wid80] and the commercially available IP-1 have also used this interconnection technique.

7.1.3   Scalable multiprocessors

The machines we have looked at so far in this chapter have been relatively small-scale systems, comprising less than twenty processors. Architectures which connect their processors via a single sequential channel, such as a bus, are limited by bandwidth constraints, electrical properties and physical wire lengths. Conversely, architectures which solve the bandwidth problem by using cross-bar switches suffer from a growth in hardware complexity which is proportional to n^2. Somewhere between these two extremes lies a family of architectures with better than n^2 hardware cost as well as communication mechanisms which can support much greater numbers of processors. These systems rely on the use of multi-stage interconnection networks for the manageability of their complexity[1]. Whilst it can be shown that there are still problems in scaling multiprocessor systems connected by multi-stage interconnection networks, quite large systems can be constructed using this style of architecture.

In the following sections we examine the architecture of three very different shared-memory multiprocessors, each of which uses one of the three types of processor-memory interconnect described previously. We examine the design decisions involved and assess their performance and scalability.

7.2   The Sequent Balance 8000

The constraining nature of common-bus multiprocessor architecture stimulates the ingenuity of designers, who then produce sophisticated solutions. The Sequent Balance is a good example of this phenomenon, as it incorporates special techniques for providing very high bus bandwidth as well as for supporting primitive locking operations.

The designers of the SB8000 started out with the knowledge that in previous multiprocessor systems each additional processor contributed only $0.8 \times$ the actual performance of each processor already in the system. Hence, points on the speedup curve for such a system would typically be 1, 1.8, 2.5, ... This diminishing return made each successive processor less and less cost effective. Therefore, careful engineering of the critical components is required in order to alleviate this problem, and the remainder of this section describes how this is achieved in the Sequent machine.

The SB8000 system is an homogeneous multiprocessor system, capable of supporting between two and twelve identical processors, based on the National Semiconductors NS32032 32-bit microprocessor. Each processor is supplied with a floating-point coprocessor and memory management hardware. All processors share a number of common memory modules via a

---

[1]Other interconnection structures, such as trees of processors, have been proposed [Lei85,IEH*85] but are beyond the scope of this book.

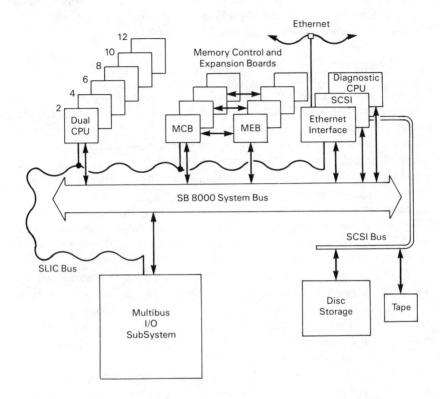

Figure 7.4 Organisation of the Sequent Balance 8000

26.7 M byte/s system bus, providing up to 28 M bytes of primary storage. All processors share a single copy of the Unix-like operating system, and in order to reduce global memory contention each processor has a private cache for storing recently used instructions and data. This is a two-way set-associative cache with an 8 K byte capacity. Transfers between main memory and the cache occur in units of 64-bits, yielding an effective hit-ratio of 95 per cent. The block structure of the SB8000 is shown in figure 7.4.

The SB8000 has an orthogonal architecture, which means that all memory, I/O and interrupt resources are accessible to all processors. These resources are allocated dynamically. Hence, a process scheduler assigns processors from the pool of processing resources, earning it the title 'processor pool' architecture. The fair distribution of work requires careful hardware and software design to ensure that there is good utilisation of all resources, especially the pool of processors. Central to this theme is a custom coprocessor chip, known as the System Link and Interrupt Controller (SLIC), which is optimised to perform tasks which normally cripple the performance of less sophisticated bus-structured multiprocessors.

7.2.1   Cache consistency

Since each processor has a private cache, the problem of maintaining cache consistency arises. It is possible for multiple copies of shared data items to exist in two or more caches throughout the system and, when a processor updates its own copy, those belonging to other processors must reflect this change. Naturally the master copy held in global memory must also be updated. Therefore the SB8000 cache employs a 'write through' technique, causing each processor write cycle to appear on the system bus. Then, when a global write cycle occurs, two things happen; firstly the correct location in global memory is updated and, secondly, all cached entries for that location are invalidated throughout the machine. This is achieved through the use of a technique known as 'bus watching', in which the control logic associated with each cache monitors every bus cycle in order to detect write cycles to memory locations cached locally. Hence, by comparing bus addresses with the addresses of blocks cached locally, it can recognise when writes to such blocks occur. Invalidating the cache entry, rather than assimilating the data on the system bus, simplifies the logic required, but means that subsequent re-reading of data is required.

In the SB8000 it has been observed that write-cycles constitute 10–15 per cent of all processor cycles and, although this is a relatively small proportion, if each processor waited for the completion of its write cycles before continuing processing, a significant amount of time could be wasted. The cache therefore incorporates a write buffer, as illustrated in figure 7.5, to permit the processing of write-through cycles to proceed in parallel with subsequent instructions.

Clearly, the write-through operation imposes a certain degree of sequentiality on the system as a whole, since the address comparison which every cache controller must perform effectively steals a cycle from all caches simultaneously. This is the price which must be paid for maintaining data consistency in a transparent multi-cache environment.

7.2.2   The SLIC

Every processor, memory controller, I/O channel and bus controller has associated with it a System Link and Interrupt Controller (SLIC) chip. The SLIC is effectively a coprocessor providing the functions required in a shared-memory multiprocessor, but not present in commercially available microprocessors (such as the NS32032). In addition to providing these extra

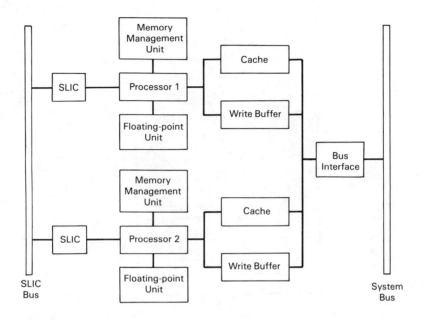

Figure 7.5 Structure of a Balance 8000 processor card

functions, the SLIC also contributes to the parallelism in the system by operating independently from the system bus.

The functions of the SLIC are three-fold. Firstly, between them the SLIC devices manage the distribution of incoming interrupts, and they do this by dynamically assigning each interrupt to the processor which is currently executing the lowest priority task. In order organise the distribution, all controllers communicate with each other across a dedicated serial bus, somewhat similar in operation to an Ethernet. The structure of a SLIC chip, and its connections to the SLIC bus, are shown in figure 7.6. It is interesting to note that some of the most time-critical functions of this shared-memory architecture are actually implemented within a message-passing multiple-coprocessor sub-system, and not through the shared memory.

The second function of the SLIC, and another time-critical function, is the manipulation of system-wide semaphores. As shown in figure 7.6, each SLIC contains a cache of semaphores. Effectively these are single-bit protection flags, through which all high-level mutual exclusion and synchronisation facilities are implemented. An important consequence of implementing processor synchronisation primitives with dedicated hardware is that spin-

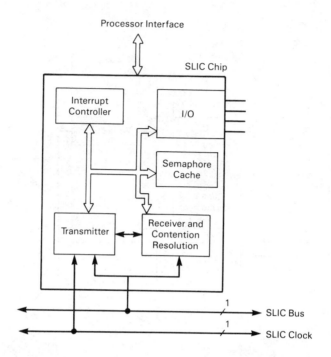

Figure 7.6 The System Link and Interrupt Controller

lock operations do not need to access global memory via the system bus. Spin-locks can present quite a heavy load on the system bus, and therefore any technique which removes this load must improve the performance of the whole system. Note however, that this migration of functionality can only improve memory bandwidth, and cannot solve the performance problem caused by the 'busy waiting' which occurs during spin-lock operations.

The third function of the SLIC is to act as a supervisory agent and communicate with other SLICs to perform system diagnostics and debugging. It can, for example, take the resources for which it is responsible 'off-line' and notify the system. Similarly, when a new processor card is inserted, the SLIC informs the other resources via the SLIC bus, and the system automatically re-configures itself without further physical modification.

The SLIC chip is implemented using 3μM CMOS gate-array technology, and the SLIC bus is implemented as a two-wire multi-drop serial link using wired-OR logic and incorporating collision-detect circuitry. The SLIC represents a very useful innovation, contributing heavily towards the efficient engineering of the sequentially accessed shared-memory of the SB8000. The other major component is of course the system bus.

7.2.3   The SB8000 system bus

Designing a shared-bus for a multiprocessor machine is a difficult task, and one made more difficult by the need to reconcile two fundamentally conflicting design criteria. The bus must provide high bandwidth and symmetrical access between all processors and system resources, including I/O sub-systems, and yet it must do so with the minimum interfacing complexity since low-cost is one of the primary reasons for choosing a bus interconnect. In order to achieve the necessary raw bandwidth to support up to twelve processors the SB8000 system bus uses a 10 MHz synchronous protocol, and to reduce the complexity of the interface hardware to less than 20 chips it uses a time-multiplexed address and data path. The interface logic is implemented in '74F series' (fast) TTL.

If each processor retained control of the bus throughout the complete duration of a memory operation, a large proportion of the bus bandwidth could be wasted. This is because while the bus can transfer a request to the memory and a response to a processor in 100 ns, the latency of each memory operation is around 300 ns. Therefore, the bus incorporates a split protocol in which processors relinquish the bus between issuing requests and receiving responses. In effect the bus masters send request packets to the bus slaves, who in turn send response packets back to the masters. Each packet transfer takes 100 ns, with the exception of a write-response, which is simply an event with no associated data, and which is implemented via the control path. Write responses can therefore occur in parallel with other bus transfers, again helping to maximise the useful bus throughput. The bus protocol also permits data transfers to take place in variable-length packets up to 8 bytes long.

Decoupling the bus protocol from the memory latency enables multiple memory controllers to be interleaved, since several requests (hopefully to different controllers) can be active at the same time. The combination of these techniques results in a quoted peak bandwidth of 40 M bytes/s and a quoted sustainable bandwidth of 26.7 M bytes/s.

A protocol which splits requests and responses can lead to situations in which multiple requests arrive at a single destination (a memory controller or I/O bus adapter) in rapid succession, and at a higher burst rate than they can be serviced. In the SB8000 this problem is solved by placing request and response queues in all destination devices. Then, having provided queues to smooth out transient peaks in the flow of requests and responses, a mechanism for preventing these queues from overflowing is required. There are two ways this problem can be approached; the first involves sending negative responses to a requesting device if there is no room in the request buffer to store an incoming request. Then, some time later, the same request must be re-tried. This is a form of 'busy waiting', since extra cycles are introduced to perform periodic checks on the status of the destination request queue. If contention for one memory module is high, these request and negative response cycles will soak up a large proportion of the available bus bandwidth. The second way only allows a request to be issued if a free place in the destination request queue exists. This means that every requester must maintain local information on the status of all destination queues. An unfortunate consequence of this is that the logical complexity if each bus requester then becomes proportional to the size of the system, and system complexity becomes non-linear. The advantage is that, even when the bus is experiencing very heavy loading, each bus cycle carries useful information. The Sequent Balance 8000 uses the latter technique in the knowledge that the slightly non-linear logical complexity has very little bearing on the actual size or cost when system sizes are limited by bus bandwidth.

7.3   C.mmp

In 1971 a project was initiated at Carnegie-Mellon University to design the hardware and software for C.mmp [WB72], a multiprocessor system using minicomputer processors (DEC PDP-11s). Once completed, the system ran for about ten years and proved to be a valuable research tool for both computer architects and users. C.mmp was intended to be *symmetrical*, so that replicated components could be treated as an anonymous pool, with no one of them being special in any way. It was also to be a *general purpose* system, in which parallelism could be exploited at both the *task* and the *process* level. The system therefore contained a pool of processors, and a number of independent tasks, each of which could contain a number of parallel (and interdependent) processes.

The symmetrical nature of the hardware can be seen from figure 7.7 which shows the configuration of the system. The 16 PDP-11 processors (P_0-P_{15}) were connected to 16 independent memory banks via a crosspoint switch (S_m) which permitted any processor to access any memory. A path through the switch was established independently for each memory request and up to 16 paths could exist simultaneously. Memory contention was handled at the inputs to the switch. The interrupt mechanism was also symmetrical; every processor being able to interrupt every other processor (including itself) with equal ease.

As a means of reducing switch and memory contention and providing faster memory access, the design permitted the inclusion of a cache memory in each processor. The problem of cache consistency, which we observed in

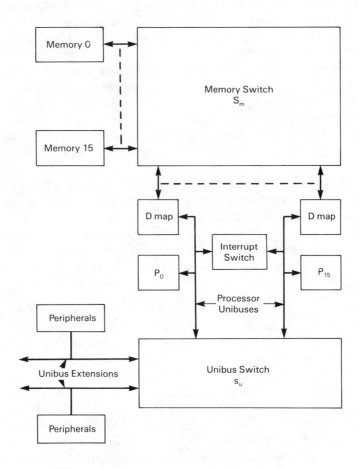

Figure 7.7 Overall organisation of C.mmp

considering the design of the IBM 3090 (volume I section 3.3.3) and the Sequent Balance (section 7.2.1), was to be solved by only creating cache entries for information taken from *read only* pages. This would have included all instructions, of course. Simulation studies showed that a small cache of 256–512 words would capture 79–90 per cent of eligible references and give an overall improvement in system performance of 10–40 per cent. In practice cost prevented the inclusion of cache stores in the system actually constructed and code sharing among all processes in a multiprocessor application proved to be a significant problem [WH78].

Symmetry in software implies that there must be no *master-slave* relationship among the processors. Thus on C.mmp any processor could execute any part of the operating system at any time, subject to mutual exclusion on accesses to shared data structures. At the user level, a job could execute on any processor, and would frequently switch from one processor to another many times during execution.

The requirement for a general purpose system proved more difficult to satisfy [WH78]. For example, it was possible to partition processors and memories but not to run the operating system kernel (Hydra) in more than one partition. The major obstacles to this were the difficulty of providing meaningful communication between what would be, in effect, two separate operating systems, and the lack of sufficient peripherals to allow each partition to have an adequate complement of devices. Access to peripherals was by a second type of switch (S_u in figure 7.7) which allowed one or more PDP-11 Unibus extensions to be connected to any one of the processors' Unibusses. In order to avoid the cost of determining dynamically which of the processors was currently managing a particular peripheral, the allocation of a Unibus extension to a processor was made on a relatively long term basis (from a fraction of a second to several hours).

7.3.1   The small address problem

The 16-bit address space of the PDP-11 allows user programs to address no more than 64 Kbytes of memory. In C.mmp the amount of memory available was much larger than this, however, amounting to 3 Mbyte. Some form of address relocation was clearly necessary, but the situation here was the reverse of that pertaining in most virtual addressing systems, where a processor can address *more* memory than is provided in hardware.

The software/hardware facility provided in C.mmp to solve this problem involved partitioning the address space of each processor into eight 4 Kword pages. A user was permitted an indefinite number of pages, but could address only eight of them at any instant. Facilities in the operating system allowed the user to designate dynamically which pages were to be addressable. Relocation of these pages into an overall 21-bit address space was achieved through the use of four sets of relocation registers, known as the D_{map} (figure 7.7). Two bits in the processor status word (inaccessible to user programs) were used to provide the additional two address bits available on the Unibus. These bits then selected one of the four sets of relocation registers and the top three bits of the 16-bit user address selected one of eight registers within the set.

At the outset of the project it was assumed that the 16-bit limitation would be offset by the ability to create multiprocess programs, and that a typical program would be organised as a large number of processes, each of which would only need to address a small amount of memory. This turned out to be true for code in many cases (although multiprocess algorithms did not always produce small programs), but less often for data. In addition, the fact that the programmer always had to be aware of page boundaries meant that the system was less than ideal. C.mmp was capable of executing at a rate of about 6 MIPS and was comparable in size to the CDC 6600. Consequently, users expected both machines to cope with problems of comparable size. As we noted in volume I section 2.2

> "There is only one mistake...that is difficult to recover from
> – not providing enough address bits..."

7.3.2   Locks and synchronisation

A multiprocessor operating system is required to schedule and coordinate the activities of the individual processors. In Hydra the information necessary to make these decisions was contained within a shared data base, and the parts of Hydra which made these decisions could be running on several processors simultaneously. In order to maintain consistency of the data base it was essential that while one processor was accessing or, more particularly, updating the data base, all other processors be prevented from accessing or changing it. The mechanism adopted involved the use of *locks* on the data base and portions of programs which accessed lockable data items were referred to as *critical sections*. On entering a critical section the program first had to check that the lock was not set, and otherwise wait, then set the lock (Dijkstra's *P* operation on a semaphore [Dij65]) and on leaving the critical section, reset the lock (Dijkstra's *V* operation). At one extreme the whole data base could be controlled by a single lock, whereas at the other extreme every data item could be individually locked. The former case would have precluded any parallel operations on the data base, of course, while in the latter case the overheads of performing the locking operations would have been prohibitive. In practice the number of critical sections in Hydra lay in the range 2–7, depending on the path taken through the scheduler. Similar mechanisms were used in user program where the synchronisation of communication between individual processes was achieved through access to lockable shared data items.

A question which immediately arises is what to do with a processor which is waiting to enter a critical section. A number of different solutions were tried on C.mmp. The mechanism which gave fastest entry to a critical section was the *spin-lock*. In PDP-11 assembly code the *P* and *V* operations for a spin-lock are as follows

```
P:   CMP SEMAPHORE         : is SEMAPHORE = 1 ?
     BNE P                 : loop if not = 1
     DEC SEMAPHORE         : decrement SEMAPHORE
     BNE P                 : if < 0, return to P
```

V: MOV #1, SEMAPHORE   : reset SEMAPHORE to 1

Thus a processor which is attempting to enter a critical section polls the value of SEMAPHORE looking for a value of 1. When it finds a value of 1 it decrements SEMAPHORE, and then checks that its value is 0 before proceeding. If the value is < 0, this implies that another processor which was also polling SEMAPHORE has gained access to the data structure and the first processor must continue to wait.

There are two major drawbacks to using spin-locks. Firstly, a processor which is polling is not doing any useful work. Secondly, it is consuming memory cycles in the bank containing the semaphore value and, if several processors are polling on the same semaphore, memory bandwidth is rapidly consumed. In the worst case the processor currently operating on the locked data structure will also be accessing this same memory bank and will be slowed down as a consequence. In more recent multiprocessor systems such as the CRAY X-MP (volume I section 7.2) and the Sequent Balance (section 7.2) this problem does not arise because the synchronisation registers are not part of main memory. The use of standard PDP-11 processors as components of C.mmp largely precluded this possibility. The spin-lock mechanism was therefore only used on small data structures, which would only be locked for a few hundred μs. For larger data structures, two alternative mechanisms were provided, the *Kernel Semaphore* and the *Policy Module Semaphore*.

In the Kernel Semaphore mechanism the P and V operations were implemented using calls to the Hydra Kernel. If a process became blocked on a P operation, because some other process was operating on the relevant data structure, the blocked process was swapped out of the processor which was then re-scheduled to run a different process. The blocked process was placed on a *blocked queue* associated with the semaphore and was swapped back in, possibly to a different processor, when its turn came. To ensure a fast restart, pages belonging to the blocked process were retained in primary memory. However, the time taken in blocking and unblocking still amounted to several μs, two orders of magnitude longer than the time taken by a spin-lock.

The *Policy Module Semaphore* was intended for user programs and was implemented by calls to a *Policy Module*. The principal difference between the *Policy Module Semaphore* and *Kernel Semaphore* was that blocked processes in the former could have their pages swapped out to secondary (disc) memory. This could delay a restart by several hundreds of μs of course, so to assist in maintaining performance and to avoid unnecessary swapping, no pages were swapped until a period of a few hundred μs had elapsed after blocking.

The C.mmp machine was a pioneering project, with features such as the symmetrical nature of the architecture surviving in to present day multiprocessors. However, problems such as the costly interconnection structure, and the inefficient implementation of process synchronisation primitives, were well-learned by the designers of subsequent shared-memory multiprocessors.

7.4 The BBN Butterfly

Our primary reason for examining this particular machine is that while many large-scale shared-memory architectures have been proposed, the Butterfly is currently the only such machine of its size, which is commercially available. We shall see that, as with all practical systems, the Butterfly achieves good performance within the range of sizes for which it is engineered but that venturing above this range with the same architecture will not necessarily produce the same results.

The origins of the Butterfly can be traced back to an earlier BBN system called Pluribus (see section 7.1.2), a multiple-bus parallel processor designed for high-reliability message processing on ARPANET. Subsequent research, into the design of a successor to Pluribus, began around 1975 with extensive support from the U.S. Defense Advanced Research Projects Agency (DARPA). Although the machine that emerged was originally intended to be used for a mixture of military and government applications, the commercial value of the Butterfly is now also being exploited. When the Butterfly was launched commercially in 1985 four machines out of an expected 10 had already been delivered to DARPA, and one of these machines was a 128-processor version.

7.4.1 Overview of the Butterfly

The Butterfly parallel processor [CGS*85,RT86] is a tightly-coupled shared-memory machine with homogeneous processing elements. The machine's primary memory is distributed amongst the processors, with each processor having either 1 or 4 M bytes of dynamic memory. The processor-memory pairs, known as processing nodes, are interconnected by the Butterfly Switch, details of which are presented later in this section. The block structure of the Butterfly architecture is illustrated in figure 7.8. Perhaps the most significant feature of the Butterfly is that it is purposefully engineered to be cost-effective over a wide range of configurations, up to a maximum of 256 processing nodes. The Input and Output are distributed amongst the processing nodes, with up to four I/O device adapters per node. These may be either IEEE 796 Multibus adapters or a proprietary adapter containing eight serial ports (4 × RS-232 and 4 × RS-449).

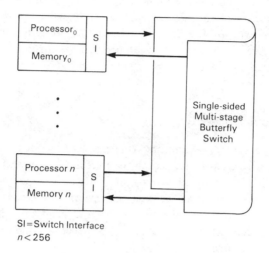

SI = Switch Interface
$n < 256$

Figure 7.8 Architecture of the BBN Butterfly

Each Butterfly card frame holds up to 16 processing nodes, and four card frames make up a rack. The largest configuration would therefore occupy eight racks. In order to maximise the system reliability for such large numbers of processing nodes each node has a private 'on-board' switched-mode power supply.

7.4.2   Butterfly processing nodes

At the heart of each processing node in the Butterfly system is a Motorola M68000 family microprocessor. This may be either a M68000, operating at 8 MHz, or alternatively if floating-point performance is important, an M86020 processor with memory management and floating-point coprocessor, operating at 16 MHz.

In section 7.2 we saw how the interprocessor communication functions required in the Sequent Balance were implemented with a custom coprocessor, and in the Butterfly a similar approach is used. Each processing node has a 16-bit user-microprogrammable bit-slice control processor, based on the AMD 2901, known as the Processor Node Controller (PNC). The PNC intercepts all memory references from the microprocessor and accesses either local or non-local memory on its behalf. The PNC also handles all incoming memory requests from non-local processors, arriving via the Butterfly Switch. With the aid of the memory management hardware the PNC translates virtual addresses into physical addresses, thus permitting the software

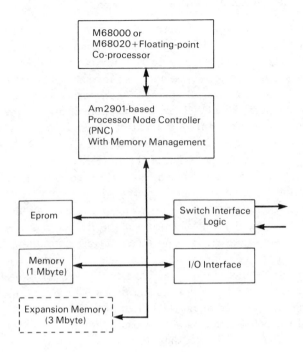

Figure 7.9 Butterfly processor node

to locate each segment of virtual memory anywhere in the system. This results in the memory of all processing nodes appearing to the application software as a single global address space.

The local memory associated with each processing node consists of 1 Mbyte of dynamic memory, expandable to 4 Mbyte with the addition of a 'daughter board'. Each processing node also has a bi-directional interface to the Butterfly Switch, and its own private Input-Output bus. The block-structure of a processing node is illustrated in figure 7.9.

From an architect's viewpoint the most interesting features of the Butterfly machine are the Butterfly Switch and the PNC, as together these two components define the time penalty associated with non-local memory accesses, and hence the intrinsic machine latency. However, because there is a time differential between local and non-local memory references, and because messages passing through the switch can interfere with one another, the way in which data are distributed throughout the shared address space also plays an important role in determining the machine's overall performance.

7.4.3　The Butterfly switch

The Butterfly switch provides a mechanism for passing messages between the Node Controllers of different processing elements. These messages normally take the form of memory cycle requests and acknowledgements, and since the assembly and dissassembly of message packets is performed by the PNC, the microprocessors perceive transparent access to both local and non-local memory. The PNCs are also capable of performing block transfer operations to facilitate the movement of blocks of memory from the local memory of one processing node to another.

The 'black box' specification of the Butterfly switch is a relatively simple one. As far as the processing nodes are concerned, it consists of an equal number of input and output ports, which need not be a power of two, although normally they would be. The ports are uniquely labelled and, to enable routing to be performed 'on the fly' as messages pass through the switch, each message incorporates a header containing the label of its destination port. The insertion of messages into the switch from different sources occurs asynchronously, and the time taken for a message to propagate from its source to its destination depends on the number of inputs to the switch and the loading on the switch during routing. The asynchronous nature of the M68000 bus enables variable round-trip delays to be hidden from the processor, although they do have an effect on system performance as we shall see shortly.

The network messages, containing non-local memory addresses, a data field and some control bits, are approximately 80-bits long and, to keep the complexity (measured here in terms of inter-stage wiring) of the switch nodes within manageable limits, the switch nodes serialise the packets into 8-bit chunks. These 8-bit chunks are piped through the switch at a rate of one chunk every 100 ns, resulting in a minimum switch latency of approximately 10 cycles per packet.

Switch topology

The Butterfly switch is a multi-stage network which uses a variant of the shuffle permutation (see section 3.3.3) to connect 4-input and 4-output exchange boxes. These exchange boxes are effectively 4×4 cross-bar switches, and to illustrate this a Butterfly switch with 16 ports is depicted in figure 7.10.

Routing within a single node is performed by labelling the four output ports uniquely in the range $\{0 \dots 3\}$, then assigning a route from each input port to the output port selected by the two least significant digits of the destination label associated with each incoming packet, as shown in figure 7.10. As the destination label for a packet passes through each switching node

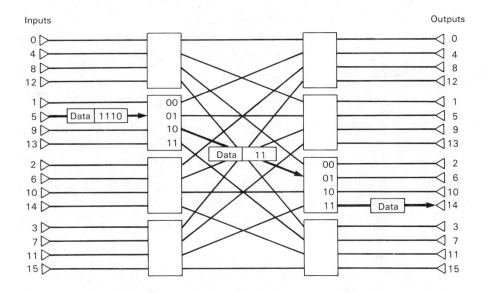

Figure 7.10 16-Port Butterfly switch

the two least signinficant digits are 'removed', thus exposing the next two digits to the routing function in the subsequent stage of the network. If at any time during the setting up of a route through the switch, a routing conflict occurs, one of the conflicting messages will proceed unaffected whereas the other must retrace its path out of the switch, to be re-transmitted after a short delay. The importance of clearing down a partially routed, but blocked, link from the point in the network where the conflict occurred back to the source node, will become apparent when we discuss the performance of the switch.

The routing function

The actual routing function used by the Butterfly switch can be expressed formally by defining it as a composite sequence of permutations, $B_n{}^i$, which is applied to an input packet of the following form. Let the input packet consist of a header containing an n-bit destination label $D = \{d_n, \ldots, d_1\}$. Let us also assume that during the routing of the packet through the switch the packet header is located at the kth stage, with an intermediate label given by $P = \{p_n, \ldots, p_1\}$. The switch network is characterised in terms of i, the *radix* of the switch nodes. The radix determines how many channels are switched within a single switch node, and this is given by $c = 2^i$. Hence, the total number of active stages in the network is given by $s = \log_{2^i} N = \frac{n}{i}$ for an N-port Butterfly switch. We can hence define $E_n{}^i$, the exchange permutation performed in each switching node on a packet with destination label D when at an intermediate label P, to be

$$E_n{}^i\left(\langle P, D\rangle\right) = \begin{array}{l}\langle\{p_n, p_{n-1}, \ldots, p_{i+1}, d_i, d_{i-1}, \ldots, d_1\}, \\ \{d_i, d_{i-1}, \ldots, d_1, d_n, d_{n-1}, \ldots, d_{i+1}\}\rangle\end{array} \tag{7.1}$$

and the shuffle permutation applied to the connections from stage k to stage $k+1$ is then

$$S_{n,k}{}^i\left(\langle P, D\rangle\right) = \langle\sigma_n^{-(n-ik)}(P), D\rangle \tag{7.2}$$

where $\sigma_n^{-x}(P)$ is the xth inverse sub-shuffle applied to P (see section 3.2). This permutation is defined formally, as

$$\sigma_n^{-(n-ik)}(P) = \{p_n, p_{n-1}, \ldots, p_{ik+1}, p_i, p_{i-1}, \ldots, p_1, p_{ik}, p_{ik-1}, \ldots, p_{i+1}\}$$

Informally, this defines a right-circular rotation of the binary representation of the least significant ik bits of P, by i places. Effectively, E_n^i and $S_{n,k}^i$ map from $\langle P, D\rangle$ to $\langle P', D'\rangle$, where P and P' are the entry and exit labels of the packet through the kth stage in the network, and D and D' are the target (destination) labels before and after the routing takes place at the kth stage in the network.

The Butterfly switch as a whole can now be defined as the composition of $E_n{}^i$ and $S_{n,k}{}^i$ over n/i stages, thus

$$B_n{}^i = \left(E_n{}^i S_{n,k}{}^i\right)_{k=1}^{\frac{n}{i}} \tag{7.3}$$

This permutation is illustrated in figure 7.10, for 16 processing nodes and $i = 2$ (4×4 switch nodes). Note, there is no shuffle permutation at the output of the switch, since the last shuffle permutation is $S_{n,n/i}^i$ which is equal to I, the identity permutation.

The logic of the Butterfly permutation indicates *how* a route through the switch is set up, but does not give any indication of how well such a network performs under differing conditions of loading. To ascertain this we must explore the available bandwidth and the probability with which packets collide during routing through the switch.

7.4.4   Performance

Assessing the performance of a general purpose parallel computer, such as the Butterfly, is an important exercise if lessons are to be learned, particularly in the area of scalability. A realistic assessment, as we saw in earlier

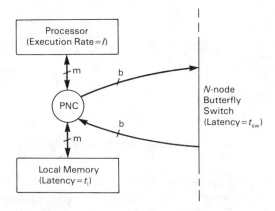

Figure 7.11 Processor memory data pathways in the Butterfly

chapters, takes account of both the architecture and the applications for which the architecture is intended. By definition a general purpose parallel computer has no single class of applications for which it is best suited, and therefore we must model not only the architecture, but also the characteristics of an arbitrary application on that architecture.

It is possible to model the behaviour of the Butterfly by characterising its structure in the form shown in figure 7.11. In this model there are N processing nodes, each of which executes instructions at a rate of I instructions per second. Memory requests originating from each processor are routed through that processor's local PNC, and are subsequently serviced either by the local memory associated with that processor, or by one of the non-local memories via the Butterfly switch. It is possible to model the performance of a Butterfly node in terms of the average time required to execute each instruction, and a significant factor here is the average time each instruction spends interacting with memory. This is determined by the average number of memory requests per instruction multiplied by the average *latency* associated with each memory operation. An important characteristic of the Butterfly is therefore how well the Butterfly switch can transport the memory requests and associated acknowledgements between the PNCs of different nodes.

The latency of *local* memory requests can be modelled, quite simply, in terms of the basic local memory access time (t_a) and a multiplying factor (λ) which represents the effect of external loading on that memory module. Hence

$$t_l = \lambda\,t_a$$

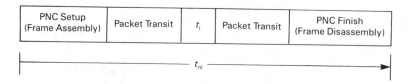

Figure 7.12 Activity-time graph for non-local accesses

The latency of *non-local* requests is a slightly more complex function since it depends critically on the transit time of the memory request and acknowledge packets through the Butterfly switch. This is illustrated in figure 7.12 which shows the component times involved in non-local operations. The setup time of the PNC consists of the time required to assemble a packet prior to insertion into the network, and this is essentially constant. However, the packet transit time depends on many factors, and therefore deserves a more thorough investigation.

The transit time of a single packet through the Butterfly switch consists of two parts. Firstly, there is the time it takes to propagate a packet through the switch mechanisms, and secondly, there is the possible time penalty associated with those packets which collide and require re-transmission.

An s-stage Butterfly switch, with a clock period of t_{cp} is capable of propagating an m-bit message in b-bit chunks, with a total delay of T_p seconds, such that

$$T_p = t_{cp} \left(s + \left\lceil \frac{m}{b} \right\rceil - 1 \right) \text{ seconds}$$

Essentially, the s switch stages operate as a pipeline of length s, switching eight bits in each clock period. In fact, the processing node controllers are also capable of performing block transfers, and these reduce the effect of s on the propagation time.

The time penalty associated with routing conflicts depends on the sum of the following time components.

1. The time to detect that a collision has occurred.

2. The time to clear down the switch setting for the blocked packet.

3. The delay inserted by the PNC before the packet is re-transmitted.

Collisions in a multi-stage routing network, such as the Butterfly, are more likely to occur in the early stages than in the later stages, and hence the

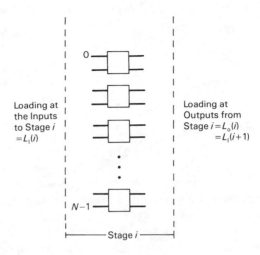

Figure 7.13 One stage in a multi-stage network

average delay between the packet header entering the switch and a routing conflict occurring (for those transfers which result in a conflict) will be less than $st_{cp}/2$. The time taken to clear down the switch setting will be equal to the time taken to detect the collision, since a 'clear down' signal must retrace the path taken during the set-up phase. We may also assume a certain delay before a blocked packet is re-transmitted, let us call this δ, which is inserted by the PNC to ensure a reasonable probability that the availability of the required route will have altered in the time between the conflict occurring and the packet being re-transmitted.

The effect that collisions have on the average non-local access time depends on the relative frequency with which such collisions actually occur, and we expect this to be a function of both the connectivity of the switch (that is, its configuration) and the connectivity of the application (in other words, the switch loading). Consider a single stage of a multi-stage network, as shown in figure 7.13, composed of simple 2×2 exchange boxes (see section 3.2). If there are x incoming messages (active inputs) distributed randomly over the N input ports to the switch, then the average input loading on each port of the switch, L_I, is

$$L_I = \frac{x}{N}$$

However, in a multi-stage network the input loading at stage $i + 1$ will be equal to the output loading at stage i, and we can hence define the loading

Table 7.1 Survival rate at each stage in a MIN with 2 × 2 nodes

0	1.000	4	.450	8	.300
1	.750	5	.399	9	.278
2	.609	6	.359	10	.259
3	.517	7	.327	11	.242

at each stage of the network as

$$L_I(i+1) = L_O(i)$$

We can complete this definition of loading, as we know that the output loading at stage i is equal to the input loading at stage i minus the *probable* number of packets blocked at stage i.

Now, the probability of losing a packet due to a blockage in a 2 × 2 switch node is equal to the probability of *both* input ports being actively loaded, multiplied by the probability of both incoming packets requiring the *same* intermediate destination label. This is equal to

$$L_I(i) \times L_I(i) \times \frac{1}{2}$$

Hence, the probability of a single output port losing a packet will be one half of this, and we can write

$$L_O(i) = L_I(i) - \frac{L_I(i)^2}{4}$$

or alternatively,

$$L_I(i+1) = L_I(i) - \frac{L_I(i)^2}{4}$$

Using this equation we can calculate the *survival rate* of a given input loading through any number of stages, and this is shown in table 7.1 for an input loading of unity. We can see from this table that if a 256-node Butterfly system were constructed using 2 × 2 exchange nodes, and then operated at 100 per cent loading, only 30 per cent of all memory references would be routed successfully to their destination labels at each attempt. Clearly, this is an unacceptably poor state of affairs, and in this simple model the effects of retries and so called 'hot spots', or frequently referenced memory modules [PN85], are not even taken into account. As a result of the poor performance of such a routing network two modifications to this basic design are used in the production version of the Butterfly. These involved halving the number of stages required for a given value of N, and reducing the maximum input loading on each port of the Butterfly switch.

We noted earlier that the number of stages in a Butterfly switch is $\log_c(N)$, where c is equal to the number of inputs to each switch node. Thus, by doubling the number of inputs to each switch node, we can halve the number of stages required in the network as a whole. Now, instead of implementing 2×2 switch nodes, we implement $c \times c$ switch nodes, these being effectively $c \times c$ cross-bar switches. We can continue this up to the point where each node switches N inputs, at which point the network becomes a full cross-bar switch. This process of node enlargement also reduces the total number of switch nodes in the network from $N/2 \log_2(N)$ to $N/c \log_c(N)$. As evidenced by table 7.1, any reduction in the number of stages traversed by a set of messages will yield an improvement in message survival rate, and this is the principle upon which the technique of enlarging the switch nodes is based.

A reduction in the number of stages in the switch network is clearly a good thing; however, by changing the number of connections to and from each switch node the probability of collisions within each node will also change. The throughput characteristics of cross-bar switches of arbitrary dimensions have been analysed by Mudge and Makrucki [MM82], who have shown that for a uniform distribution of output port addresses, and a probability, r, of each input in a $c \times c$ cross-bar switch being active, the expected bandwidth of the switch is $BW_c(r)$.

$$BW_c(r) = c \left[1 - \left(1 - \frac{r}{c} \right)^c \right] \tag{7.4}$$

Hence, the survival rate of requests passing through a $c \times c$ cross-bar switch is $S_c(r)$.

$$S_c(r) = \left[1 - \left(1 - \frac{r}{c} \right)^c \right] \tag{7.5}$$

Interestingly, as the size of a cross-bar switch grows, the survival rate tends towards an asymptotic value $S_\infty(r)$.

$$S_\infty(r) = 1 - e^{-r} \tag{7.6}$$

So, for a fully loaded cross-bar switch with $5 \le c \le \infty$, the survival rate ranges between 67.2 per cent and 63.2 per cent.

We can now use equation 7.5 to model the throughput of a Butterfly switch by applying it recursively over $s = \log_c(N)$ stages, using the following rule for evaluating the loading (r_i) at stage i $\{0 \le i \le s\}$,

$$r_{i+1} = \begin{cases} S_c(r_i) & i \ne 0 \\ S_c(l) & i = 0 \end{cases} \tag{7.7}$$

where l is the input loading to the whole network. Recall that the BBN Butterfly switch is constructed from switch nodes with a value of $c = 4$, and

Table 7.2 Packet survival vs. switching radix

i	c	$S_c(1)$
1	2	.7500
2	4	.6836
3	8	.6564
4	16	.6439

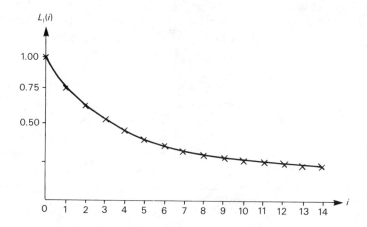

Figure 7.14 Survivability of packets traversing a Butterfly switch ($c = 4, l = 1.0$)

hence in order to evaluate the effectiveness of using $c > 2$ we may compare $S_{(c>2)}(1)$ with $S_2(1)$. This has been done for values of c which are powers of two, and in the range $\{2 \leq c \leq 16\}$, and the results are shown in table 7.2.

Progressing from switch nodes with c inputs to $c + 1$ inputs per switch node divides the number of stages in the network by half, and this more than makes up for the slight decrease in survivability of packets traversing 4×4 switch nodes in comparison with 2×2 switch nodes, and this technique does therefore improve throughput.

Using equations 7.5 and 7.7 we can produce a survivability curve for a Butterfly switch constructed from $c \times c$ switch nodes, given any value for l, and such a curve is illustrated in figure 7.14 for $l = 1.0$ and $c = 4$.

The second method of improving the throughput of a multi-stage interconnection network, which is also implemented in the Butterfly switch, is *switch de-rating*. This involves operating the switch at a reduced input loading in order to limit the losses due to routing conflicts. The input loading can be reduced in one of two ways, either the switching elements can

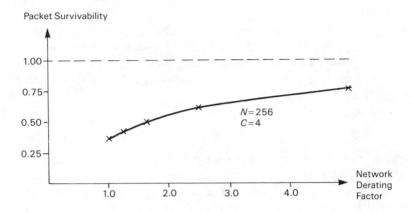

Figure 7.15 Relationship between packet survivability and switch derating factor for a 5-stage network

be engineered to operate faster than requests can be generated from the processing nodes, or extra links can be inserted in the network to provide more than N links at each stage. The latter technique is also useful from a reliability point of view, since the extra links mean there is more than one route from each input to each output, and hence failure of any one link will not affect the connectability of any pair of processing nodes. The Butterfly incorporates an additional stage in the network to provide two paths from each source node to each destination node. This increases the number of stages by one, but the de-rating of the switch reduces the average loading by approximately one half. The effect of de-rating a multi-stage network is shown graphically, in figure 7.15, from which it is apparent that derating the switch produces a marked increase in survivability.

Manufacturer's performance measurements of the Butterfly, running Matrix Multiplication and Gaussian Elimination algorithms, indicate that for systems containing 128 processing nodes the overhead due to switch contention is a very small part of the total execution time (approximately 2 per cent) [CGS*85]. The same benchmarks indicate that the overhead incurred due to switch propagation time is also quite low (approximately 3 per cent). It must be stated that both of these algorithms contain a high degree of uniformity, and that block transfers of the rows and columns of the matrices involved could influence the performance of the switch. Furthermore, the loading on the switch during these operations must have been well within the peak capability of the switch, since the occurrence of collisions was remarkably low.

It is clear that the performance of the switch will affect the performance of the machine as a whole, and that the rate of non-local requests is central to this theme. However, through a combination of optimised switch architecture and careful engineering it is possible to produce a multi-stage interconnection network for connecting together relatively large numbers of microprocessor nodes in a distributed shared memory environment, and make it work relatively efficiently.

7.5 Summary

Shared-memory multiprocessors are probably the most conventional form of MIMD architecture; they do not alter the model of computation, and they can be used simply to provide high performance multi-user systems if that is what is required. Small-scale shared-memory systems can be built quite easily using high performance buses, as witnessed by the availability of machines such as the Sequent Balance and the Encore Multimax/Ultramax. Large-scale shared-memory multiprocessors can encounter significant problems related to access contention to the shared-memory modules, and several techniques have been devised to overcome these problems.

As far as commercial systems of this kind are concerned the Butterfly machine is the currently largest. However, several other machines using this type of architecture have been proposed, and are currently being developed. These include the IBM RP3 project [PBG*85,PN85], and the associated NYU Ultracomputer project [GGK*83].

The extension of the shared-memory model to very large systems is, at the time of writing, still an active research area with the problem of access contention under conditions of heavy switch loading yet to be resolved.

8 Message-passing Multiprocessors

The connection of a number of parallel processors by means of a common shared store suffers from two fundamental problems. Firstly there is the difficulty of providing adequate memory bandwidth to support large numbers of processors, all of which in principle could be contending for the same memory module. Secondly, where processors attempt to coordinate their activities through *synchronisation variables* held in common memory, the inefficiencies due to processors idling in a tight loop, and the saturation of vulnerable links in the processor-memory network can lead to poor performance.

Sophisticated solutions to these problems have been proposed, for example the *fetch & add* operators in the NYU Ultracomputer [GGK*83], and *combining switches* in the IBM RP3 design [PN85]. However, these techniques inevitably introduce additional hardware complication and expense, and their cost effectiveness is yet to be established.

A radically different approach to MIMD processing must be sought if these fundamental problems are to be avoided, and perhaps the most natural alternative is simply to design systems in which processors *do not share variables*. An immediate consequence of enforcing such a rule is that there is no requirement for generally accessible shared memory, and the attendant difficulties are therefore avoided. However, if the facility for sharing variables is removed, some other mechanism for passing values between processes must be provided. The key to this alternative communication mechanism is the *message-passing* paradigm, used for many years in multiprocessing operating systems but only recently applied to parallel architectures.

In a message-passing architecture processors communicate by *sending* and *receiving* messages. The processors in such systems normally operate asynchronously, and so the transfer of information requires the sending and receiving processes to *synchronise*. As a rule, for two processes to communicate one must perform a Send_Message operation and the other must perform a Receive_Message operation. If the actual times at which these operations are initiated are t_S and t_R respectively then, if $t_S < t_R$ the sending process must wait for the receiving process to catch up, and if $t_S > t_R$ the receiving process must wait. We refer to $|t_S - t_R|$ as the *wait-time* associated with a communication event, and its value is clearly dependent on the temporal behaviour of the application and the speed with which messages are transferred from process to process.

In a shared memory multiprocessor the link between two cooperating processes is effectively the address of the shared variable(s) through which they communicate. In a message-passing system the link between cooperating processes exists in the form of a *naming convention* within the Send_Message and Receive_Message operations, and here two alternatives are possible. An obvious naming convention would be for each message-passing operation to name explicitly the partner process (and/or the processor on which it resides) for that operation. For example, assuming that processes P1 and P2 exist, a message could be sent from P1 to P2 by the execution of the following code.

```
Process.1                    Process.2
   :                            :
Send(P2,message)             Receive(P1,message)
   :                            :
```

An alternative naming convention can be implemented by directing messages through *named channels*. In this case, for two processes to communicate, they must both quote the *same* channel identifier in their respective message-passing operations as follows.

```
Process.1                    Process.2
   :                            :
Send(chan_X, message)        Receive(chan_X,message)
   :                            :
```

When contemplating message-passing systems from a theoretical viewpoint it is usually sufficient to consider processes, channels and communication operations as existing without reference to any specific implementation restrictions. In practice however, this is an over-simplification. The general structure of a message-passing multiprocessor system is depicted in figure 8.1, from which it can be seen that there are two primary components; the processing elements (PEs) and the message transfer system (MTS).

Consider a system in which there are n processors, and m application processes. There are likely to be many circumstances under which $m > n$, and so we must expect each processor to provide a large (but necessarily finite) number of *virtual processors* to which these processes can be mapped directly. By multiprogramming a number of virtual processors on each physical processor the wait-time experienced by each virtual processor, during inter-process communication, can be overlapped with other useful processing on that physical processor. Whilst these techniques have been used in single-processor systems for many years, it is important to address the implications of multiprogramming for the message transfer system. For example, with both naming strategies mentioned previously it is possible for

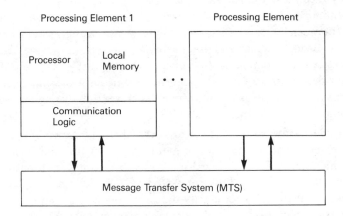

Figure 8.1 A generic message-passing multiprocessor architecture

communication events to occur between processes (effectively virtual processors) which reside on the *same* or *different* physical processors, and the MTS protocol must deal with both of these situations.

8.1 Design issues for message-passing architectures

Observing that the processing elements in a message-passing multiprocessor are essentially equivalent, in function and form, to a conventional uniprocessor, it is easy to see why the majority of innovation and design effort is normally expended on the MTS and the inter-process communication protocols. As we saw in chapter 6 the granular efficiency of an MIMD system depends on the ratio of computation time per communication event to the communication overhead per communication event. Traditionally, the task of preparing and sending an inter-process message has been notoriously slow, leading to excessive communication overheads. However, this state of affairs need not, and indeed has not, persisted. The primary reason why message-passsing is considered slow and expensive is that the processing elements in early message-passing systems were implemented using conventional processors. A simple examination of the programming model of these processors indicates that they embody none of the concepts of message-passing and so these must be simulated in software.

If we refer back to chapter 6 and relate the simulation of a message-passing processor to the fundamental parameters of granular efficiency, it becomes apparent that the simulation of communication leads to large values for d and l (the proceed/wait decision time and intrinsic communication latency respectively). For example, in the MUSS operating system [FT79], the sending and reception of messages is supported via operating system calls (between named processes). Typical operating system implementations of Send_Message and Receive_Message execute several hundreds of instructions per communication event. Consequently, one of the most important design issues for high performance message-passing multiprocessor systems is the minimisation of software intervention during process communication.

At the hardware level there are several design issues which affect the performance of inter-process communication. Of particular significance is the connectivity of the physical processor inter-connection network. There are two choices; either a fully-connected or a partially-connected network of processors. If the network is only partially connected then messages travelling between arbitrary pairs of processing elements may have to make several passes through the MTS, being forwarded each time by an intermediate processor. This *store-and-forward* technique is common in local and wide-area networks where the exigencies of cost dictate the use of sparse communication networks. However, store-and-forward may steal CPU cycles (as well as memory cycles) from each intermediary, effectively decreasing the efficiency of the processors and increasing the net cost of each message. This is taken to the extreme in transputer-based systems (see section 8.2) whereby the programmer must implement the store-and-forward mechanism explicitly.

Modifying conventional programming languages to exploit shared memory in MIMD systems requires very little in the way of language enhancements, and those which are required are normally quite straightforward to implement. The primary reason for this is that there remains a *global state* to which all processors have access, and which a designated processor can initialise and interrogate throughout program execution. Hence, examining the state of a parallel application code is conceptually identical to examining the state of a sequential application code. In a message-passing system there is, by definition, a *distributed state* which is only accessible via the MTS. This can complicate the diagnosis of errors, and even the detection of errors.

The programming language (and perhaps also the programmer) must also be responsible for at least an initial *placement* of processes on to virtual processors. A poor placement is typically one in which processes which communicate a significant volume of information are placed at some distance. The best placement will minimise the total distance travelled by all bits of communicated information. A poor placement will lead to reduced performance over the best-case placement, and for that reason should be avoided.

The placement problem can be formalised by identifying the *distance* between pairs of communicating processes. Let the set of all physical processors $\mathcal{P} = \{p_1 \ldots p_n\}$, and let the set of all virtual processors (processes) $\mathcal{V} = \{v_1 \ldots v_m\}$. Communication between two processes running on a pair of physical processors (i, j) takes a time which is proportional to their physical separation $d_{i,j}$. The actual placement of processes on to processors can be defined as a mapping *place*: process $\rightarrow$ processor, which is a many-to-one mapping. Hence, the physical separation of two processes (i, j) is given by $d_{place(i),place(j)}$. Each communication event can be defined as a triple (i, j, w) where i and j are the source and destination processes and w is the *quantity* of information associated with that event. If the set of all communication events occurring during program execution is $C = \{(i_1, j_1, w_1), \ldots, (i_l, j_l, w_l)\}$, then the total cost of all inter-process communication can be defined as T

$$ T = \sum_{(i,j,w) \in C} w.d_{place(i),place(j)} $$

The problem of placement is hence a problem of *minimising* T, often a task which cannot be performed prior to program execution. The minimisation of T requires explicit knowledge of all process interactions, including which processes communicate and how much information is transferred during each event. Since such information is not normally available in practice, a less than optimal placement may have to be accepted. Alternatively, a dynamic placement may be used whereby the placement alters during program execution through the *migration* of processes. Dynamic schemes are only effective when there is a significant amount of locality in the pattern of communication since it relies on the assumption that if a pair of processes communicated heavily during the interval $T - t$ to T then they are likely to do so again in the interval T to $T + t$. Migration is typically initiated when the cumulative cost of communication between a pair of processes exceeds a certain threshold. The choice of which process should migrate is often a difficult one, since communication with other processes may also be affected by a change of placement.

As we saw in chapter 6 the latency of communication is an important factor in determining the actual speedup achievable for a given degree of application parallelism in a shared-memory architecture; in a message-passing system the same principle holds. In effect the only difference from a performance point of view is that in the message-passing style of architecture the scheduling of processes on to processors is restricted by the often prohibitive cost of moving processes between processors.

The remainder of this chapter describes a number of message-passing architectures, which for reasons of taxonomy are divided into those which communicate via *fixed degree* networks and those which communicate via *variable degree* networks.

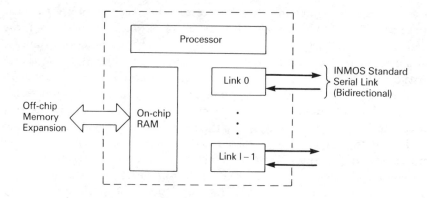

Figure 8.2 Conceptual structure of the transputer

8.2   Transputer-based systems

A description of the internal architecture of the transputer is difficult to
justify without reference to **occam**, the primary language for which it is
designed, since the architecture of the transputer is optimised specifically
for executing **occam** processes. The language **occam** [INM84,Ros84,BS89]
has been designed specifically with inter-process communication and explicit
process parallelism in mind, and this should be borne in mind when reading the following description of the transputer architecture. Section 9.1.2
presents an overview of the **occam** language, and in section 9.2.2 an example **occam** program is developed.

The transputer [Whi85] is one of several 32-bit VLSI processors that
have been specifically designed for use in concurrent message-passing systems. The conceptual structure of the transputer (see figure 8.2) contains
the three essential ingredients for a self-contained element of a message-
passing system, notably *processor, local memory* and *communications*. The
general philosophy of the transputer is one of providing a family of compat-
ible components which are able to communicate with the minimum of external logic, irrespective of their individual internal clock rates. To this end
individual transputers communicate via point-to-point *links*, implemented
using an asynchronous bit-serial protocol. Each transputer has a fixed
number of such bi-directional links, nominally four, and hence any processor inter-connection network of fixed degree i ($i \leq 4$) can be constructed
from these devices. In transputer-based multiprocessors the serial communication links and their inter-connection topology together constitute the
message transfer system.

The architecture of the transputer is defined by reference to the pro-

gramming language **occam** [INM84] (see section 9.1.2). Occam possesses
the necessary language attributes for expressing algorithms in a manner
suitable for distributed parallel processing on networks of transputers. It
enables the whole computation to be expressed as a static collection of processes which operate concurrently and communicate through named channels. The placement of **occam** processes on to transputer processors is
the explicit responsibility of the occam program, and processes would not
normally be expected to migrate. The static structure of occam processes
permits the transputer hardware to remain simple and uncomplicated. This
means, for example, that the domain of each process is known at compile
time and consequently hardware for segment based memory protection is
not required.

In the following sections we examine the implementation of the transputer architecture and the influence which **occam** and concurrency have
had on the design of the programming model and instruction set of the
transputer. We then discuss the ways in which large transputer-based multiprocessors can be constructed, and examine an example system.

8.2.1 Architecture of the T414

Overview

The T414 is a 32-bit microprocessor implementation of the general transputer structure outlined in figure 8.2. It has 2 Kbytes of on-chip RAM
and four standard INMOS full duplex, serial links. The block structure of
the T414 can be seen from figure 8.3. The on-chip memory consists of 512
32-bit words of 50 ns cycle-time static RAM. The fixed-point processor is
capable of executing code at a peak rate of one 8-bit transputer instruction
every 100 ns, when isssuing instructions held in the on-chip RAM. The external 32-bit memory interface is capable of addressing up to 4 Gbytes and
has a peak data transfer rate of 25 Mbytes per second, equivalent to one
32-bit word every three processor cycles. No external memory interfacing
logic is required with the T414 since this is contained on-chip in the form
of a programmable set of memory control signals. The T414 is thus able to
provide refresh signals for a variety of dynamic memory devices, as well as
signals suitable for use as row and column address strobes.

Each of the four links provides two **occam** channels, one in each direction, operating at frequency of 5, 10 or 20 Mbits/sec[1]. The data transfer
protocol is word length independent enabling the T414 to interface to other
devices in the transputer family which may have differing word lengths.
The links operate autonomously, enabling the transmission and reception
of messages to be overlapped with instruction processing. This is an im-

---

[1]The standard link frequency is twice the input clock, or 10 Mbits/sec.

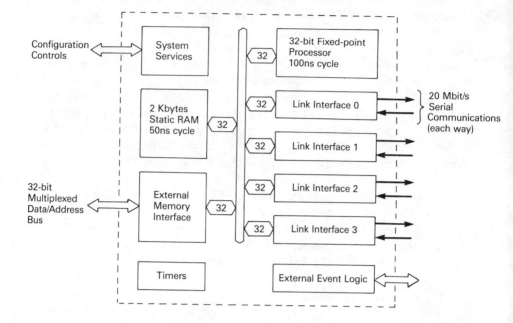

Figure 8.3 Block structure of the T414 transputer

portant feature of the transputer, for it enables the performance-degrading effects of message-passing latency to be transparent to the processor. Of course this can only be achieved when there are sufficient parallel processes. The T414 also contains a timer which permits **occam** programs to perform real-time functions. For example, the current process can be delayed until the timer reaches a certain value.

The T414 contains approximately 150,000 transistors fabricated in a 1.5 micron twin-tub CMOS process, and dissipates less than 500 mW. The device accepts a clock signal of 5 MHz, from which it generates its own internal processor clock.

Instruction set architecture

Instruction set architecture (ISA) encompasses both the programming model (or user's view) and the architectural constructs required to support that model in hardware. The design of an instruction set architecture intended for use in concurrent systems will be influenced heavily by the need to support concurrency and communication, so one must first consider the major influences which were brought to bear during the design of the transputer.

Of the many influences on the design of the ISA for the transputer, the following five are of particular importance.

1. There should be hardware support for concurrency, and in particular for inter-process communication and process management.

2. Object code should be word length independent to permit the integration of a variety of devices within the transputer family.

3. Source code should run unchanged between transputer networks of differing sizes.

4. **Occam** is the lowest semantic level that any programmer should need to see, and hence the instruction set can be optimised to give prejudicial support to **occam**.

5. **Occam** processes and procedures are declared statically, and therefore process workspaces can be allocated statically and do not need runtime memory protection.

Programming model

The programming model of the transputer is extremely simple, in keeping with the **occam** philosophy, and effectively implements a stack architecture. The entire state of the currently active process consists of just six machine registers, plus the code and workspace for that process. This is illustrated in figure 8.4.

Due to the non-recursive nature of **occam** the depth of stack required to evaluate an arbitrary expression can be computed at compile-time, and temporary variable space within the workspace can be allocated accordingly. The three registers Areg, Breg and Creg together constitute the top three locations of an evaluation stack. The Wptr register is used as a base from which all local variables belonging to a process can be addressed. The Iptr register addresses the next sequential instruction to be executed by the current process. The Oreg register is used to build word length values from word length independent instructions, the precise functioning of which is discussed shortly.

When the current **occam** process is not in the process of evaluating an expression only the Wptr and Iptr registers contain volatile process context. This simple arrangement of internal architecture means that scheduling and de-scheduling processes at such positions can be extremely fast.

Instruction format

The instruction format of the transputer is optimised for minimum static and dynamic code space requirements. It comprises a single 8-bit instruction

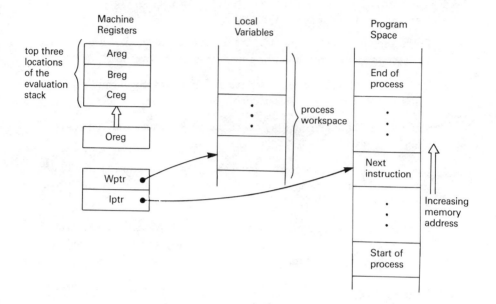

Figure 8.4 Transputer programming model

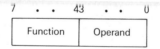

Figure 8.5 Transputer instruction format

format partitioned as two 4-bit fields representing *function* and *operand*, as shown in figure 8.5. Thirteen of the sixteen functions encode the most popular transputer instructions directly. These include instructions for loading variables on to the evaluation stack, storing values back to memory, adding constant values to the top of stack value, and performing certain control transfer operations. Table 8.1 outlines these direct functions.

All instructions place the contents of their 4-bit *operand* field in the least significant four bits of the operand register (Oreg). Oreg is then used as the operand for the function specified by the *function* field. All instructions except *pfix* and *nfix* clear Oreg upon completion of their function. The *pfix* and *nfix* instructions differ from the rest in that they shift Oreg four places to the left *before* inserting their data. The *nfix* instruction additionally

Table 8.1 transputer instruction set – direct functions

function code	mnemonic	number of cycles	description
2	*pfix*	1	prefix
6	*nfix*	1	negative prefix
F	*opr*	–	operate
4	*ldc*	1	load constant
7	*ldl*	2	load local
D	*stl*	1	store local
1	*ldlp*	1	load local ptr
8	*adc*	1	add constant
C	*eqc*	2	equals constant
0	*j*	3	jump
A	*cj*	4(2)	conditional jump (untaken)
3	*ldnl*	2	load non-local
E	*stnl*	2	store non-local
5	*ldnlp*	1	load non-local ptr
9	*call*	7	call
B	*ajw*	1	adjust workspace

negates Oreg prior to the shift. Any literal value between MostNeg (10...0) and MostPos (01...1) can be loaded in to Oreg by using a sequence of such prefix instructions. It is primarily this aspect of the transputer instruction set, together with the memory addressing convention, which makes the transputer word length independent.

The *opr* instruction implements a call on a microcode routine identified by the contents of Oreg. This greatly extends the range of possible instruction codes in the transputer, resulting in a total of over 100 instructions[2]. Naturally the encoding of the indirect functions is chosen so that the most frequently used of these functions can be specified without resorting to *pfix* or *nfix* instructions.

---

[2]From the large number of instructions, and the multi-cycle mode of execution, one could reasonably infer that the transputer is not a true RISC architecture.

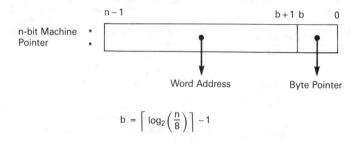

Figure 8.6 Byte addressing in the transputer

Memory organisation

The 4 Gbytes of memory addressable by the transputer is organised as a single linear address space. This memory is *byte addressable* through the use of *pointers*, consisting of a word address concatenated with a byte pointer (figure 8.6). Only if the number of bytes per word is a power of two can ordinary arithmetic be performed on pointer values. The on-chip memory and the external memory are both integrated within the same address space.

Process scheduling

In an architecture optimised for the concurrent processing of a set of processes on an arbitrary number of processors there is a fair probability that each processor will be required to manage more than one process. As we saw in chapter 6, each communication event will cause at least one process to become un-runnable, necessitating a context switch in at least one processor. In order to maintain a balanced architecture the time taken for a processor to swap contexts should be a small fraction of the average process grain-time. Looked at another way, a processor with a lengthy context switching time can only support correspondingly large grain-times for a given granular efficiency. It is this consideration which led to the adoption of hardware support for process management and context switching in the transputer.

At the heart of the transputer's process management functions is a process scheduler held in microcode. The occam processes that it manages can be in one of two states, either *active* or *inactive*, and each state has a number of sub-states, as shown in figure 8.7. The active processes waiting to be executed are automatically linked into one of two *run-queues* by the microcode of the instruction which caused the suspension of processing. These two queues implement two levels of priority in the scheduling

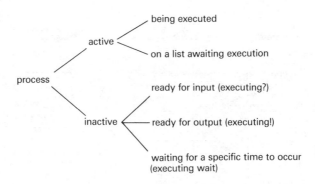

Figure 8.7 Transputer processing states

algorithm, and naturally the scheduler will choose to run a high priority process if one is runnable. Furthermore if a high priority process becomes runnable whilst a low priority process is executing, the low priority process is preempted and replaced by the high priority process. Switching to a high priority process takes slightly longer than switching from a high priority to a low priority process, or between two low priority processes, since there is a greater quantity of volatile context in the processor registers which must be saved. The list structures maintained by the transputer are illustrated in figure 8.8.

Each transputer also maintains two timers, a low priority timer which increments every 64 μs, and a high priority timer which increments every 1 μs. A single time-slice lasts for 1024 high priority time periods, and low priority processes are de-scheduled at the first suitable moment after two time-slices have been completed. High priority processes are never preempted. When a process is de-scheduled its Iptr is stored at location (Wptr−1) and the process is linked to the back of the relevant run-queue. When a process becomes halted as a result of a local channel I/O operation the process workspace pointer is simply placed in the word of memory allocated to the channel, effectively linking the waiting process to a single-element list identified implicitly by the channel address. When a matching communication event occurs the microcode re-links the halted process to the appropriate run-queue[3]. The transputer also provides instructions to *initiate* and *terminate* processes.

---

[3]The least significant bit of the workspace pointer is always zero, and is therefore used to store the process priority. The priority then identifies the correct run-queue.

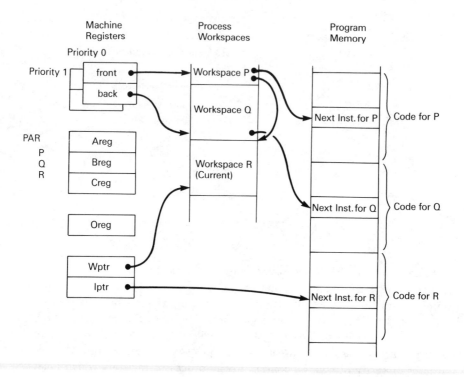

Figure 8.8 Process-management lists in the transputer

Performance

The T414 transputer operates at a peak rate of one instruction executed per processor cycle, but this asymptotic limit is unlikely to be sustained in practice. There are several reasons for this, the most important being that many instructions take more than one cycle, as indicated in table 8.1. Fixed-point arithmetic instruction times are shown in table 8.2, clearly indicating the effect on performance of the interative (microcoded) multiply and divide instructions.

If the **occam** code is held in on-chip memory four instructions can be fetched every 50ns. However, if the code is stored externally then the processor may incur additional cycles during instruction fetching. The extent of this delay is determined by **e**, the number of *extra* cycles required for external memory references. If e is less than 4 then, assuming that there are no control transfers, each external cycle takes less time than the execution of the instructions fetched and there will be no additional delay. If $e \geq 4$ then a delay of at least $(e - 3)/4$ will be incurred. Control transfers will of

Table 8.2 T414 fixed-point timings

operation	processor cycle times
add	1
subtract	1
multiply	38
divide	39

course make the average delay longer than this, since some fetches will not result in the execution of all four instructions.

Context switching times

Perhaps one of the most impressive features of the transputer is the speed with which it can swap processes when a communication event causes a hold-up. When a high priority process is suspended, and there are no further high priority processes to schedule, a low priority process can be scheduled in just 17 processor cycles[4]. Interrupting a low priority process to schedule a high priority process entails preserving the evaluation stack, and consequently takes a maximum of 58 processor cycles. Switching between two low priority processes only occurs at specific points in the microcode where it is known that the evaluation stack is empty, and again this takes only a small number of cycles.

Communication performance

Communication between two processes that are co-resident (on the same transputer) occurs via single words of memory. The communication protocol involves inspecting the channel location to ascertain whether a partner process is already waiting to communicate. This results in either the current process being de-scheduled or the waiting process being linked to the relevant run-queue. By implementing both the communication primitives and the process scheduler in microcode, communication incurs a relatively small overhead.

Communication between two processes that reside on adjacent processors takes place via an INMOS serial link, normally operating at 10 MHz. Messages are transmitted as a sequence of data packets, each of which must be acknowledged by an acknowledge packet. The transmission protocol is asynchronous, enabling communicating transputers to be driven from different clocks, and is implemented as a single wire for each occam channel. Each link consists of a pair of channels, one in each direction, and data

---

[4]These timings assume that no memory references go off-chip.

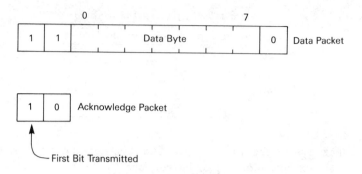

Figure 8.9 INMOS link protocol

packets for one direction are multiplexed with acknowledge packets for the other direction on the same wire. The link protocol can be seen in figure 8.9. Acknowledge packets are used both to signal reception of the data packets and maintain flow control.

Transputer links are formed by cross-connecting the LinkIn and Link-Out signal of two standard links. Over physical distances of less than 300mm a series terminating resistor of 56 Ω, in conjunction with 100 Ω impedance transmission lines, will maintain an adequate signal quality provided the total line delay is less than 0.4 bit-periods (nominally 40 ns). Since the link protocol is asynchronous the relative skew, caused typically by different rising and falling edge times of the link signals (through signal buffers for example), must be kept within a close tolerance. This has implications for *configurable* transputer arrays in which the connectivity of the links is determined by gating the link signals according to a predefined topology.

8.2.2   The T800 floating point transputer

In 1987 INMOS produced a second generation transputer, the T800. This is essentially identical to the T414 except for a larger on-chip memory and an on-chip floating-point unit. In addition, the link communication rate of the T800 can be set at 5, 10 or 20 Mbits/s, corresponding to peak data transmission rates of 670, 1250 and 2350 Kbytes/s respectively, when operating concurrently in both directions. Extra instructions are also provided to support floating point data types and to support graphics operations directly.

The programming model of the T800 is only slightly more complex than that of the T414, as illustrated in figure 8.10. The floating-point unit obtains all operands from a floating-point evaluation stack consisting of three registers AF, BF and CF. When a low priority process is interrupted in or-

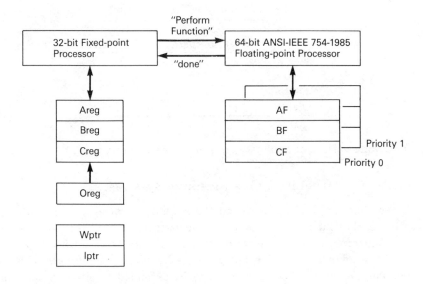

Figure 8.10 T800 programming model

der to schedule a high priority process the contents of the floating-point evaluation stack are preserved in a duplicate set of floating-point registers to minimise interrupt latency.

A form of parallelism similar to that found in the CDC 6600 and the IBM System/360 Model 91 occurs in the T800. The fixed and floating-point units operate independently and so a limited amount of implicit overlap of instructions within a single instruction stream can occur. Synchronisation between the fixed and floating-point units occurs when data is moved in or out of the floating-point unit. This permits address (integer) calculations to proceed in parallel with floating-point value calculations.

The floating-point ALU is microcoded, and uses a three-bit cyclic multiplication algorithm and a two-bit cyclic division algorithm [Gos80], resulting in the floating-point operation times shown in table 8.3. These operation times produce benchmarked performance [INM] of 4000 K Whetstones per second for single length arithmetic on 20 MHz devices.

The temptation to construct very large multiprocessor systems from such high performance microprocessors as the T800 is irresistible; a simple calculation indicates that 1000 T800 transputers operating at 30 MHz have a peak aggregate floating point execution rate of 2.25 GFLOPS (2.25×10^9). However, both the T414 and the T800 transputers can only be connected together using network topologies of fixed degree (≤ 4) so the task of linking large numbers of transputers to form a *general-purpose* structure, suitable

Table 8.3 T800 floating-point timings

operation	processor cycle times	
	single length	double length
add	7	7
subtract	7	7
multiply	13	21
divide	19	34

for a wide variety of applications, could present problems[5].

8.2.3   Constructing multi-transputer systems

Given that the limiting factor on the possible topology of transputer networks is the four point-to-point links on each transputer, it is worth considering the range of regular networks that can be constructed with degree four.
Perhaps the most obvious topology is the *two-dimensional mesh* which, depending on the edge connections, can be extended to either a *cylinder* or
torus (see the DAP interconnection structure on page 55). A fully connected
torus will have problems communicating with the outside world, however,
since every available link will be in use.

If processes in non-adjacent transputers wish to communicate they must
do so via intermediate processors, which must themselves be programmed
to perform message routing since the link protocol does not support store-
and-forward directly. The number of links traversed by a message in transit
between an arbitrary pair of processors is referred to as the *path length*, and
in a two-dimensional mesh this is exactly $2(n^{1/2} - 1)$ hops for an n processor
system. In general, for a k dimensional square mesh, the upper bound on
path length is $k(n^{1/k} - 1)$ hops.

It would appear at first glance that a square mesh in three dimensions
cannot be constructed from processors with just four links, as each node in
a three-dimensional (3D) mesh must have at least six links (up, down, left,
right, back and front). However, a *chain* of exactly two transputers has six
spare links, and can therefore be used to implement a single node in a 3D
square mesh. Such a square mesh has a maximum path length of exactly
$4\left(\frac{n}{2}\right)^{1/3} - 2$ hops.

Near-neighbour mesh topologies are very efficient for algorithms with
predominantly local communication patterns, but for algorithms with little

---

[5]As feature sizes reduce, the amount of logic which can be put in a single chip will
increase. Subsequent generations of the transputer are likely to exploit the extra area by
incorporating more links, more memory and possibly more floating-point units. Note that
with a six-link transputer a 64-processor binary k-cube architecture could be constructed
directly.

communication locality an upper bound distance between processors that is better than $O(n^{1/3})$ may be required. In chapter 3 (section 3.3.1) the binary k-cube network was shown to have a maximum path length of $k = \lceil \log_2 n \rceil$, and this is less than $4\left(\frac{n}{2}\right)^{1/3} - 2$ for all values of n for which a perfect square 3D mesh can be constructed. Clearly cubes of dimension one, two, three and four can be constructed from transputers, but k-cubes with $k > 4$ cannot be constructed directly. Instead, a network known as the *cube-connected cycle* can be used to model the binary k-cube, where nodes have degree which is logarithmic in n, from processing elements which actually have a fixed degree. Each node in the k-cube is constructed from a ring (or cycle) of $c = k/2$ transputers ($c > 2$). A network containing 2^{2c} nodes is hence created with a maximum path length between any two nodes of $2c$. Within a node the maximum distance between any pair of transputers is $c/2$, and this routing distance may be incurred at any node visited on a path between an arbitrary pair of nodes. Consequently, the maximum distance between any pair of transputers is limited to c^2 hops, which means that the upper bound on path length is $O(\log^2 n)$. This is a graph-theoretic distance, and is not directly related to the physical wire lengths. In practice the 300mm limit on transputer link lengths places a strict upper bound on the size of system that can actually be constructed using k-cube topologies without using reconstituted link protocols.

Another topology which has fixed degree and logarithmic path length, but which has wire lengths which grow more slowly, is the *ternary tree*. A binary tree comprises nodes with links to two offspring nodes and a parent node. A ternary tree is a simple extension to this which makes use of all four links on a transputer by having three offspring nodes instead of two. At the leaves of the tree there will be a large number of unconnected links, and these could be used for I/O or to link two trees (of similar depth) together. The maximum path length of a ternary tree is simply twice the depth of the tree, and is therefore $2\lceil \log_3(2n + 1) - 1 \rceil$, which is $O(\log n)$.

An alternative to having one of the above fixed topologies is to have a *configurable* array of transputers from which any of the previously described networks can be constructed. The logical structure of such an architecture is depicted in figure 8.11 and essentially consists of n transputers and a $4n$-input to $4n$-output full permutation network. Assuming one could build a full permutation network for the required value of n, it would then be possible to configure all $n!$ possible permutations of link connections. Computing the configuration control signals has been shown to take $O(n \log n)$ time[6], but since the number of permutations that is likely to be of real interest is only a small proportion of the total number of possible permutations the

---

[6]A parallel algorithm for calculating permutation descriptors in $O(\log^4 n)$ time also exists [OT68].

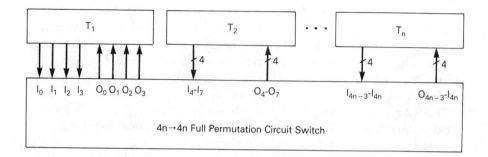

Figure 8.11 Structure of a configurable transputer network

power of a full permutation network is unlikely to be required in practice.

Several research designs for configurable transputer systems have been produced and these include the ESPRIT Supernode project for which the T800 was originally developed, the Alvey ParSiFal project and the IBM VICTOR machine [WBB*87]. The primary goals of these projects is to produce transputer systems capable of being configured as one of a number of important topologies, and particularly in the case of the VICTOR machine to be *partitionable* into a number of distinct networks. These are also the goals of the Meiko Computing Surface, a recent commercial product based on transputer technology.

8.2.4　The Meiko Computing Surface

The Meiko Computing Surface was first demonstrated in July 1985 at the SIGRAPH Conference in San Francisco, and became commercially available in the third quarter of 1986. It is a modular and expandable system organised as a reconfigurable array of transputer-based computing elements, I/O elements, and storage elements. These elements are supported by a library of circuit boards, each optimised for a specific function.

A Computing Surface consists of a number of Modules each containing up to 40 boards housed in two 19-inch racks. All inter-board links within a Module are routed via the System backplane, and links between Modules are provided by special inter-Module link boards. There is no theoretical limit on the number of Modules, and hence transputers, that can be contained in a Computing Surface, although the upper bound on the inter-Module link wire length ultimately constrains the configurations which can be extended indefinitely. Modules contain a private power supply and use forced-air cooling, dissipating up to 3.1 kW each. The structure of the Computing Surface is illustrated in figure 8.12.

The system backplane in each Module supports a Supervisor bus as well as the link connectivity, and this provides for low bandwidth communication between all computing elements in the system. It has a single Bus Master, which is nominally a Local Host board, and is capable of resetting and examining the internal state of all transputers, reporting errors, and configuring the link connectivity. Application software can also use the Supervisor bus as a communication pathway, and this could be particularly useful for transmitting debugging information.

The board library

The boards in the library supported by the Computing Surface each contain one or more *computing elements*, a *supervisor bus interface*, a *link network interface* and optionally some specific I/O function. Each computing element consists of a single transputer (either a T414B or a T800) and a certain amount of external private memory. The link network interface is supported by custom VLSI circuit switches, although the network connectivity can also be configured manually using polarised jumper cables. Special purpose I/O boards, such as graphics display elements, are provided as part of the system rather than as peripherals in order to provide an integrated programming environment for both the computing and I/O sections of an application.

Local Host board

The Local Host board consists of one transputer, 3 Mbytes of RAM with error detection logic, 128 Kbytes of EPROM, an IEEE-488 bus controller, a Supervisor bus interface, two RS-232 asynchronous serial communication ports and a link network interface. At least one Local Host is required in each Computing Surface Module. It is responsible for monitoring hardware and software errors, controlling the reset and post-mortem analysis of the other transputers in its Module, and configuring the link routing switches.

Quad Computing Element board

The computing power of the Computing Surface derives from the massive replication of transputers, each with a significant amount of private off-chip memory. These transputers are located in groups of four on Quad Computing Element (QCE) boards. Each processor on a QCE board contains either 256 K, 1 M, 2 M or 4 M bytes of error-checked RAM, a Supervisor bus interface, and a link network interface. Each QCE has a maximum connectivity requirement of up to sixteen INMOS links (two wires per link),

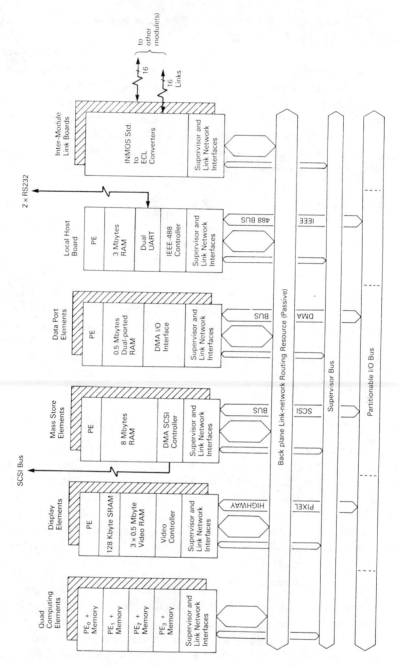

Figure 8.12 Structure of the Meiko Computing Surface

although the placement of logical processors on physical processors maximises the locality of link configuration within a board in order to minimise the usage of backplane routing.

Display Element board

Computer graphics is an application where significant computing power is often required. In addition, many computationally intensive applications produce results which are best displayed pictorially. To support these applications the Computing Surface provides a Display Element board which consists of a single transputer, a Supervisor interface, a link network interface, 128 Kbytes of static RAM and a display controller with a 1.5 Mbyte frame buffer.

Mass Store board

The interfacing of Computing Surface Modules to external I/O devices, such as disk drives, is performed by the Mass Store (MS) boards. Each MS board contains a single transputer with its Supervisor bus and link network interface, plus 8 Mbytes of RAM and a 3 Mbyte/s DMA SCSI interface. Multiple MS boards can be configured in a system, permitting very high aggregate I/O bandwidths to be achieved.

Inter-Module Link board

The limitations on the physical length of standard INMOS links means that links between Modules must be supported in some other way. This is achieved by providing special Inter-Module Link boards, each of which provides sixteen *hardened* links that can be connected to any other Inter-Module Link board in the system (normally in a different Module). These hardened links are implemented using differential ECL drivers, and can operate over distances of up to twenty feet. The sixteen hardened link interfaces are connected to a link network interface which allows them to be allocated to the transputers within their local Module via the backplane routing resource. The Supervisor buses in adjacent Modules can also be connected via the Inter-Module Link board to enable a single Master to configure a multi-Module system.

Data Port board

Certain types of I/O device are supported directly in transputer technology, for example the IMS M212 is a 16-bit transputer with an on-chip disk interface. Special purpose I/O devices, or devices which require very high data transfer rates, are not supported directly in silicon. The Computing Surface board library therefore contains a board which provides a mechanism for interfacing such devices.

A Data Port board comprises two data port elements. Each element consists of a single transputer, with the usual link network interface and Supervisor bus interface, 0.5 Mbytes of 20 Mbyte/s dual-ported memory, and an I/O interface controller. The link to a special-purpose I/O device is implemented via an 80 Mbyte/s 32-bit common bus located on the Module backplane. Each I/O controller manages DMA transfers in or out of the dual-ported memory in parallel with normal processing in the transputer. The common I/O bus consists of a 32-bit data pathway, together with some control and signals, and has a peak bandwidth of one word every 100 ns.

Effectively the I/O bus acts rather like a 32-bit link, except that multiple destination processors can receive the same data simultaneously. The data port elements would normally communicate with special purpose boards such as frame grabbers, graphics output devices, multiple head disk subsystems, or possibly high bandwidth channels to other processing equipment.

Link Network Structure

Ideally there should be a complete connectivity between all transputer links in a configurable transputer array. In practice, however, implementing this is firstly very costly and secondly not extensible. One could, for example, use a Beneš network (see section 3.3.3) or a switch similar to the Memphis switch of the IBM GF11, but the logic required to implement these switching functions is not linearly proportional to the number of connected ports and therefore could not be accommodated on the computing element boards. The routing method chosen for the Computing Surface involves two components in each Module; the *backplane routing resource*, and the *link network interface chips*. A manually configured system does not require the link network interface chips, and is adequate for systems with a fixed or infrequently changing topology.

A Computing Surface Module fully populated with Quad Computing Elements can contain as many as 160 transputers, each of which has four bi-directional links. In order to be able to connect every possible set of links one would require a backplane routing resource with at least 1280 signals. This is beyond the limits of current packaging technology, and so a restricted routing resource is provided. The precise details of the capabilities and limitations of this restricted routing resource are not in the public domain, although the manufacturers claim not to have found a network of degree four which cannot be mapped on to the available routing resource.

The link network interface chips are full custom CMOS devices which essentially contain a cross-bar switch. They permit connections between the links on a board and the backplane routing resource to be set up under control of the Supervisor bus. Up to four of these 84-pin packages can be accommodated on each Quad Computing Element board. By allocating the user's virtual processors to the processors of the physical processors statically, it is possible to place them so as to maximise the connectivity of processors which are on the same board, thus minimising the backplane routing resource requirements.

8.3 Hypercube multiprocessors

When a message-passing processor supports a small number of point-to-point links, statically configurable architectures with store and forwarding capability (whether in software or hardware), such as the Computing Surface, are the norm. Such architectures can be configured so that the maximum path length varies from $O(n^{1/2})$ to $O(\log n)$. However, message-passing processing elements which have *at least* $\log_2 n$ point-to-point links can be used to construct a binary k-cube network; a network known for its high connectivity and $O(\log n)$ path length.

Much of the original work on hypercube architectures[7] was done at Caltech by Seitz [Sei85,Sei83] (see also [SB77]), and from there the concept of a cube-connected ensemble of message-passing processing elements was taken up by Intel and a number of start-up companies most notably in the USA.

8.3.1 Cosmic Cube and the Intel iPSC

The Cosmic Cube [Sei85] is an experimental MIMD machine which dates from around 1980. It consists of 64 processing nodes connected in a binary 6-cube. Each node has a level of hardware complexity that could be integrated in a single chip using 1 micron feature size technology. The processing element comprises an Intel 8086 with an 8087 floating-point co-processor, 128 Kbytes of parity-checked RAM, 8 Kbytes of boot ROM, and six full-duplex asynchronous communication channels each operating at 2 Mbits/s. The Cosmic cube is very much an experimental machine, although benchmarks on a restricted class of physics related problems indicated a performance roughly ten times that of a VAX 11/780 and something less than 1/10th that of a CRAY-1.

The Intel Personal Scientific Computer (iPSC) is a commercial derivative of the Cosmic cube architecture, and systems containing up to 128 processors (7-cube) can be configured. Each node in the iPSC is an independent single-board computer containing an Intel 80286 processor wi

---

[7] The terms *hypercube*, *boolean k-cube* and *binary k-cube* are essentially interch

point coprocessor, 512 Kbytes of RAM and 64 Kbytes of
each node there are eight serial communication channels
eight Intel 82586 communication coprocessors (normally
interfaces). The software overhead for message-passing,
tails a certain amount of control processing, is such that
transmitting a zero length message takes roughly 120 μs. This highlights one
of the major problems of implementing MIMD systems with conventional
microprocessors, they do not support equally all features of the abstract
machine seen by the user. For example, atomic operations such as ADD
and COMPARE are supported directly in hardware but communication
operations such as SEND and RECEIVE are not, and must therefore be
simulated.

The Inmos transputer does not suffer from this simulation overhead,
nor does it require half a circuit board of logic per processor to implement
a memory interface as in the BBN Butterfly, although the four link re-
striction currently rules out cube-connected transputer arrays. The second
generation iPSC incorporates hardware mechanisms to improve the latency
of message passing by introducing a circuit-switched protocol for long messages. This uses a message header to set up a hardware switch at each
node it traverses, after which the body of the message is streamed through
without software intervention. This improves the latency of a zero length
message between nearest neighbours by about a factor of three [ISC87].

8.3.2 The NCUBE/10

In November 1985 a startup company called NCube Corp. announced the
availability of the the NCUBE/10, a custom VLSI implementation of the
Cosmic cube style of architecture [JRW86]. The NCUBE/10 contains from
16 to 1024 processors organised from a 4-cube to a 10-cube network. Each
NCUBE processor is contained in a single 160,000-transistor HMOS chip
fabricated using a 2.5 micron minimum feature size process. A processing
element consists of just seven chips; a processor plus six 256K $\times$ 1 dynamic
RAM chips.

The architecture of the NCUBE processor is similar in many respects
to the T800, except for the presence of eleven links rather than four. Internally the NCUBE processor contains a 32-bit integer ALU with shifter,
16
gisters, 13 special-purpose registers, a 64-bit IEEE
t unit, an instruction cache, a memory interface and
erial channels. The extra link on each processor is
uted I/O.

anised as a four-stage pipeline and is able to execute
er instructions at a peak rate of one every 200 ns.
structions (branching within the cache) take 500 ns

and conditional branches take 600 ns. However, the floating-point performance of the NCUBE is at most 0.5 MFLOPS per processor compared with 1.5 MFLOPS for a 20 MHz IMS T800.

Perhaps the most impressive feature of the NCUBE is its physically compact construction. The small amount of memory in each processing element means that 64 processing elements can be accommodated on a single printed circuit board and hence 1024 elements are contained in a single rack on just 16 boards. Consequently all communication signals are less than 24 inches long.

8.3.3 The FPS T series

In an attempt to combine the power of the transputer with the connectivity of the binary k-cube, Floating Point Systems designed a transputer-based system, containing additional communication logic, capable of being configured as a 14-cube. Each processing element contains a single transputer together with a pipelined vector coprocessor and 1 Mbyte of memory. The peak performance of each node is 16 MFLOPS, and hence the peak performance of a full 14-cube would be 0.26 TFLOPS (Tera-FLOPS, or 10^{12} FLOPS). However, the size and power consumption would be somewhat large, and to quote Lloyd Turner (president of FPS) [Mok86]

> "If the customer has an application for the T/40000, we'll provide the building."

8.4 Summary

Message-passing multiprocessors do not suffer from the problem of access contention found in shared-memory systems, and thus the parallelism of message-passing architectures is not restricted. However, several problems do exists. For example, distributing the load of m parallel processes across n physical processors (where $m > n$) is not a simple task. If the load is badly distributed the system will have the performance characteristics of a single processor. There is also the problem of debugging a system of distributed processes in which the means of access to variables within each process is through a network of processors, some of which may be in an unknown state. Finally, the cost of communicating between processors in a message-passing system is usually much greater than in a shared-memory environment, and this means that fine-grained computations cannot be supported efficienctly.

9 Multiprocessor Software

In the quest for high performance *single processor* architectures, software is important, but does not play a critical rôle. By this we mean that the languages and algorithms designed for one generation of high performance architectures can often be inherited by a subsequent generation since the *architectural model* remains sequential, and any changes can usually be hidden from the application. Certain machines augment the sequential model by introducing data-parallel operations, for example vector processors such as the CRAY-1 and the CYBER 205. These machines require vectorising compilers in order to mask their augmented model of computation from the application code, but processing is otherwise similar.

In the quest for high performance *multiprocessor* systems, however, software is arguably a more critical component than hardware. The reason for this is that the exploitation of parallelism in multiprocessors normally requires the application parallelism to be specified explicitly by the programmer in the form of a number of *independent streams* of instructions. Conventional languages are incapable of expressing programs in this form, and even if they were, conventional algorithms are not tailored to exploit this form of parallelism. The exploitation of multiprocessor architectures therefore requires not only efficient inter-processor communication hardware, but new algorithms and new languages.

In chapters 7 and 8 we discussed the architecture of shared-memory and message-passing multiprocessors respectively. These two broad classes of architecture define a dichotomy of programming languages and algorithms, each suited to one or other class of machine. This is only true for reasons of efficiency, since a message-passing machine can be programmed to simulate a shared-memory machine, and vice versa.

In this chapter we introduce briefly two representative languages which have been devised for multiprocessor systems, and then discuss two case studies in the design of parallel algorithms for multiprocessors.

9.1 Languages for multiprocessors

Shared-memory architectures lend themselves to software environments in which variables can be accessed by a number of processors operating concurrently, and it is through these shared variables that process communication takes place. Conversely, message-passing architectures lend themselves to software environments in which processors (and hence user processes) may only access purely local variables, with communication occuring via the explicit sending and receiving of inter-process messages.

In the following sections we examine the ways in which the two languages **Ada** and **occam** support parallel processing, looking in particular at how they *describe* parallelism and at their mechanisms for *coordinating* parallel activities.

9.1.1   Ada

In the search for a language suitable for programming embedded systems which have long life-cycles, and therefore a strong need for maintainability, the U.S. Department of Defense established a Higher Order Language working group in 1975. Several proposals for a new language were evaluated, and in May 1979 a language from Honeywell Bull in France was chosen. By 1982 an ANSI Standard for the new language had been established (ANSI MIL-STD-1815). The new language was named after Augusta Ada, Countess of Lovelace (1815–1852), who worked with Charles Babbage and is often considered to have been the first computer programmer.

Embedded systems typically comprise a number of closely cooperating parallel tasks. Before the advent of **Ada**, many hardware systems had been constructed for this purpose, but languages suitable for expressing the cooperation between tasks were not widely available. Consequently, software development was ad hoc, and much effort was wasted in producing software packages which were similar in many respects but which relied on incompatible languages and systems. The primary goals of **Ada** were to improve programmer productivity and software portability, and although the language contains many diverse features it is the support for declaring concurrent tasks, and communicating between them, which is of relevance to this text.

Much of the syntax of **Ada** is reminiscent of **Pascal**, with the major difference being the support for *modular* programs and multi-tasking. Declarations appear at the head of each program module, defining types, variables and subprograms (procedures and functions). These declarations are of two types. Those declared in the *implementation part* of a module, or in the *private part* of the module specification, are local to that module and cannot be accessed from another module. However, those declared in the *public part* of a module are visible from outside that module. Each module has an associated identifier, which is visible throughout the context of the module declaration, and this identifier can be used to prefix the names of local objects when accessed from a different module.

There are two types of module in **Ada**: the *package* and the *task*. **Ada** programs can be partitioned into packages for the purpose of introducing high level structure. Thus, for example, a group of subprogram units (such as numerical routines) can be grouped together in a package, and this not only makes the resulting program easier to read but makes the packaged subprograms reusable. The essential idea behind packages is to disassociate the definition of a logical entity from the parts of a program in which it is referenced. Packages containing only declarations are permitted, and so groups of variables accessed from a number of subprogram units (or concurrent tasks) can be placed in a package for the sake of clarity. Packages can be thought of simply as a textual convenience, permitting the programmer to structure a large piece of software without really introducing any additional computational features.

The second type of module is the *task*, and this is of much greater significance to the computer architect since it is the sole means of introducing parallelism into an **Ada** program. In **Ada**, every task is defined within the declarative part of an enclosing program unit. This enclosing program unit is referred to as the *parent unit*, and it is involved implicitly in the initiation and termination of its enclosed sub-tasks. Here is a small example of a task definition; as is the case with all program units, it comprises a specification part and a body.

```
   THE_PARENT:
     declare   - - parent's declarations
        time : natural;
        error_flag : boolean;
        task WATCHDOG; - - task specification;

        task body WATCHDOG is
          - - this is the body of the task
          loop
            time := time + 1.0;
            if error_flag then
              PUT("Error detected at T = ");
              PUT(time,5);
              NEW_LINE;
            end if;
          end loop;
        end WATCHDOG;

     begin
     - - here is the body of the parent unit
     end THE_PARENT;
```

A fundamental notion in **Ada** is that all tasks declared within the declaration part of a program unit begin executing, in parallel, from the moment the parent unit begins executing. The conditions for termintation of a parent task can be defined recursively as the conjunction of the termination of all sibling tasks with the termination of the parent body. Hence, since sibling tasks may themselves have further sibling tasks declared within them, all such nested tasks must terminate before the parent can terminate. The trivial example shown above will therefore *never* terminate since the WATCHDOG task loops indefinitely.

It is also possible to declare a **task type**, and this is a convenient way to create multiple instances of the same task which are to run in parallel. For example, one could simulate the behaviour of an ICL DAP processing element as a single task which could then be replicated 4096 times to simulate the behaviour of a complete array. This could be written as

```
task type DAP_PE is
   entry EXECUTE_INSTRUCTION(inst : in inst_parcel);
end DAP_PE;

task body DAP_PE is
   loop
      accept EXECUTE_INSTRUCTION(inst : in inst_parcel) do
         - - simulate one local instruction
      end accept;
   end loop;
end DAP_PE;
```

The following declaration will then create a 64 × 64 array of DAP_PE tasks.

```
DAP : array(0..63, 0..63) of DAP_PE;
```

The specification of the DAP_PE task type defines an *entry point* called EXECUTE_INSTRUCTION, and within the body of DAP_PE there is an accompanying **accept** statement which defines the sequence of actions which must be obeyed when the task accepts an entry at that entry point.

When each of the 4096 instances of DAP_PE is started up they continue processing up to the **accept** statement, and then pause until another task initiates a *rendezvous* with that task at that entry point. This is achieved by executing the following statement within a parallel task.

```
DAP(x,y).EXECUTE_INSTRUCTION(the_instruction)
```

In this statement, the EXECUTE_INSTRUCTION(the_instruction) part names the entry point and defines the parameter to be passed from the *calling* task to the *called* task during the rendezvous, and DAP(x,y) names the called task. The semantics of **Ada** stipulate that the calling process becomes *suspended* the moment it initiates a rendezvous, becoming active again only when the associated **accept** statements have been executed to completion. This is most important because it defines a mechanism for ensuring mutual exclusion. During a rendezvous between two tasks only the called task is active, and it is therefore safe for it to access data which are also operated on by the calling task. It is possible to write **Ada** programs in which tasks share data *without* enforcing exclusive access, since the scope rules of **Ada** permit data to be visible across the boundary of two parallel tasks, although under these circumstances the results of unsafe computations are undefined.

Ada is therefore very much a language for tightly-coupled, shared-memory multiprocessor architectures, typified by the Sequent Balance, the BBN Butterfly, and newer architectures such as the Motorola M88100 RISC processor. **Ada** can of course be implemented on a single processor machine, but this in itself cannot guarantee safe update of shared variables.

One point which is worth noting about **Ada** tasks is their inherent asymmetry. In particular, the calling task must name the called task explicitly, but the called task has no way of specifying with which task it will rendezvous. This defines two categories of task: *active* and *passive*, in which active tasks call upon the services of passive tasks, and passive tasks provide these services by defining suitable entry points. It is important that the passive tasks do not have to name the task with which they rendezvous, since this enables them to provide a generic service to any or all of the tasks to which they are visible.

Passive tasks also have the ability to express *non-deterministic choice*, whereby one of a number of possible entry points within a single passive task is a candidate for the next rendezvous. The choice of which entry point is selected depends on which entry point has an outstanding active task waiting to rendezvous. The following example of a simple first-in-first-out queue illustrated this mechanism.

```
task QUEUE_MANAGER is
    entry ENQUEUE(value : in queue_item);
    entry DEQUEUE(value : out queue_item);
end QUEUE_MANAGER;

task body QUEUE_MANAGER is
    queue : queue_structure; - - local declaration of queue
begin
```

```
loop
  select
    when not empty(queue) =>
      accept DEQUEUE(value : out queue_item) do
        - - remove item from queue
        - - assign item to value
      end DEQUEUE;
  or
    when not full(queue) =>
      accept ENQUEUE(value : in queue_item) do
        - - insert value into queue
      end ENQUEUE;
  end select;
end loop;
end QUEUE_MANAGER;
```

As one can see from this simple example, it is possible to specify *conditions* which must be satisfied before an entry point becomes a candidate for selection, and this is a feature found also in the the non-deterministic choice construct of **occam** explained in section 9.1.2.

Since only one task can rendezvous with the QUEUE_MANAGER at a time, this ensures exclusive access to the queue data-structure during queue operations. In order to schedule the rendezvous correctly there is a *task wait queue* associated with each entry point, and active tasks which attempt to rendezvous with an entry point which is not ready to accept get placed in this queue. **Ada** supports a strictly FIFO scheduling policy for queued rendezvous. Hence the implementation of the **select** statement simply requires the passive task to scan the task wait queues in search of a waiting active-task descriptor. This of course requires a sequence of machine instructions to find a suitable task with which to rendezvous, followed by a sequence of instructions to schedule the halted task upon completion of the rendezvous. If we now refer back to the speedup model introduced in section 6.2, we can see that the first sequence of instructions represents the *decision time* associated with the rendezvous (the basic synchronisation event), and that the second sequence of instructions represents the *context switching time*. We may reasonably surmise that since these times will be long in comparision with the time to execute a single machine instruction (in most machines) few **Ada** systems will be able to support fine-grain computations efficiently.

9.1.2 Occam

In many ways **Ada** is a complex language; it supports a sizeable number of syntactic structures and extensive data types. In extreme contrast to this we find **occam**, a language with a philosophy of 'keeping things simple'. However, simplicity is just a syntactic convenience (or inconvenience, depending on one's point of view), and the major conceptual difference between **Ada** and **occam** is that whilst in **Ada** data can be shared between tasks, in **occam** the same is *not* true.

Occam is essentially a *distributed* processing language. In **Ada** data can be communicated through shared variables (although this is not intended to be the primary means of communication), and synchronisation is enforced via the rendezvous mechanism. However, in the case of **occam**, data can be communicated between processes only by explicitly sending a message from one process to the other via *named channels*.

Occam programs are constructed from three primitive processes. These primitive processes perform *assignment, input* and *output*. For example,

```
v := e    assign expression e to variable v
c ! e    output expression e to occam channel c
c ? v    input from occam channel c to variable v
```

Each occam channel provides one-way communication between two concurrent processes. Synchronisation between processes is performed by the channel communication protocol which ensures that the communication event occurs only when both the receiving and the transmitting processes are ready to communicate.

These primitive processes can be combined to form meaningful programs using *process constructors*. For example, the most obvious way to construct a program from a number of primitives is to execute them in sequence (in the same way that individual statements are assumed to execute in a conventional sequential programming language). There is an explicit SEQ constructor for expressing the sequential execution of processes, thus

```
SEQ
    process.1
    process.2
```

The natural dual of the SEQ construct is the PAR construct in which all component processes can be executed in parallel. Occam also supports a construct for choosing one of a number of alternative processes to execute. This ALT construct takes a list of guards, each with an associated process, and executes the process associated with the *first* satisfied guard. Each guard is a logical conjunction of a boolean expression and an (optional) input primitive, similar in many respects to a **select when** statement in **Ada**. For example, one may write

```
ALT
    (n > 0) & chan1 ? var1
        process.1
    (n < 0)   chan2 ? var2
        process.2
```

Conditional (IF) and iterative (WHILE) constructs are also provided, but since these are equivalent to similar constructs found in sequential programming languages they are not discussed further. The constructs discussed above are also processes in their own right, and can be composed to form nested process-structures of arbitrary depth.

If it is required that several copies of a single process be executed under one of the SEQ, PAR or ALT scheduling disciplines a *process replication* constructor can be used. This performs an analogous function to the **task type** construct in **Ada**. The syntax of process replication requires the specification of an activation variable (i), and a lower bound and range for the possible values taken by the activation variable, thus

```
SEQ i = 0 FOR n
    process.1
```

or

```
PAR i = 0 FOR n
    process.1
```

or

```
ALT i = 0 FOR n
    process.1
```

A replicated SEQ construct creates n copies of process.1 which are subsequently executed in sequence, terminating on completion of the nth process. A replicated PAR construct again creates n copies of process.1, but may (if there are sufficient hardware resources) execute them in parallel. The PAR construct terminates when *all* component processes have terminated. A replicated ALT construct causes one of n versions of process.1 to be created and executed, with the choice depending on the first of n guards to be satisfied.

Replication can also be applied to communication channels to permit the declaration of *vectors* of channels, thus channels link[0]...link[n-1] can be declared by writing:

```
[n]CHAN OF ANY link:
```

An essentially unlimited number of channels can be declared provided they connect processes executing on the same transputer. However, the fixed number of inter-transputer links together with the direct mapping of one occam channel to one physical transputer link, means that only four channels are available for connecting processes which reside on adjacent transputers.

There is greater symmetry in occam channels than there is in **Ada** rendezvous, since in occam the communicating processes must both name a unique unidirectional channel in order to effect the transfer of a message. There is still some asymmetry in that only the receiving process can express non-deterministic choice over the channel from which it is willing to accept a message.

This summary of occam and its relation to the transputer is necessarily brief, and serves only to highlight the language features which support concurrency. The interested reader should consult the *occam Programming Manual* [INM84], the *occam 2 Reference Manual* [INM88], or Brookes and Stewart [BS89] for more detailed tutorials on programming in occam.

9.2 Multiprocessor algorithms

This book is concerned primarily with the design and analysis of high performance parallel computer architectures. However, since the design of any system is heavily infuenced by its intended use, it is appropriate to consider not only the hardware structures and programming language interface but also one or two representative application algorithms. The analysis of parallel algorithms can yield useful information, particularly about the *quantity* and *granularity* of parallelism, and from this one can quantify the expected execution time for a particular input data size. By comparing this with the expected execution time of an equivalent sequential algorithm one obtains a value for the expected *absolute speedup*. These metrics can also be used in conjunction with system performance models, such as the one outlined in section 6.2 to predict speedup and efficiency. Results of these analyses indicate to the computer architect the areas in which the system as a whole is performing adequately and, more importantly, the areas in which it is not.

In the following sections we investigate two multiprocessor algorithms: the first is intended for use in shared-memory systems supported by languages such as **Ada**, and the second is intended for use in distributed memory systems supported by languages like occam.

9.2.1   Sorting on a shared-memory architecture

Sorting is an important activity in computing, and one which is often cited as a model problem for parallel machines. It has been shown that any sequential sorting algorithm based on pair-wise comparisons must have a time complexity of $\Omega(n \log n)$. Numerous methods for reducing this by using multiple processors have been devised, for example Batcher's *bitonic merge* algorithm [Bat68] sorts n items in $\Theta(\log^2 n)$ time using a network of $n \log_2 n (\log_2 n + 1)/4$ simple comparators. For a survey of parallel sorting algorithms the reader should consult [BDHM84].

In this section we consider the development of a simple parallel sorting algorithm, using the well-known sequential *Quicksort* algorithm as a basis from which to begin. In some ways one's choice of initial sequential algorithm is influenced by the architecture of the multiprocessor system being used. For example, we know that in a shared-memory system a number of tasks can sort independent sections of a common data structure simultaneously. We mentioned earlier that an analysis of parallel algorithms should yield information which is useful to the designer of parallel architectures. This completes a circular argument, and serves to stress that the design of parallel algorithms is an iterative, and often an intuitive, process.

The Quicksort algorithm is an efficient (internal) sequential sorting algorithm which contains independent sub-computations, and thus has potential for parallel processing. The simplest variant of the Quicksort algorithm can be defined as follows;

1. Given an array $K[l \ldots u]$ of keys, partition the array such that the value originally at position $K[l]$ is at position $K[i]$, and all values ranked below $K[i]$ are in locations $l \ldots i-1$, and all values ranked at the same level or higher than $K[i]$ are in locations $i+1 \ldots u$

2. If $i - l > 2$ then perform step 1 on the sub-array $K[l \ldots i - 1]$

3. If $u - i > 2$ then perform step 1 on the sub-array $K[i + 1 \ldots u]$

There are two points to note here: firstly, steps 2 and 3 both require step 1 to be completed before they can proceed. Secondly, steps 2 and 3 are completely independent, and therefore can execute in parallel. This is an example of *non-linear recursion*, where each procedure (or task) creates more than one recursive (and independent) call on itself. Figure 9.1 shows the temporal relationships between a number of such calls.

Let us now consider how this could be implemented on a shared-memory architecture using **Ada**. Following this we outline some techniques with which one can analyse the behaviour and performance of this algorithm. Since we are considering an implementation on a shared-memory architecture no *decomposition of data* is required. However, we must partition the

parallelism

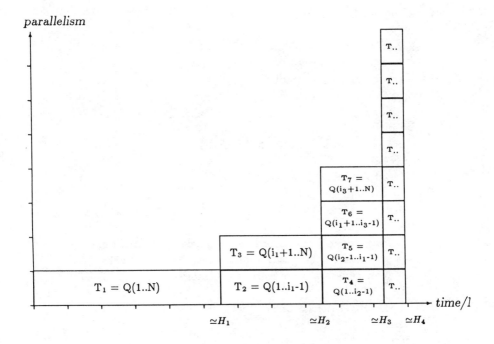

Figure 9.1 Idealized parallel decomposition of Quicksort, where H_k is the harmonic series given by $\sum_{i=1}^{k} i^{-1}$

computation to define the unit of parallelism, and devise a scheme whereby the tasks can coordinate their activity.

We have already identified the recursive calls to the Quicksort procedure as potential parallel tasks, and so let us define a **task type** which performs a Quicksort on a sub-array of unsorted keys given lower and upper bounds on array index defining the set of keys to be sorted. The Quicksort task operates by repeatedly executing a loop until it is told by the MANAGER that there is no more work. Within each loop a Quicksort task obtains a pair (l,u) from the MANAGER by executing a rendezvous with the MANAGER at the DISPATCH entry point. After this rendezvous (l,u) defines a range of keys which the task must take responsibility for sorting during that iteration of the loop. The condition for termination is if the MANAGER dispatches a pair (l,u) for which l=u. If this is not the case then the sub-array must be partitioned according to the Quicksort method, and this can generate two further pairs (l,i-1) and (i+1,u) which each define a sub-range of the given sub-array which can be parallelised still further. These are entered into the queue of pairs by executing one rendezvous with the MANAGER for each valid pair, at the RECEIVE entry point.

```
task type QUICKSORT;

task body QUICKSORT is
    i, l, u : integer; busy : boolean;
    - - any other local variables
begin
busy := true;
while busy loop
    - - get some work from the MANAGER
    MANAGER.DISPATCH(l, u);
    - - test to see if sort is complete
    if l = u then
        busy := false
    else
        - - Partition K[l...u] according to Quicksort algorithm,
        - - and let i be the position of the new sorted element.
        - - Now generate more work if necessary.
        if i /= l then
            MANAGER.RECEIVE(l, i-1);
        end if;
        if i /= u then
            MANAGER.RECEIVE(i+1, u);
        end if;
    end if;
end loop;
end QUICKSORT;
```

The manager of the tasks maintains a queue of pairs (l,u) which describe sub-arrays which need to be sorted. The code for the task manager is very similar to the FIFO queue example described on page 173. The only difference is that the items to be queued are pairs of integers rather than values of type 'queue_item'. The ENQUEUE entry point is renamed RECEIVE, and the DEQUEUE entry pointy is renamed DISPATCH. In addition, the MANAGER task must detect when the array of keys has been completely sorted, and inform the QUICKSORT tasks. Failure to do this would result in deadlock, and hence non-termination of the algorithm.

```
task MANAGER is
    entry DISPATCH(l, u : out integer);
    entry RECEIVE(l, u : in integer);
end MANAGER;
```

```
task body MANAGER is
  sorted : integer;
  the_workers : array (1 . . number_of_sorters) of QUICKSORT
begin
sorted := 0; - - must terminate when sorted = size
- - now dispatch the first task explicitly
accept DISPATCH(l, u : out integer) do
  l := 1; u := size;
end accept;
while sorted /= size loop
  select
    when not empty(work_queue) =>
      accept DISPATCH(l, u : out integer) do
        - - get next (l, u) pair from queue
        sorted := sorted + 1;
      end accept;
  or
    when not full(work_queue) =>
      accept RECEIVE(l, u : in integer) do
        - - put the (l, u) pair into the queue
      end accept;
  end select;
end loop;
for sorted in 1..number_of_sorters loop
  accept DISPATCH(l,u : out integer) do
    l := 1; u := 1; - - this will terminate the sorter tasks
  end accept;
end loop
end MANAGER;
```

This piece of code requires some explanation. The QUICKSORT task type is used to generate a *fixed number* of QUICKSORT task instances; the actual number will depend on how much physical parallelism there is in the the target hardware. For example, when running on a single processor, there is absolutely no advantage in generating more than one QUICKSORT task. The manager task detects termination by counting the number of sorting operations it dispatches to the workers, and since each dispatched task results in exactly one item being placed in its correct position, providing a direct mechanism for detecting when the parallel sorting operation is complete.

This parallel version of Quicksort uses a task decomposition scheme known as *recursive divide-and-conquer*. This scheme can be particularly

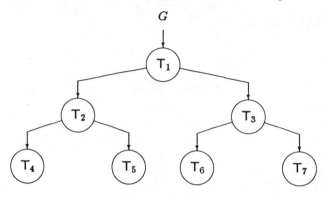

Figure 9.2 Task graph for parallel Quicksort

effective at generating large quantities of parallelism since the parallelism can grow exponentially. However, as is the case with this example, much of the work done in each task is related to the creation of tasks (that is, the decomposition itself), and as the number of tasks mushrooms towards the end of the computation the amount of *real* work done per task becomes quite small. In a practical parallel sorting algorithm one would not decompose the problem down to the most trivial case (as we have done here), but stop generating tasks when an optimum value for u-l is reached and revert to a sequential sorting algorithm.

Let us now examine this parallel algorithm from the point of view of deriving an expression for the expected execution time on a parallel machine with a given number of processors. Observing figure 9.1 one can see that the total execution time depends on the length of the path from the initiation of the root task to the termination of the final leaf task. This can be represented as a *task graph G*, as shown in figure 9.2, in which T_i denotes task i and T_i has execution time t_i. In the parallel Quicksort algorithm the values of t_i depend on the distribution of values within the range of keys to be sorted since at each stage the algorithm chooses a supposedly *median* value from the values to be sorted and ranks the remainder with respect to this value.

Some definitions

Given a set of tasks $T_1, T_2, \ldots, T_n$ that are partially ordered in their execution sequence by a precedence relation $<$, we call T_i a *predecessor* of T_j (and T_j a successor of T_i) if $T_i < T_j$. In terms of scheduling, this means that T_j must not begin executing until T_i has terminated. If $T_i < T_j$ and there is no task T_k for which $T_i < T_k$ *and* $T_k < T_j$ then T_i is an *immediate predecessor* of T_j (and T_j an immediate successor of T_i). Tasks with no predecessor are *initial* and tasks with no successor are *final*.

Using these notions we can define formally the task graph G to be the set of nodes $T_i\{1 \le i \le n\}$ in which there is a directed arc from T_i to T_j if T_i is an immediate predecessor of T_j. A set of tasks is said to be *independent* if for any tasks T_i, T_j in the set, neither $T_i < T_j$ nor $T_j < T_i$. The *width* of G (written $width(G)$) is the maximum of the sizes of all independent sets of tasks. We also define a *chain* of tasks to be a task graph in which the tasks are totally ordered, and then the *length* of the chain is the number of tasks in the chain. The depth of a graph G is the maximum length of all the chains in G.

Estimating execution times

A probabilistic analysis of the execution times for statically decomposed tasks (where the decomposition is not computed 'on-the-fly') has been given by Robinson [Rob79], and here we apply his techniques to our example.

Let t_G be a random variable which represents the execution time of graph G, and let F_G be the cumulative distribution function (c.d.f.) for t_G. In order to make statements which express t_G and F_G in terms of the individual task execution times t_i, and task c.d.f's F_i, the task graph must be *simple*. A simple task is defined as follows. Let $C_1, C_2, \ldots, C_m$ be all chains from initial to final tasks in G. We define an expression E_i for all chains C_i containing tasks $T_{i_1}, T_{i_2}, \ldots, T_{i_k}$, such that $E_i = x_{i_1} x_{i_2} \ldots x_{i_k}$, and then G is said to be *simple* if the polynomial expression $E_1 + E_2 + \cdots + E_m$ can be factored such that each x appears only once. Simple task graphs correspond to parallel programs in which task creation always takes the form

```
PAR(P1; P2; P3;...; Pn)
```

and where the sub-tasks P1 to Pn do not synchronise with any task except at their initiation and termination.

If we assume that the execution times of all m_j tasks at level j in a simple task graph G, of depth L, are identically distributed with mean μ_j and standard deviation σ_j, then on k processors, where $k \ge width(G)$, the upper and lower bounds on the expected execution time, denoted $E(t_G)$ can be derived using Order Statistics [Dav70, pp.46–48], [Rob79], and are given by equation 9.1.

$$\sum_{j=1}^{L} \mu_j \le E(t_G) \le \sum_{j=1}^{L} \left(\mu_j + \frac{m_j - 1}{\sqrt{2m_j - 1}} \sigma_j \right) \qquad (9.1)$$

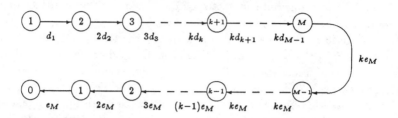

Figure 9.3 State-transition diagram for parallel Quicksort

The conditions under which this equation applies describe an important but rather restricted class of parallel algorithms. For example, $k \geq width(G)$ implies that there are enough processors to absorb *all* task parallelism all of the time, and in most cases this is unrealistic . A more satisfactory analysis technique for dynamically decomposed algorithms (such as the Quicksort derived earlier) is that of using *queueing models* [Kle75].

It is possible to analyse divide-and-conquer algorithms like Quicksort by considering the divide and conquer phases separately (even though the two phases may be interleaved). Given k processors as before, and a level of partitioning which results in M leaf tasks (sequential Quicksort procedures), the sequential creation and execution of M tasks can be represented by a state-transition diagram, as illustrated in figure 9.3.   Note, although each Quicksort task is theoretically capable of creating two sibling tasks in *parallel*, enforced sequential access to the task queue means that in practice they are created sequentially.

In figure 9.3 each state is identified by a state variable which in this case is defined as the number of tasks in the task queue (initially one). The times to decompose and execute tasks are assumed to be exponentially distributed with means of d_i^{-1} and e_M respectively, where i is the instantaneous task queue length. Hence, the mean time to decompose and execute M tasks on k processors can be found by summing the mean state-transition times from the start of the Quicksort algorithm to its termination. The mean execution time is then $E(T)$

$$E(T) = \sum_{i=1}^{M-1} (\min(i, k) d_i)^{-1} + e_M^{-1} \left(\frac{M - k}{k} + \sum_{i=1}^{k} i^{-1} \right) \qquad (9.2)$$

In any realistic model of execution time on a parallel architecture the mean decomposition time d_i must take account of the time to access a shared queue, which in most cases will be a function of k.

These short examples hopefully serve to illustrate typical techniques that can be used to analyse the execution time of parallel algorithms without entering into lengthy details which can be found in existing texts.

9.2.2 Matrix multiplication using message-passing

In this section we look at the design and implementation of a *distributed* numerical algorithm for computing the product of two square matrices, and use the **occam** language to illustrate how message-passing primitives form a key element in these types of algorithm.

Consider the multiplication of two $n \times n$ matrices a and b to produce a result matrix c. The method of computing c can be defined by the following equation.

$$c_{ij} = \sum_{k=1}^{n} a_{ik} b_{kj} \; ; \; i, j \in \{1 \ldots n\} \tag{9.3}$$

The first, and most obvious, point to note about this algebraic specification of matrix multiplication is that it defines a set of n^2 *independent* computations. Secondly, each independent computation is a dot-product operation comprising $2n$ dyadic operations (multiply and accumulate) on a total of n pairs of input values. However, there are only $2n^2$ input values in a and b, compared with $n^2 \times 2n$ dot-product input operands, so clearly each matrix element from a and b must be *used* in n independent calculations.

Since the total number of arithmetic operations is $2n^3$, and the total number of memory accesses needed to satisfy the operand requirements is also $2n^3$, the memory bandwidth and CPU bandwidth requirements are perfectly matched. This is only true, however, if the rates of memory and CPU processing are equal. If one introduce parallelism into the evaluation procedure the balance becomes upset. Consider what happens if we use n^2 processors to compute all c_{ij} concurrently. The minimum theoretical computation time, assuming purely sequential processing for each c_{ij}, is just $2n$. If the memory bandwidth is not increased by a factor of n^2 then the utilisation of processors will be less than unity, and the parallel processing efficiency will be poor.

One solution to this problem is to provide highly parallel access to shared memory as in the BBN Butterfly, the IBM RP3, and many others. A concommitant problem is then the arrangement of memory access patterns to ensure that memory bank collisions do not cause undue interference between processors. This is a problem that has been studied widely, in particular by Lawrie, Chang and Kuck [Law75,CKL77]. The cost of providing the required bandwidth to a shared memory structure is sometimes too great, and then other techniques must be sought.

An alternative suggested by Kung [Kun82], known as *systolic process-ing*, gets round the problem of memory bandwidth by using each value retrieved from memory several times. Systolic systems operate by pumping each operand value through an array (a systolic array) of processing elem-ents, in such a way that each value is *used* at each processor it encounters. Systolic arrays normally perform the same computation at each PE in the array, and the movement of information between PEs is normally consid-ered to be synchronous. Input and output from the array occurs only at the boundary of the array. This conceptual view of systolic arrays, in which there exists a common clock, is useful for analysing their logical behaviour although in practice the distribution of a common clock across indefinitely large 2-D array structures is not feasible. Systolic arrays are typified by $\Theta(k)$ processing elements connected by a regular static network containing $\Theta(k)$ unidirectional links. From an **occam** programming point of view this is ideal since it corresponds directly with the notions of **occam** channels and processes. Let us now consider a systolic implementation of matrix multi-plication using a two-dimensional systolic array, and then devise a suitable implementation using **occam**.

In figure 9.4 the outline of a systolic matrix multiplier is illustrated, showing an array of PEs, their communication pathways, and the order and placement of input operand values. One can see that for both the a and b matrices a *wavefront* of values flows into the array at the Northern and Western perimeters. The staggering of the rows and columns along each input perimeter ensures that the correct values meet in the correct processing element. To make the array work properly, a real implementation of this scheme would contain a mechanism for inserting zero values before (and after) each staggered a and b vector where required. For clarity these are omitted from figure 9.4.

Verification of correctness

The regularity of many systolic arrays permits the designer to verify for-mally that the systolic implementation meets the specification of the al-gorithm. In the scheme presented in figure 9.4 the array operates syn-chronously by propagating the a values one array-position Eastward and the b values one array-position Southward on each clock cycle. At every proces̲ ̲ which at least one pair of non-zero values has been re-um (which is initially zero) is incremented by the product b values.

$\cdots$ $\{1 \leq i \leq n, 1 \leq j \leq n\}$ the local sum c_{ij} after $2n - 1$ $\cdots$ $c_{ij} = \sum_{k=1}^{n} a_{ik} b_{kj}$.

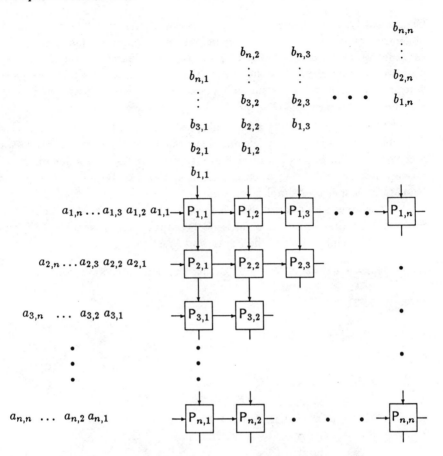

Figure 9.4 A systolic matrix multiplication scheme

Proof

The alignment of input values entering the Northern and Eastern perimeters is such that values a_{ik} and b_{ki} $\{1 \le k \le n\}$ are delayed from entering the array for $i-1$ clock cycles. Hence, at processor P_{xy} in clock cycle t the local values of a and b, denoted $a(x,y)$ and $b(x,y)$ are given by the following two equations, assuming $L = \max(x,y)$.

$$a(x,y) = \begin{cases} 0 & \text{if } t < i \\ a_{y,L-t} & \text{if } t \ge i \end{cases} \tag{9.4}$$

$$b(x,y) = \begin{cases} 0 & \text{if } t < i \\ b_{L-t,x} & \text{if } t \ge i \end{cases} \tag{9.5}$$

Consequently, after L clock cycles, processor P_{ij} receives its first pair of non-zero values; a_{i1} and b_{1i}. During the subsequent n clock cycles the sequence of pairs $(a_{i2}, b_{2j}), (a_{i3}, b_{3j}), \ldots, (a_{in}, b_{nj})$ passes through P_{ij}. By observation it is clear that the summation of the products of these pairs will produce a value equivalent to $\sum_{k=1}^{n} a_{ik} b_{kj}$. Since this is assigned to c_{ij} the specification is met. □

The leading and trailing zero values, not shown in figure 9.4, are necessary only because this is a synchronous systolic array, so when one processor receives input all processors receive input. With an asynchronous message-passing protocol, such as **occam** channels, this can be avoided and this leads to a cleaner and simpler solution.

We now define an **occam** process for a single PE which takes input from its North and East links, performs a local computation and passes the input values to its neighbours via the South and West links.

```
PROC element(CHAN OF REAL North, South, East, West)
  REAL a, b, sum;
  SEQ
    sum := 0;
    SEQ i = 0 FOR N
      SEQ
        PAR
          North ? a
          West ? b
        sum := sum + (a * b)
        PAR
          South ! a
          East ! b
:
```

This process contains an iterative loop which receives a and b values in parallel (to avoid possible deadlock, and maximise communication bandwidth). Since the process performing the parallel input of a and b values does not itself terminate until *both* values have been received, no zero values need to be inserted to forcibly align the two input streams at each position in the array. For example, processor $P_{4,1}$ will not begin executing the first sum:=sum+(a * b) statement until it has received $a_{4,1}$ and $b_{1,1}$. This only occurs after processors $P_{1,1} \ldots P_{3,1}$ have each computed their first iteration. It is the **occam** channel protocol which ensures that computations begin when their data are available, and this form of processing is usually referred to as *data-driven* processing.

An array of element processes can be declared by first defining vectors of channels, and then initiating n^2 processes from within a *harness* process, thus

```
VAL n IS 100:
[n+1][n+1]CHAN OF REAL NS, WE:
PAR
   PAR i = 1 FOR n
     PAR j = 1 FOR n
       element(NS[i][j-1], NS[i][j], WE[i-1][j], WE[i][j])
   - - Read a and b values from memory and input
   - - to WE[0][1..n] and NS[1..n][0] respectively.
```

This simplistic scheme omits the check for boundary conditions on the Southern and Western boundaries, where processors would otherwise attempt to output to non-existent processors: this could be prevented by the addition of a simple test in each element process. For clarity the sequencing of input values and the removal of output values has also been omitted from this example.

Process placement

Placing n^2 processes on less than n^2 physical processors could pose something of a problem. The transputer, which is the target hardware for occam, can support many processes in each processor, but at present has only four hard links (eight channels). This is a problem which is apparent to all transputer-based systems, such as the Meiko Computing Surface, the PARSYS SN1000 series (formerly ESPRIT project 1045), and many smaller systems. The actual placement of processes is dictated largely by the physical topology of the transputer array, except in machines which have the ability to *reconfigure* the links.

An array of $n \times n$ element processes can placed on an array of less than n^2 transputers in several ways. For example, the array could be divided into strips of rows or columns w processes wide, thus placing $w \times n$ processes in each transputer, leading to a requirement for at least $2(w+n)$ unidirectional channels going into or out of each transputer.

If each transputer is given responsibility for a $p \times p$ square sub-array, then at least $4p$ channels are required for each transputers. For a fixed size array of transputers, say $m \times m$, the number of channels required per transputer is $p = 4n/m$. However, in conventional terms, the input problem size, N, is equal to n^2. Hence, we can say that the number of channels required per processor is $\Theta(N^{1/2})$. This conflicts somewhat with the $O(1)$ hardware links provided on the transputer devices. It is therefore common for occam programmers to write a *routing harness* which maps k ($k > 4$) soft channels down to just eight unidirectional hard channels, effectively *multiplexing* the communication bandwidth at the program level.

The inter-transputer communication bandwidth requirements of the systolic matrix multiplication algorithm are proportional to the *perimeter* of each sub-array, and the computational requirements are proportional to the *area* of the sub-array. In the transputer, communication and computation in different processes can occur simultaneously, and therefore if the actual time spent communicating through the off-chip links is not greater than the total computation time of p^2 `element` processes then the utilisation of each transputer will be determined only by the granular efficiency of each `element` process. If the reverse is true, then the utilisation of each transputer will naturally be limited by a communication bottleneck. Therefore, in transputers there are two efficiency consideration: firstly, the granular inefficiency introduced when two processes communicate within the same transputer, and secondly the inefficiency which arises due to the communication between chips.

Let us for the moment assume a unit delay for communicating a value between two `element` processes, and examine the performance of this distributed matrix multiplication algorithm. The time taken to propagate a and b values to $P_{n,n}$ (the process farthest away from the source of input), denoted here by t_{pg}, is equal to the number of inter-process hops from the input perimeters (North and West) to the bottom right-hand corner, multiplied by the communication time per hop. This is given by equation 9.6.

$$t_{pg} = (n - 1)(t_{calc} + t_{prop}) \tag{9.6}$$

In this equation, t_{calc} refers to the time taken to evaluate

```
s := s + (a * b)
```

and t_{prop} refers to the time taken to evaluate

```
PAR
    South !  a
    East  !  b
```

Note, we do not include the time taken to input the a and b values since that activity is overlapped with the reception of a and b values in an adjacent processor. The time from the initiation of the first element computation (that in $P_{1,1}$) to the termination of the last element computation (that in $P_{n,n}$), on an $n \times n$ array, is given by $T(n)$ and is equal to the propagation time t_{pg} plus the time to complete n iterations of the main loop in the element process. Hence,

$$T(n) = (2n - 1)(t_{calc} + t_{prop}) \qquad (9.7)$$

The granular efficiency of this parallel computation (see equation 6.2 on page 97), denoted η_g, is given by

$$\eta_g = \frac{1}{1 + \left(\frac{t_{prop}}{t_{calc}}\right)} \qquad (9.8)$$

The absolute speedup or *gain* of a parallel algorithm is defined as the ratio of the execution time of the *best* equivalent sequential algorithm to the execution time of the parallel algorithm, expressed as a function of the exploited parallelism. In the case of matrix multiplication, the best sequential algorithm which does not parallelise within the dot-product operation has an execution time T_s which involves n^3 multiply-accumulate operations, each of which takes a time of t_{calc}.

$$T_s = n^3 t_{calc} \qquad (9.9)$$

Consequently, we can write down a simple equation for the parallel processing gain, $G_{\parallel}$, on this algorithm thus

$$G_{\parallel} = \frac{n^3 t_{calc}}{(2n - 1)(t_{calc} + t_{prop})}$$

which is equivalent to

$$G_{\parallel} = \eta_g \left(\frac{n^3}{2n - 1}\right) \qquad (9.10)$$

This concludes our discussion of speedup and efficiency for this systolic algorithm. Among the points worth noting are that relative speedup $(G_{\parallel}/\eta_g)$ is $O(n^2)$ on n^2 processors, which is $O(N)$ for input of size N. This is characteristic of systolic arrays, and means that the array can be scaled up in proportion to the size of the input without any degradation in performance.

9.3   Summary

In this chapter we have looked at multiprocessor software from two viewpoints. Firstly, by considering languages for multiprocessors, and secondly by considering algorithms for multiprocessors. Following on from our treatment of multiprocessor systems in chapters 7 and 8, in which the distinction between shared versus distributed memory is emphasised, we have examined a typical language and a typical algorithm for each of these two classes of machine. Although this is a very coarse classification of multiprocessor systems, the general principles have been expounded. We also looked briefly at some techniques for estimating the execution times of parallel algorithms, under both static and dynamic decomposition schemes. Those interested in pursuing this line of study further, should consult Quinn [Qui87] which contains a chapter on the design of parallel algorithms, and chapters on each major class of problem. Quinn also presents bibliographic notes on most aspects of parallel algorithms. Kleinrock [Kle75] describes the theory behind queueing networks, and their application in analysing the throughput of certain types of computing system. Many of these techniques can also be applied to parallel systems.

This book has aimed to introduce the reader to a variety of topics that are relevant in the field of high performance architectures. We began by looking at the architecture of SIMD array processors, their interconnection techniques (which are also applicable to MIMD systems), and their programming methods. We have studied the architecture of some large scale SIMD systems, such as the DAP and the Connection Machine, and examined their performance at a number of levels. The second half of this book has been devoted to multiprocessor architectures, from their design principles to example systems, and finally to some of the software implications of such architectures.

It is likely that parallel processing will take on greater significance as the implementation technology of multiprocessor systems matures. As we have seen from chapter 7, these systems can range is size from small (less than 32 processors) systems connected using a single high performance bus, up to quite large systems (more than 128 processors) connected using multi-stage networks. Bus-connected systems can provide a significant cost advantage in multi-user applications, rather than genuinely concurrent applications, since relatively low communication bandwidth can be tolerated. We have seen that to support genuinely concurrent applications a significant degree of concurrency in the processor interconnection mechanism is essential.

The architectures described in volume I all have the same basic goal; to make a single stream of instructions execute as fast as possible without significant modification at the source code level. This naturally involves techniques which optimise the placement of information (storage hierarchies) and the exploitation of low-level parallelism (parallel functional units and pipelining). Vectorising compilers are used to bridge the semantic gap between what the programmer specifies and how the machine is capable of realising that specification. Sometimes this gap is too wide, and users are obliged to insert compiler directives into their programs. The types of architecture described in this volume are qualitatively different in the sense that the semantic gap between the architecture and a sequential program is so wide that a different approach to programming is required. Architects and users of these array processors and multiprocessors have evolved their own languages (or language variants), some of which we have outlined in this book. We have hopefully convinced the reader that the task of creating software for parallel computers is not simply a problem of re-coding existing algorithms. Furthermore, the automatic conversion of existing applications to run n-times faster on an n-processor machine is a non-trivial task, and one which at present limits the commercial applicability of parallel systems to existing software. However, in many cases, the availability of highly parallel systems encourages the development of solutions to problems previously considered either impractical or too expensive.

Bibliography

[Aus79]   J.H. Austin. *The Burroughs Scientific Processor*, pages 1–31. Volume 2, Infotech Intl Ltd., Maidenhead, 1979.

[Bac78]   J. Backus. Can Programming be Liberated from the von Neumann Style? *Communications of the ACM*, 8:613–641, 1978.

[Bat68]   K.E. Batcher. Sorting networks and their applications. In *Proceedings of the Spring Joint Computer Conference*, pages 307–314, AFIPS Press, Reston VA, 1968.

[Bat74]   K.E. Batcher. STARAN Parallel Processor System Hardware. In *Proc. AFIPS-NCC*, pages 405–410, 1974.

[Bat76]   K.E. Batcher. The FLIP Network in STARAN. In *Int. Conf. Parallel Proc.*, pages 65–71, 1976.

[Bat77]   K.E. Batcher. Multi-dimensional Access Memory in STARAN. *IEEE Transactions on Computers*, C-26:174–177, 1977.

[Bat80]   K.E. Batcher. Design of a Massively Parallel Processor. *IEEE Transactions on Computers*, C-29:836–840, 1980.

[BBK*68]   G.H. Barnes, R.M. Brown, M. Kato, D.J. Kuck, D.L. Slotnick, and R.A. Stokes. The ILLIAC IV computer. *IEEE Transactions on Computers*, C-17:746–57, 1968.

[BDHM84]   D. Bitton, D.J. De Witt, D.K. Hsaio, and J. Menon. A taxonomy of parallel sorting. *ACM Computing Surveys*, 16(3):287–318, September 1984.

[BDW85]   J. Beetem, M. Denneau, and D. Weingarten. The GF11 Supercomputer. In *Proc. 12th Annual Symposium on Computer Architecture*, pages 108–115, 1985.

[Ben64]   V. Beneš. Optimal Rearrangeable Multistage Connecting Networks. *Bell System Technical Journal*, 43(4):1646–1656, 1964.

[Ben65]   V. Beneš. *Mathematical Theory of Connecting Networks and Telephone Traffic*. Academic Press, New York, 1965.

194

[BS89]   G.R. Brookes and A.J. Stewart. *Introduction to occam 2 on the Transputer.* Macmillan, London, 1989.

[CGH*72]   B.A. Crane, M.J. Gilmartin, J.H. Huttenhoff, P.T. Rus, and R.R. Shively. PEPE Computer Architecture. In *IEEE Compcon*, pages 57–60, 1972.

[CGS*85]   W. Crowther, J. Goodhue, E. Starr, R. Thomas, W. Milliken, and T. Blackader. Performance measurements on a 128-node Butterfly parallel processor. In *Proc. 1985 International Conference on Parallel Processing*, pages 531–540, 1985.

[CKL77]   D. Chang, D.J. Kuck, and D.H. Lawrie. On the Effective Bandwidth of Parallel Memories. *IEEE Transactions on Computers*, Vol. C-26(5):480–490, May 1977.

[Dav70]   H.A. Davis. *Order Statistics.* Wiley, New York, 1970.

[Den68]   P.J. Denning. The working set model for program behaviour. *Communications of the ACM*, 11:323–33, 1968.

[Dij65]   E.W. Dijkstra. *Cooperating Sequential Processes.* Academic Press, New York, 1965.

[Fal76]   H. Falk. Reaching for the gigaflop. *IEEE Spectrum*, 13(10):65–70, 1976.

[Fen81]   T.Y. Feng. A Survey of Interconnection Networks. *IEEE Computer*, 12–27, Dec. 1981.

[Fly72]   M.J. Flynn. Some Computer Organisations and their Effectiveness. *IEEE Transactions on Computers*, C-21:948–960, 1972.

[FT79]   G.R. Frank and C.J. Theaker. The Design of the MUSS Operating System. *Software – Practice and Experience*, Vol. 9:599–620, 1979.

[FW60]   G.E. Forsythe and W.R. Wasow. *Finite-difference Methods for Partial Differential Equations.* Wiley, London, 1960.

[GGK*83]   A. Gottleib, R. Grishman, C.P. Kruskal, K.P. McAuliffe, L. Rudolph, and M. Snir. The NYU Ultracomputer — Designing a MIMD Shared Memory Parallel Machine. *IEEE Transactions on Computers*, C-32(2):175–189, 1983.

[GL73]   G.R. Goke and G.J. Lipovski. Banyan Networks for Partitioning Multiprocessor Systems. In *1st Annual International Symposium on Computer Architecture*, pages 21–28, 1973.

[GM63]   J. Gregory and R.C. McReynolds. The SOLOMON computer. *IEEE Transactions on Electronic Computers*, EC-12:774–81, 1963.

[Gos80]   J.B. Gosling. *Design of Arithmetic Units for Digital Computers*. Macmillan, London, 1980.

[Gro75]   H.A. Grosch. Grosch's law revisited. *Computerworld*, 8(16):24, April, 1975.

[GS82]   A. Gottleib and J.T. Schwartz. Networks and Algorithms for Very-Large-Scale Parallel Computation. *IEEE Computer*, 27–36, January 1982.

[HB84]   K. Hwang and F.A. Briggs. *Computer Architecture and Parallel Processing*. McGraw-Hill, Singapore, 1984.

[Hil85]   W. Daniel Hillis. *The Connection Machine*. MIT Press, Cambridge, MA, 1985.

[HJ81]   R.W. Hockney and C.R. Jesshope. *Parallel Computers*. Adam Hilger, Bristol, 1981.

[IEH*85]   R.N. Ibbett, D.A. Edwards, T.P. Hopkins, C.K. Cadogan, and D.A. Train. Centrenet – A High Performance Local Area Network. *Computer Journal*, Vol. 28(3):231–242, 1985.

[INM]   *IMS T800 Architecture, Technical note 6*. INMOS Limited, Bristol.

[INM84]   *occam Programming Manual*. INMOS Limited, UK, 1984.

[INM88]   *occam 2 Reference Manual*. Prentice-Hall International, UK, 1988.

[ISC87]   *iSCurrents*. Intel Scientific Computers, Fall/Winter 1987.

[JD86]   T. Johnson and T. Durham. *Parallel Processing: the challenge of new computer architectures*. Ovum Ltd, London, 1986.

[JRW86]   D. Jurasek, W. Richardson, and D. Wilde. A Multiprocessor Design in Custom VLSI. *VLSI Systems Design*, 26–30, June 1986.

[KEM*78]   D. Katsuki, E.S. Elsam, W.F. Mann, E.S. Roberts, J.G. Robinson, F.S. Skowronski, and E.W. Wolf. Pluribus — An Operational Fault-Tolerant Multiprocessor. *Proc. IEEE*, Vol. 66(10):1146–1159, October 1978.

[Kle75]   L. Kleinrock. *Queueing Systems*. Volume 1, Wiley, New York, 1975.

[Knu73]   D.E. Knuth. *The Art of Computer Programming (3 vols.)*. Addison-Wesley, Reading, MA., 1973.

[KS82]   D.J. Kuck and R.A. Stokes. The Burroughs Scientific Processor (BSP). *IEEE Transactions on Computers*, C-31(5):363–376, 1982.

[Kun82]   H.T. Kung. Why systolic architectures? *Computer*, 15(1):37–46, 1982.

[Law75]   D.H. Lawrie. Access and alignment of data in an array processor. *IEEE Transactions on Computers*, C-24:1145–1155, 1975.

[Lei85]   C.E. Leiserson. Fat-Trees: Universal Networks for Hardware-Efficient Supercomputing. In *Proc. International Conference on Parallel Processing*, pages 393–402, 1985.

[Lis88]   A.M. Lister. *Fundamentals of Operating Systems*. Macmillan, London, fourth edition, 1988.

[LM87]   G.J. Lipovski and M. Malek. *Parallel Computing: theory and comparisons*. John Wiley & Sons, New York, 1987.

[MGN79]   G.M. Masson, G.C. Ginger, and S. Nakamura. A Sampler of Circuit Switching Networks. *IEEE Computer*, 12(6):32–48, 1979.

[MI79]   D. Morris and R.N. Ibbett. *The MU5 Computer System*. Macmillan, London, 1979.

[MM82]   T.N. Mudge and B.A. Makrucki. Probabilistic Analysis of a Crossbar Switch. In *Proc. 9th Annual International Symposium on Computer Architecture*, pages 311–320, 1982.

[Mok86]   N. Mokhoff. Hypercube architecture leads the way for commercial supercomputers in scientific applications. In *Computer Design*, pages 28–30, May 1986.

[Moo59]   E.F. Moore. The shortest path through a maze. In *Proceedings of the International Symposium on the Theory of Switching*, pages 285–292, 1959.

[OT68]   D.C. Opferman and N.T. Tsao-Wu. On a Class of Rearrangeable Switching Networks, Part I: Control Algorithms, & Part II:

Enumeration Studies and Fault Diagnosis. *Bell System Tech. J.*, Vol. 50(5):1579–1618, May-June 1968.

[PBG*85]   G.F. Pfister, W.C. Brantley, D.A. George, S.L. Harvey, W.J. Kleinfelder, K.P. McAuliffe, E.A. Melton, V.A. Norton, and J. Weiss. The IBM Research Parallel Processor Prototype (RP3): Introduction and Architecture. In *Proc. International Conference on Parallel Processing*, pages 764–771, 1985.

[Pea77]   M.C. Pease. The Indirect Binary *n*-Cube Microprocessor Array. *IEEE Transactions on Computers*, C-26(5):458–473, May 1977.

[Per87]   R.H. Perrott. *Parallel Programming.* Addison-Wesley (International Computer Science Series), Wokingham, England, 1987.

[PN85]   G.F. Pfister and V.A. Norton. "Hot-Spot" Contention and Combining in Multistage Interconnection Networks. In *Proc. International Conference on Parallel Processing*, pages 790–795, 1985.

[Qui87]   M.J. Quinn. *Designing Efficient Algorithms for Parallel Computers.* McGraw-Hill (Computing and Artificial Intelligence Series), New York, 1987.

[Red73]   S.F. Reddaway. DAP – a distributed array processor. In *1st Int. Symp. Comp. Architecture*, pages 61–65, 1973.

[Red79]   S.F. Reddaway. The DAP Approach. In C. R. Jesshope and R. W. Hockney, editors, *Infotech State of the Art Report: Supercomputers*, pages 311–329, Infotech Intl Ltd, Maidenhead, England, 1979.

[Rob79]   J.T. Robinson. Some analysis techniques for asynchronous multiprocessor algorithms. *IEEE Transactions on Software Engineering*, SE-5(1):24–31, January 1979.

[Ros84]   A.W. Roscoe. Denotational Semantics for occam. In *Proc. NSF/SERC workshop on concurrency*, LNCS, Springer, 1984.

[RT86]   R. Rettberg and R. Thomas. Contention is no Obstacle to Shared-Memory Multiprocessing. *Communications of the ACM*, Vol. 29(12):1202–12, December, 1986.

[Rus78]   R.M. Russell. The CRAY-1 Computer System. *Communications of the ACM*, 21:63–72, 1978.

Bibliography

199

[SB77] H. Sullivan and T.R. Brashkow. A Large Scale Homogeneous Machine I & II. In *Proc. 4th Annual International Symposium on Computer Architecture*, pages 105–124, 1977. *hypercube*

[SBM62] D.L. Slotnick, W.C. Borck, and R.C. McReynolds. The SOLOMON computer. In *AFIPS Conf. Proc.*, pages 97–107, 1962.

[SBN82] D. P. Siewiorek, C. G. Bell, and A. Newell. *Computer Structures: Principles and Examples.* McGraw-Hill International, Japan, 1982.

[Sei83] C.L. Seitz. Experiments with VLSI Ensemble Machines. *Journal of VLSI & Computer Systems*, 1(4):311–334, 1983. *hypercube*

[Sei85] C.L. Seitz. The Cosmic Cube. *Communications of the ACM*, 28(1):22–33, 1985. *hypercube*

[Sie79] H.J. Siegel. Interconnection Networks for SIMD Machines. *IEEE Computer*, 12(6):57–65, 1979.

[SM81] H.J. Siegel and R.J. McMillen. The Multistage Cube : A Versatile Interconnection Network. *IEEE Computer*, 65–76, Dec. 1981.

[TMC86] *Introduction to Data Level Parallelism.* Thinking Machines Corporation, technical report 86.14 edition, 1986.

[Ung58] S.H. Unger. A computer oriented towards spatial problems. In *Proc. Inst. Radio Eng.*, pages 1744–50, 1958.

[Var62] R.S. Varga. *Matrix Iterative Analysis.* Prentice-Hall, Englewood Cliffs, New Jersey, 1962.

[VC78] C.R. Vick and J.A. Cornell. PEPE architecture — present and future. In *AFIPS Conf. Proc*, pages 981–1002, 1978.

[Wak68] A. Waksman. A Permutation Network. *J. Assoc. Comput. Mach.*, 15:159–163, 1968.

[WB72] W.A. Wulf and C.G. Bell. C.mmp - A multi-mini-processor. *Proc. AFIPS Fall Joint Comp. Conf.*, 41:765–777, 1972.

[WBB*87] W.W. Wilcke, R.C. Booth, D.A. Brown, D.G. Shea, F.T. Tong, and D. Zukowski. *Design and Application of an Experimental Multiprocessor.* Technical Report RC 12604, IBM Research Division, March 1987.

[WH78]   W. Wulf and S.P. Harbison. Reflections in a Pool of Processors: An Experience Report on C.mmp. In *Proc AFIPS NCC*, 1978.

[Whi85]   C. Whitby-Strevens. The transputer. In *Proc. 12th Annual International Symposium on Computer Architecture*, pages 292–300, 1985.

[Wid80]   L.C. Widdoes Jr.   The S-1 Project: Developing High-Performance Digital Computers. *IEEE Compcon '80*, 282–291, Spring 1980.

[WKI86]   T. Watanabe, H. Katayama, and A. Iwaya. Introduction of the NEC Supercomputer SX System. In S. Fernbach, editor, *Supercomputers: Class VI Systems, Hardware and Software*, pages 153–168, North-Holland, Amsterdam, 1986.

Index

access permissions, 45
active data structures, 59
Active Memory Technology, 57
activity bits, 48
Actus, 67
Ada, 170–174
    application of, 177
    nondeterminism, 173
    packages, 170
    rendezvous, 172
    tasks, 170
adaptive routing, 64
addressing:
    BBN Butterfly, 129
    in CM-1, 61
    in CM-1 network, 63
    in networks, 24
    in transputers, 147, 152
    predictability of, 83
ADI, 76
algorithms, 73–81
alpha notation, **71**
ALT, 175
alternating direction implicit, *see*
    ADI
Alvey ParSiFal project, 160
AMD 2901, 128
Amdahl's Law, 83
ANSI MIL-STD-1815, 170
application:
    characterisation, 92–94
    of array processors, 73–81
    of multiprocessors, 177–191
arbitrary permutations, 36
arithmetic permutations, 28
arithmetic:

bit-parallel, 49
bit-serial, 48–49
    performance of DAP, 56
ARPANET, 127
array processor organisation, 8–11
array processors:
    algorithms for, 73–81
    control mechanisms, 8
    control of ILLIAC IV, 11
    design issues, 7–8
    languages, 67–72
    performance issues, 15–21
    scalability of, 20
asymmetry of tasks, 173
asynchronous networks, 23
Augusta Ada, 170
average down time, 106
average vector length, 18

backplanes, 61
banyan network, 39
Batcher's bitonic merge, 178
BBN Butterfly, 40, 127–140, 173,
    185
    processing nodes, 128–129
    the switch, 130–132
Beneš network, 36–37, 38, 40
beta reduction, *64*, 71–72, 73
binary k-cube, 33, 96, 159
bipartite graphs, 25, 28
bit vectors, 48
bit-parallel word-serial, 16
bit-serial processing, 16
bit-serial word-parallel, 48
blocking networks, 40, 64, 131
boolean processors, 48

Briggs F.A., 94
BSP macro-pipeline, 13
Burroughs Scientific Processor, 11,
        12–15, 21
bus-connected multiprocessors, 111–
        115
butterfly permutation, 27–28, 38
Butterfly switch, 127

C.mmp, 122–127
CDC 6600, 2, 4
CDC 7600, 2, 4, 12
chain network, 31
Charles Babbage, 170
Chebychev acceleration, 76
chequer board algorithm, 76
chordal ring network, 11, 32
circuit switching, 23
CM-Lisp, 59, *67*, 70–72, *79*
        alpha notation, 7⊥
        beta reduction, 71–72
CMOS, 60, 148
coarse-grain processes, 89
column highway, 45
combining switches, 141
communication overheads, 143
comparing architectures, 18
completely connected networks, 32
complexity of hardware, 105
conflict resolution, 24, 65
        shared bus systems, 113
Connection Machine, 21, 58–66
        alpha notation, **71**
        beta reduction, 71–72
        CM-Lisp, 70–72
        design philosophy, 58–59
        hypercube network, 62–66
        message format, 63
        network performance, 65–66
        physical construction, 61
        pin-boundedness, 105
        processing elements, 61–62
        programming, 70–72

        routing algorithm, 63
        system architecture, 59–61
        technology, 60
context-switch time, 95, 174
        in transputers, 155
control point, 58
control vectors, 11, 68
Cosmic Cube, 35, 165
cosmic radiation, *106*
cost/performance:
        c.f. Grosch's Law, 85
        CRAY-1S v. Butterfly, 85
Cray Seymour, 44
CRAY X-MP, 84
CRAY-1, *4*, 15, 18, 55, 69, *85*, *165*,
        169
CRAY-2, 84
CRAY-3, 84
cross-bar switch, 5, 15, 22, 30, 36,
        164
        cost of, 22, 104
        routing function, 30
cross-point calculation, 77
CYBER 205, *4*, 15, 18, 56, 69, *85*,
        169
cycle-stealing, 44, 144
cyclic arrays, 7
cyclic geometry, 69

DAP, 43–58
        array unit, 45–48
        bit-serial mode, 48
        boundary geometry, 53, 69
        clock period, 53
        comparative speed, 51
        control vectors, 68
        data-shift instructions, 53
        Fortran, *67*, 68–70
        historical significance, 21
        host interface, 47
        instruction buffer, 48
        instruction set, 50–53
        loop-catching, 48

memory structure, 47
    performance, 17, 53–57
    processing elements, 48–50
    registers, 45
    system architecture, 44–45
DAP-3, 57, 68
DARPA, 127
data alignment, 73
data sharing, 109
data-forwarding, 58
data-level parallelism, 44, 66, 67,
    73, *83*
dataflow architectures, 94, 95
decision time, 95, 174
decomposition, 70, 73
decomposition of tasks, 181
dependencies, 93, 94
direct methods, 76
distributed memory:
    in array processors, 9
    in CM-1, 60
    in ILLIAC IV, 11
    in the DAP, 53
    multiprocessors, 88
DO loop, 51
dynamic networks:
    banyan, 39
    characteristics, 31
    general, 35–36
    indirect binary n-cube, 40
    multistage cube, 40
    omega, 39

ECL, 163
efficiency:
    MIMD models, 96–104
    of beta reduction, 74
    of process placement, 190
    of SIMD systems, 20
    prediction of, 177
Encore:
    Multimax, 112
    Ultramax, 140

environmental factors, *106*
ERDA Class IV, 85
ESPRIT Supernode project, 160
ETA[10], 84, *85*
Ethernet, 166
exchange permutation, 26–27, 33

fan-out, 21
fault diagnosis, 106
fault tolerance:
    in networks, 64
fault-tolerance, 105–108
fine-grained processes, 89, 92, *97*,
    174
finite difference methods, 75
flow-dependence, 99
Flynn limit, 83
Flynn M.J., 3
Fortran, 51
    DAP, 68–70
    matrices, 68
    vectors, 68
FPS T/40000, 167
full connection networks, 40, 111

gain equation, 104
    systolic multiplication, 191
Gantt charts, 97
general exchange switch, 37, 38
GF11, 41, 107
Goodyear Aerospace STARAN, *see*
    STARAN
granular efficiency, **97**, 104, 143,
    190
granularity, 73, **89**, 92, *177*
    effect on performance, 103
    in transputers, 152
graph algorithms, 79
Grosch's Law, 85
guarded commands, 175

Honeywell Bull, 170
Hwang K., 94

hybrid switching, 23
hypercube:
    bandwidth, 34
    complexity, 34
    multiprocessors, 165–167
    networks, 33
    routing functions, 33

IBM:
    GF11, 41, 107
    RP3, 140, 141, *185*
    System/360, 4, 58
    System/370, 4
    VICTOR, 160
ICL:
    2900, 43
    DAP, 16
identity permutation, 29, 33, 132
ILLIAC IV, 11–12, 21, 32, *43*
indirect binary n-cube network, 40
indirect methods, 76
INMOS links, 155
instantaneous parallelism, 93
instruction buffering, 48
instruction issue logic, 84
instruction sets:
    DAP, 50–53
    transputer, 148–153
integration, 43
Intel 8086, 165
inter-process communication, 169
interconnection networks, 22–41,
        84
    as graph structures, 23, 29
    BBN Butterfly switch, 130–132
    Connection Machine, 59
    design of, 23
    for array processors, 23
    for MIMD systems, 86, 111
    for multiprocessors, 23
    in SIMD systems, 9
    loading, *88*
    operating mode, 23

    redundancy, 107
    routing algorithms, 41
    switching method, 23
    the ILLIAC IV network, 12
interleaved memory, 8, 14
IP-1, 115
iPSC, 165

Jacobi's method, 76

Kleinrock L., 192
Kung H.T., 186

languages:
    Ada, 170–174
    for array processors, 67–72
    for multiprocessors, 169–177
    Occam, 175–177
latency, 95, 144
    in the Butterfly, 129
    sensitivity to, 96, 99
    tolerance of, 96, 99
least-recently-used, 113
linear second-order PDEs, 75
Lipovski G.J., 105
Lisp, 59
load balancing, **90**, *97*
loci of control, 84
Lockheed SUE processors, 115
lockstep arrays, 7, 11
logic-in-memory machines, 59
loop-catching, 48, 51
lower-broadcast, 37

M-SIMD machines, 84, 85
Makrucki B.A, 137
Malek M., 105
matrix multiplication in parallel,
        185–191
MCU registers, 45
mean time between failures, 106
Meiko Computing Surface, 160–165,
        189
    board library, 161–164

supervisor bus, 161
memory access conflicts, 14
Memphis Switch, 41, *see GF11*
message transfer system, 142
message-passing, **141**
message-passing systems:
    design issues, 143–145
    hypercube architectures, 165–167
    multiprocessors, 89
    process placement, 144
    taxonomy, 145
microcode, 151
microprocessor revolution, 21
MIMD architectures, 4
MIMD network requirements, 24
MIMD performance models, 91–108
MIMD performance:
    Butterfly switch, 132–140
    latency limitations, 95
    realistic, 103
    realistic gain, 104
    speedup bounds, 102
MIMD systems:
    categorisation, 88–89
    context-switch time, 95
    decision time, 95
    design issues, 86–91
    fault-tolerance, 105–108
    granularity of, 89
    interconnection problem, 86
    justification, 84
    latency of, 95
    message-passing, 89, 143–145
    reliability, 105–108
minimum path length, 79–81
MISD architectures, 4
model problem, 76
modular programming, 170
Moore's algorithm, 79
Mosaic, 35

Motorola:
    M68000, 128, 130
    M68020, 128
    M88100, 2, 173
MPP, 21, 61
MTBF, 106
MU5 Exchange, 112
Mudge T.N., 137
multi-stage networks, 35, 36–41, 116
multiprocessor granularity, 89
multiprocessors:
    algorithms, 177–191
    c.f. multicomputers, 84
    languages, 169–177
multiprogramming, 90, 142
multiprogramming overheads, 103
multistage cube network, 40
MUSS, 144

naming conventions, 142
NCUBE/10, 166
    pin-boundedness, 105
near-neighbour grid, 46, 60, 158
NEC SX Series, 15
network addressing, 24
network characteristics, 23–24
network connectivity, 165
    full, 22
    of transputer systems, 158
    partial, 22
network contention, 64
network control mechanisms, 40–41
network control signals, 23
network links, 23
network nodes, 23
network performance, 65–66
network topology, 29–41, *73*
    BBN Butterfly switch, 130
    boundary connections, 11, 53
    of CM-1, 62–66
    of DAP, 69

ring-structured, 30
    ternary trees, 159
NEWS grid, 60, 62, 74, *78*, 186
nondeterminism, 98, 173
novel architectures, 84, 94
NYU Ultracomputer, 140, 141

Occam, 146, 175–177
    application of, 177, 185
    channels, 147, 177
    harness processes, 189
    primitive processes, 175
omega network, 39
operating systems, 113
order statistics, *183*

packet survival rate, 136
packet switching, 23, 112
    in CM-1, 60
PAR, 175
parallel algorithms:
    design of, 87
    for multiprocessors, 177–191
    matrix multiplication, 185–191
    sorting, 178–185
parallel data structures, 67
parallel functional units, 2, 83
parallel systems:
    predicted market growth, 2
    from transputers, 158–160
    MIMD characteristics, 95–96
parallelism:
    data-level, 44, 67, 73, *83*
    explicit, 169
    in CM-1, 59
    in CM-Lisp, 71, 81
    in data structures, 67
    in hardware, 2–3
    in SIMD languages, 67–72
    in SIMD systems, 20
    instantaneous, 93
    matching h/w & s/w, 86
    MIMD gain, 104

profiles, 93, 97
static v. dynamic, 90, 91
taxonomy of, 3–4
PARSYS SN1000, 189
partial differential equations, 75–79
Pascal, 67, 170
PCB routing, 81
PDP-11, 112
PEPE, 21
perfect-shuffle permutation, 25–26
performance:
    Butterfly switch, 132–140
    cross-bar switches, 137
    MIMD potential, *84*
    models, 16–19
    of communication, *89*
    of MIMD systems, 91–108
    transputer communications, 155
permutations, **23**, 25, 62
    arbitrary, 36
    BBN Butterfly switch, 131–132
    butterfly, 27, 38
    exchange, 26, 135
    identity, 29
    perfect-shuffle, 25
    shift, 28, 30, 31
    transputer networks, 159
Perrot R.H., 87
petit cycles, 64, 65
pipelining, 58, 83
planar geometry, 69
Pluribus, 115, 127, 127
PMS, 4
portability, 67
precedence relations, 182
process migration, 90, 145
process placement, 144, 189
process replication, 176
process scheduling, 90
process synchronisation, 109
processing elements:

BBN Butterfly, 128–129
bollean, 61
boolean, 48
BSP arithmetic units, 12
in Connection Machine, 61–62
in MIMD systems, *86*
in the DAP, 48–50
sequential, 85

quantum chromodynamics, 107
queueing models, 184
Quicksort, 178
Quinn M.J., 87

real-time response, 91
recirculating networks, 35
rectangular mesh network, 31
recursive divide-and-conquer, 181
reliability, 105–108
rendezvous, 172
resilience, 106
ring network, 31
RISC architecture, *151*, *173*
routing conflicts, 65
routing:
    in Butterfly switch, 131
    algorithm complexity, 41
    cause of conflicts, 24
    conflicts, 24, 40, 64, 134
    functions, 23, 24–29, 25
    in CM-1 network, 63
    solution to conflicts, 138
row highway, 45
RP3 project, 140, 141, *185*

scalability:
    of array processors, 20
    of hypercubes, 35
    of MIMD systems, 104–105
    sequential limitations to, 86
    shared bus systems, 114
scalable multiprocessors, 116
scheduling of processes, 97

scoreboard, 2
SECDED, 107
Seitz C.L., 165
self-routing networks, 41
semaphores, 88
SEQ, 175
Sequent Balance 8000, 112, 116–122, 173
sequential processors, 85
shared bus structures, 31, 36
shared-memory:
    bandwidth problems, 141
    BSP memory modules, 12
    cost of, 15
    DAP-host, 44
    in array processors, 9
    MIMD design issues, 109–116
    multiprocessor systems, 88
shared-variables, 89
shift permutation, 28–29, 30, 31
shuffle permutation, 132
shuffle-exchange networks, 38–40
SIGRAPH Conference, *160*
silicon, 1
SIMD architectures, 4
SIMD language features, 68
SIMD network requirements, 24
SIMD performance:
    DAP performance, 17
    efficiency bounds, 18–19
    performance models, 16–19
    raw performance, 17
    realistic, 18
    space-time diagrams, 18
    throughput equations, 16
    two-state machines, 18
    utilisation equations, 16
single-bit processors, 48
single-chip processors, 2
single-stage networks, **35**
SISD architectures, 4
software:

for array processors, 73–81
SOLOMON, **21**, 43
SOR, 76
sorting in parallel, 178–185
space-time diagrams, 97
speed-of-light, 84
speedup:
    absolute, 177
    best-case MIMD, 100–101
    defined by Amdahl's Law, 83
    in SIMD systems, 20
    in SISD systems, 83
    linearity, 85
    MIMD model, 96–104
    Minsky's conjecture, 85
    realistic figures, 103
    superlinear, 108
    through parallelism, 92
    worst-case MIMD, 99–100
spin-lock, 114
square-mesh network, 53
Stanford S-1, 115
star network, 31, 112
STARAN, 21, 61
state multiplexed architectures, 96
state-transition diagram, 184
static networks:
    characteristics, 30
    chordal ring, 32
    completely connected, 32
    general, 31–35
    rectangular mesh, 31
    ring network, 31
    star network, 31, 112
    the chain, 31
    three-cube, 32
    topology, 31
    tree networks, 31
static state architectures, 96
store-and-forward, 64
structural notation, 4
sub-shuffle permutation, 26

successive over-relaxation, 76
super-linear speedup, 108
super-shuffle permutation, 26
switch de-rating, 138
switching nodes, 23
switching radix, 138
symbolic algorithms, 79
synchronisation, 21
    via shared-memory, 88
synchronous networks, 23
systolic arrays, 186

T414 transputer, 147–156
T800 transputer, 156–158
task graphs, 183
taxonomy:
    in general, 3–4
    message-passing systems, 145
    of MIMD systems, 88–89
telephone networks, 24
templates, 13
ternary trees, 159
Texas Instruments ASC, 53
three-cube network, 32
time-sharing, 92
transmission delays:
    BBN Butterfly switch, 130
    in hypercubes, 34
    INMOS links, 156
    SIMD clock speed, 21
    the ILLIAC IV clock problem,
      11
transputer, 144, 146–165
    configurable arrays, 159
    instruction format, 150
    instruction set, 148–153
    memory interface, 152
    performance, 147, 154–156
tree networks, 31
triple-modular-redundancy, 107

upper-broadcast, 37
utilisation:

without multiprogramming, 91

variation in parallelism, 93
VAX 11/780, 165
vector efficiency, 97
vector registers, 58
vectorisation, 18, 69, 83, 169
virtual memory, 44, *91*
virtual processors, 142
virtual store interrupts, 91
VLSI:
    Computing Surface switches,
      161
    NCUBE implementation, 166
    technological push, 86
    the transputer, 146
von Neumann bottleneck, 66, 83

wait-time, 141
Whetstones, 157
wiring cost, 105
word-parallel bit-serial, 16, 48
working-set model, 91
workload, 90
workstations, 92

Xectors, **70**, 81
XREF, 71